AF553356

NEOLIBERAL STATE AND ITS CHALLENGES

Edited by

Bhupen Sarmah
Joydeep Baruah

NEOLIBERAL STATE AND ITS CHALLENGES
Edited by Bhupen Sarmah and Joydeep Baruah

First Published, 2014

ISBN 978-93-5002-301-3

Published by
AAKAR BOOKS
28 E Pocket IV, Mayur Vihar Phase I, Delhi 110 091
Phone : 011 2279 5505 Telefax : 011 2279 5641
info@aakarbooks.com; www.aakarbooks.com

Printed at
Sapra Brothers, Delhi 110 009

Contents

PART III
Neoliberalism, Class and Power Structure

Preface

The collection of papers offered in this volume was presented at a seminar organised by the Omeo Kumar Das Institute of Social Change and Development (OKDISCD), Guwahati held during December 20-21, 2011 at Guwahati, Assam. The seminar attempted serious deliberations on some of the pressing issues of contemporary statehood and statecraft, both theoretical and practical. The seminar discussed, inter alia, at length the state in the context of the post-colonial era, its crises in governance including various manifestations of 'internal colonialism' and subsequent contestations, its crises in maintaining the legitimacy and concomitant process of militarisation, relations and frictions amongst the state, market and 'civil society' and attendant class configurations.

Evidently, the post-colonial state has been theorised by almost axiomatically projecting the state as the 'prime mover' with enormous legitimate power of intervention in the socio-political and economic life of the citizens. Backed by a global consensus for a strong interventionist role and drawing legitimacy from the prolonged anti-colonial movement, the state in the post-colonial democracies was envisaged to construct modern nations as well as economies through a process of development, primarily marked by rapid industrialisation, required agrarian reforms and provisioning of sufficient political space to accommodate aspirations of the diverse sections of the society, to reverse the 'colonial order' in its totality. Such development projects and the associated processes of social engineering, notwithstanding essentially statist in orientation, were by and large argued as 'class neutral' in the contemporary discourse. Building upon the argument of the 'relative autonomy of the state', a consensus was established that the society, incapable of regulating itself, needs to be directed from above, and hence, the state needs to be essentially all pervasive.

Nevertheless, theorisation of the state in the 1960s and 70s witnessed a remarkable shift as the state itself unfolded its oppressive nature. The statist development paradigm further aggravated inequality and exclusion with a distinct class bias. The net outcome of the state-led social engineering and its class bias expectedly influenced academic discourse on the state. The academics sought answers, besides relative autonomy, to sharply focused questions of class character of the state and the forms and nature of internal colonialism in practice. No wonder that the idealised post-colonial state and its legitimacy, therefore, had to confront with, besides academic attack, political mobilisation and social movements.

Consequently, theorisation of the state in the changing context started accepting the increasing political assertion of the civil society in the form of social movements questioning legitimacy of the paradigm of statist development. With an alternative perspective of participatory development, the state vs. civil society debate underpinned a series of vital issues such as gender, ecology, democratic decentralisation, human rights and civil liberties to be adequately addressed by the academic discourse.

The theoretical contestations that started in the 1960s and 70s against the overall 'statist development paradigm' and its failure in producing the desirable 'social outcome' found even stronger ideological armoury in the theory of contemporary neoliberalism from the 1980s onwards. The distinctive features of neoliberalism in its present form, essentially, entail a divide between the 'state' and 'market' as 'institutions' where the market is typically identified as 'efficient' over the state. Ideally, it is believed, the market is 'perfect' when it is allowed to operate 'freely', and any interventions in the form of 'regulations', including those coming from the state, are regarded as unwarranted limits to 'freedom' of optimising agents participating in market transactions. It has been argued that the result of such superfluous interventions is obvious — the market fails and the outcome deviates from potential optimum. Therefore, all failures of the so-called 'statist development paradigm' was, in general, attributed to diverse forms of 'market imperfections' caused by myriad state interventions across different sectors of the economy.

In typical political economy analysis 'output' and 'employment' are viewed as two most significant economic variables. In fact, the authority of controlling these two variables is considered as a critical distinctive feature in typifying a regime. Under the statist development paradigm, the state—as an institution—is envisaged to exert major control over these two critical variables through a sizeable 'public sector' and also through a substantial 'public investment'. Expansionary fiscal policy in general and public expenditure in particular, therefore, are suspected as the overarching presence of the state in the sphere of market functioning.

Neoliberal discourse, hence, favours 'monetarism', as opposed to 'fiscalism' and advocates in favour of even further financial liberalisation. The contribution of contemporary events in the 1970s and 80s to this neoliberal faith in monetary policy is, however, well-conceivable. Given the post-colonial re-ordering of the global economy, the industrial capitalism in the West needed to search for an alternative to 'financial capitalism' for sustaining accumulation. For unbridled accumulation to take place, evidently, financial capitalism required, inter alia, a globally integrated financial market and 'national monetary policy', thus, became a major concern which can influence this integration to happen.

The implications of this transformation have been far reaching. Firstly, it is important to critically look at how the global order under the emerging phase of finance capital essentially estranged 'economic sovereignty' from 'political sovereignty'. It is not hard to see that the decisions regarding so-called critical variables such as 'output' and 'employment' no longer remained under the control of a 'politically sovereign state'; rather they became integral to the overall business goals and policies of the class of global financiers. This resulted in the gradual waning of the stylised apparatus of 'statist development' like that of 'national planning'. Secondly, when capital became no longer tied to any particular territory, the class of the 'national capitalists' too gradually disappeared and began to merge with the class of the 'global capitalists'. Thirdly and most importantly, in order to 'oversee' that the global finance capital functions well, a set of institutions were created over and above the 'state' to which a 'politically sovereign state' had to submit at least some of its 'economic sovereignty'. Manifestly, all these have necessitated and generated intense theoretical reconsiderations about the issues and aspects of the state, sovereignty and nationality.

Crucial in this context is to recognise that the recent debate on 'market versus state' has also been viewed as a debate between 'efficiency' and 'equity' or 'social justice'. The neoliberal discourse on development axiomatically believes that market-led economic growth and social justice are compatible, realisable, and commendable. The genesis of the argument lies in the philosophical foundation in idealising 'justice', rather than hard economic facts. It is well established that the 18th century liberalism premised on 'individual right' and 'freedom' as against the 'state intervention' was inspired by the contemporary experiences of the state in the 17th and early 18th century Europe. Essentially, classical liberalism, as it is called, contested and rejected the notions, common at that time, of hereditary privileges, state religion, absolute monarchy and the so-called 'divine right' of kings.

It is interesting to note the role played by the idea of 'rationality' espoused during the enlightenment in putting individual rights and freedom at the centre-stage of 18th century liberalism. The idea that individuals are both 'moral' and 'rational' was diametrically opposed to the idea that individuals are by nature 'violent' and 'evil', and thus, the very idea of 'rational human beings' helped to crystallise the 'contractarian' argument that society is an association of rational individuals with a desire for 'order' and 'cooperation' rather than 'disorder' and 'conflict'. This, in turn, was influential in legitimising the 'liberal democratic state' replacing Kingdom and Monarchies in the later half of the 18th century. The fact that the liberal philosophy was opposed to any form of 'concentration of power', no wonder, economists of the 18th century had to articulate a 'perfectly competitive market' as an institution for 'social ordering'.

Recognisably, the classical liberalism underlined the consistent relations between the 'individual liberty' and 'private property' (i.e. the higher the private property the higher is the freedom to decide what to do with them) — a relation often so intimate that sometimes both were equated and used interchangeably. The market order based on private property was, therefore, viewed as the embodiment of individual freedom and protection of that order was treated as protection of freedom. Quite clearly, here the underlying idea was that dispersal of power emanating from the free market economy based on the institution of private property essentially safeguards liberty of subjects against the so-called evil encroachment of the state. Notwithstanding, the classical liberalism did provide a 'legitimate ground' for the state to exist. It was recognised that 'rules' and their 'observance' is critical to fair play of the game in the market and the state was assigned with responsibility to 'design' and 'observe' the rules and also to come to terms in case of any 'violations'.

A More fundamental and philosophical question, however, was whether such a 'social order' can be defended on grounds of 'social justice' since one of the central themes of political economy has always been 'distributive justice'. Classical liberalism held that so long as individuals' liberty and freedom are not intruded given the fulfilment of the condition that no individual is allowed to 'influence' the outcome in his favour the social order can be considered as 'just'. In fact, the question of 'social justice' has been a dominant subject in the study of economics in general and welfare economics in particular. For quite some time 'majority rule' supposed to hold the key to typify 'socially just order'. However, later on the famous Pareto rule—'making at least one individual better off without making none worse off'—provided a far more acceptable basis for characterising social justice.

One has to turn to Rawls, though, for a fuller exposition of the *theory* of justice to see the point in the discussion. In his *Theory of Justice* (1971), Rawls proposes his two principles—principle of 'egalitarianism', i.e. equal liberty to all and principle of 'difference', i.e. inequalities are to be so arranged as to optimise the benefits of the most underprivileged. His definition of justice as 'fairness' puts a precedence of the first principle over the second—observed inequalities are acceptable and justified provided all individuals are ensured equal freedom and opportunities. To be precise, according to Rawls, wage inequality between a manager and a menial is justified when both were provided with equal freedom and the opportunity to become a manager.

It is worthwhile to understand that the idea of social justice so defined always contains an element of structural inequality. Although the rich getting richer at the cost of the poor is strictly unjustified and thus despised, the poor getting rich at the cost of the rich is also ruled out on the same ground. What is justified is either the poor getting rich provided the rich remaining rich or rich getting richer provided poor remaining poor or at the very best both becoming better off together. The notion of 'social justice' within the liberal philosophy, thus, favours a status quo and there is no incentive for radical altering of the existing social, political and economic arrangements.

It was only during the post World War I period when idealised interconnection between private property and private liberty came into critical review. Great economic depression challenged the ability of the free market to produce unfailing equilibrium and the idea of the welfare state had to emerge out of the under-employment equilibrium and potentially unstable social order, and as a consequence, faith in the state prevailed over the market. The period witnessed political philosophers like Mill questioning whether personal liberty can flourish without private property. It may be argued that the necessity of such an investigation was contingent upon the 'structural inequality' justified under liberalism. One of the central philosophical queries of the welfare state, in fact, has been the limit to private liberty caused by inequalities in private property and resultant instability in the social order. It is, therefore, not surprising that this transition from 'rightness' to 'goodness' has been central in Keynesian and post-Keynesian discourses. Needless to point out that Keynes was concerned with 'allocative justice' rather than 'distributive justice'.

Present-day neoliberalism entails reverting back to the *free* market from the *welfare* state even more forcefully. While conditions of classical liberalism, viz. free market, private property and private liberty have been kept intact, the contingencies have undergone remarkable changes. Unlike classical liberalism where free market order based on private property and private liberty were placed vis-à-vis oppressive kings and monarchs, these are placed vis-à-vis presumably the welfare state in the current neoliberal phase. Obviously, the 'relative autonomy' of the welfare state theorised during the post-depression period is at stake and as such, the state has to reflect a distinct class bias. Caught in the whirlpool of global finance capital, a neoliberal state is faced with many challenges. Today, a neoliberal state must negotiate between the predatory profit-making interests of global financiers and legitimate rights of its citizens. The necessary metamorphosis of the neoliberal state is, in fact, the consequence of tensions and frictions of these two opposites, and as the neoliberal state undergoes the process of metamorphosis the 'structural inequalities' get entrenched, permeated and engrossed in favour of the class interests of the global financial capitalists.

Admittedly, intellectual war against an ideology needs to be launched on its strongest points. The seminar that was organised on the *Neoliberal State and its Challenges* at the institute discussed many facets and foundations of the neoliberal state. As stated earlier, the seminar deliberated at length on the theorisation of the post-colonial state, state and democracy, development state and its manifestations, class biases of the neoliberal state and crisis of legitimacy of the neoliberal state.

The eleven papers offered in this volume have been divided into three sections to make a thematic yet comprehensive reading on the subject.

The first section 'Neoliberal Way' contains one paper titled *Neoliberalism and Illiberalism in South Asia* by Neil DeVotta. Drawing on the maladies that have been caused by neoliberalism in South Asian countries the paper goes on to argue that the neoliberal way of governance invariably breeds corruption and malpractices of myriad kinds which can best be described as 'illiberalism'. The paper attempts to take a stab at that by briefly discussing the crisis of governance in South Asia and its possible relationship to the neoliberal policies that hold sway in the region. Demonstrating the extent of 'illiberal ways' in which the South Asian countries are governed the paper tends to argue that neoliberalism has perhaps reached an apogee in its course given the crises it faces in recent times, while admitting the peculiar tenacity of it to linger on even then.

The second section 'Neoliberalism and the State' comprises six papers. The first paper by Samir Kumar Das titled *Developmental State and its Sovereign Gaze* discusses how neoliberal processes have undermined the 'sovereignty' of the state. The paper attempts at examining the Foucauldian dichotomy between 'sovereignty' and 'governmentality'. With the help of a series of experiences of displacements in different parts of India, the paper focuses on how new 'technologies of governance' has resulted in 'governmentalisation of sovereignty' where the latter has been argued as 'an economy of gaze that the sovereign casts with its mission of 'developing' its subjects'. The second paper *Demise of the Developmental State or a Redefinition: Lessons from the State of Andhra Pradesh* by Radhika Kumar tries to look at the various ways in which neoliberalisation perceives the state and the extent to which states concerned have imbibed these tenets or otherwise modified the same. The paper examines the state of Andhra Pradesh in India which has been one of the first to undertake reforms following negotiation on a structural adjustment loan from the World Bank in 1996. The successive electoral victory of the Telugu Desam Party in the 1990s was seen as a mandate for liberalisation. The state thus seemed to have found the right fit in terms of conducting economic reforms aggressively as also continuing with populist measures. It is this electoral and economic formula that the paper interrogates together with attempts at mapping the contours of the state, i.e. its nature and attributes in the larger context of neoliberalisation. In the third paper *Return of the State: End of Neoliberalism? An Inquiry into the Indian Governmentality* by Santanu Rakshit tries to investigate whether neoliberalism has started withering away in recent times. Describing neoliberalism as the 'expression of International Finance Capital' the paper attempts to find the trace of the hegemony of neoliberalism and its seeming fading out from economic, social and political spaces in India. Given the growing recognitions of malevolent outcomes of neoliberal pursuits the paper rightfully interrogates the seemingly benevolent market expression of the Indian state in terms of the 'governmentality' or 'development management'. The fourth paper *Challenges of the Welfare State under Neoliberalism* by Asok Kumar Ray discusses various challenges offered by neoliberal 'governmentality' to the welfare state. He argues that a 'governmentalised' state creates a reasonable amount of discomfort to the post-colonial welfare state. The romantic height given to the non-state actors in such a form of the state are often contested as these are regulated by the state or international funding agencies. The non-state actors in most cases thus play instrumental roles instead of countervailing the political power of the state. In the fifth paper *Rise of Finance Capital and Decline of the Nation-State* by Sudipta Bhattacharyya analyses how the policies of neoliberalism found some ideological justification among a section of Indian population and how India passed through a transition from Nehruvian liberalism to a regime of neoliberalism which he calls, quite radically though, a 'gangster' neoliberalism. He argues that the process of neoliberal globalisation in many ways has largely alienated the people from local identity. At the same time there has been a steady decline in the nation-state and centrist policy in India. Worldwide there has also been a decline in socialist ideology. Therefore when the local identity is being endangered, there were no other positive alternative identities available to absorb the lost identity. The alienated people in most of the countries reacted in a negative way, which found identity in religion or other ethnic grouping, e.g. caste, tribe, language, etc. The sixth and last paper in this section *Political Economy of Neoliberal Urban Order in India* by Joydeep Baruah makes an attempt to outline and understand India's policy towards urbanisation in particular and overall development in general. The paper reveals how the shift from 'urban dispersal' to 'urban renewal' is very much in conformity with the shift from 'equity' to 'efficiency'. Drawing upon the enactment and repeal of the Urban Land Ceiling Act, the paper throws light on how the neoliberal state is compelled to function at the best of the capitalist class thereby marking a fundamental departure from so-called relative autonomy.

The third section 'Neoliberalism, Class and Power Structure' consists of four papers. In the first paper *Is a Free Market in Land Just?* Indraneel Dasgupta examines the ethical foundations of the case for a free market in land from the perspective of distributive justice. Beginning with the Lockean justification for private property in general and then extending the argument to the private property in land, the paper shows that an ideological commitment which valorises privatisation of the land market suffers from two cardinal errors which constitute the intellectual landscape of neoliberalism. First, it involves an acceptance of the efficiency claims of the market in precisely that sphere where such claims are, logically and empirically, least warranted. Second, it involves an *a priori* defence of market determination of that form of property income which is ethically least defensible (and least defended). In the second paper *Investment-Induced Displacement: Analysing the Neoliberal Power Structure*, Felix Padel argues that a total disconnect exists between policy and practice regarding Resettlement and Rehabilitation where as at least forty million villagers have been displaced by 'development projects' since India's independence. Two problems have been identified. On the one hand, new 'generous' R & R policies and packages turn out to be anything but, since they do not offer land for land, and cash compensation soon morphs into debt in the hands of village people not used to handling bank accounts and loan offers. On the other hand, social impact assessments are barely carried out at all, forming at best a very subsidiary component in some Environment Impact Assessments, but without any weight or substance. The paper argues that the very development projects that leave vast majority of masses destitute are financed by a financial system based on debt which serves the interests of big corporations and those running the World Bank/IMF cartel. The third paper in the section *Land Acquisition Laws and the State in the Neoliberal Era: Some Observations on the Constitutional Imperatives, Legislations and Judicial Interventions* by V. Krishna Ananth makes an attempt to place in context the various provisions and injunctions—Constitutional and Statutory—in the area of land acquisition from a historical perspective and locates its relevance in the context of the neoliberal state. The paper shows how the constitutional connotation of 'public purpose' has undergone changes during the last sixty years and what substantial changes have taken place in the process with the state asserting its powers for purposes that are quite the opposite and the challenges to these. The last paper in this section *Will Neoliberal Policies and Regulations Resolve Our Water Sector Dilemmas? Learning from Maharashtra and Gujarat* by P.K. Viswanathan examines how the neoliberal policies have influenced the water sector reform in India, particularly, in Maharashtra and Gujarat. In doing so, the paper focuses on three issues: the national and state-level responses towards the neoliberal policies and their immediate outcomes on reforms in the water sector, whether the neoliberal policies and the regulatory systems as evolved in the contexts of developed countries would help resolve the burgeoning challenges and conflicts confronting the water sector in India and the critical issues and challenges that the policies and regulatory systems face in achieving the goals of integrated water resources development and a sustainable water future for the country. The paper observes that the policy responses and regulatory reforms in the case of Maharashtra have been somewhat proactive in sensitising the issues concerning allocation and distribution of water across competing sectors.

Nevertheless, the legislations and regulatory systems that came into being have failed to internalise the ground realities concerning the critical issues of equitable distribution and conservation of water. The paper argues that the incompatibility between the neoliberal policies and the water sector interventions in the Indian context may be explained in terms of India's experimentation with the macro economic policy reforms without recognising the need for internal restructuring.

The eleven papers organised in three sections, thus, provide a thorough criticism of the neoliberal state and adequately address diverse challenges faced by it. We sincerely believe that the volume would make a wholesome read and in conclusion we wish to thank the participants of the seminar for their rich and passionate interactions and most importantly the contributors for their active involvement in making this volume a reality. We would like to thank Professor Atul Sarmah, Chairman of the Institute for his inspiring inaugural address at the seminar. We take this opportunity to thank all our esteemed colleagues at the Institute for engaging us with deep and provocative discussions on numerous occasions. Finally, we would like to place on record our gratitude to Mr. K.K. Saxena of Aakar Books for agreeing to bring out the volume in its present form. We hope that the readers will find the volume intellectually stimulating and rewarding.

Guwahati
August 14, 2013

Bhupen Sarmah
Joydeep Baruah

PART I
Neoliberal Way

1

Neoliberalism and Illiberalism in South Asia

Neil DeVotta

Neoliberalism is premised on the belief that economic growth and social justice are compatible, realisable, and commendable. Yet what we increasingly see in South Asia is a monomania on economic growth that de-emphasises social justice and thereby also undermines liberal democracy. This is best evidenced by how those seeking to institute neoliberalism often resort to ham-handed practices, such as, banning or suppressing trade unions or tolerate increased corruption and malgovernance, which neoliberalism has partly facilitated and exacerbated.

All South Asian states have dealt with corruption in various forms, but neoliberal programmes, while generating selective prosperity, have magnified corruption in blatant and conspicuous ways and undermined good governance. There is a crisis of governance facing South Asian states, and this is in no small measure related to how the social justice component of neoliberalism has been divested from economic growth.

This paper will evaluate the ways in which neoliberalism has adversely affected liberalism in South Asia with a special focus on neoliberalism's impact on Sri Lanka, both in terms of its ethnic problem and malgovernance.

Whither Neoliberalism?

Depending on which scholars one privileges, neoliberalism ranges from being a theory to an ideology.[1] Either way, it is premised on the belief that "human well-being can best be advanced by the maximisation of entrepreneurial freedoms within an institutional framework characterised by private property rights, individual liberty, unencumbered markets, and free trade."[2] The thinking behind neoliberalism has been influenced by the likes of Friedrich Hayek and Milton Friedman[3] and its current avatar is attributed to the policies unleashed by Margaret Thatcher and Ronald Reagan in the late 1970s and 80s—although the reforms introduced in Chile under Augusto Pinochet and to a lesser degree in Argentina under the military leadership were used to justify its spread. If one adds Deng Xiaoping to this list, the irony is that neoliberalism's vanguards were not democrats, but repressive autocrats.[4]

The implosion of the Soviet Union and the argument that the Cold War represented "the end point of man's ideological evolution and the universalisation of Western liberal democracy as the final form of human government"[5] also projected neoliberalism as a sine qua non for not just countries that were part of the Soviet ambit but for all those aspiring towards higher socio-economic progress.

David Harvey, who considers neoliberalism to be an economic theory not necessarily tethered to traditional or modern liberalism, offers one of the best and detailed definitions of the term:

> Neoliberalism is in the first instance a theory of political economic practices that proposes that human well-being can best be advanced by liberating individual entrepreneurial freedoms and skills within an institutional framework characterised by strong private property rights, free markets and free trade. The role of the state is to create and preserve an institutional framework appropriate to such practices. The state has to guarantee, for example, the quality and integrity of money. It must also set up those military, defense, police and legal structures and functions required to secure private property rights and to guarantee, by force if need be, the proper functioning of markets. Furthermore,

> if markets do not exist (in areas such as land, water, education, health care, social security, or environmental pollution) then they must be created, by state action if necessary. But beyond those tasks the state should not venture. State interventions in markets (once created) must be kept to a bare minimum because, according to the theory, the state cannot possibly possess enough information to second guess market signals (prices) and because powerful interest groups will inevitably distort and bias state interventions (particularly in democracies) for their own benefit.[6]

The type of capitalism associated with neoliberalism, however, is "prone to destructive booms and slumps, to financial crises that wipe out household savings and government fiscal strategies alike, to polar extremes of wealth and poverty, and to a continuing reckless consumption of the global commons."[7] Its spread across the global south to even the most destitute states has also led to "a political order constituted first and foremost on the defence of private property, in which the reach of democratic and electoral accountability stops at the entrance to the gated communities and tax havens of the super-rich, whether they hail from Omaha or Beijing."[8]

On the one hand, neoliberal policies have increased competition, encouraged wealth creation even in poor societies, controlled hyperinflation, done away with inefficient and unproductive parastatals, reduced bureaucracies, curtailed tariffs, and stabilised currencies. On the other hand, these same policies have increased disparity between the so-called haves and have-nots so as to cause serious concern among policymakers. For instance, Dominique Strauss-Kahn, when IMF Director, warned that "More unequal countries have worse social indicators, a poorer human-development record, and higher degrees of economic insecurity and anxiety" and warned that increased economic disparity within countries "wear down the social fabric."[9] Add a "youth bulge" and the combination of factors may be conducive to massive uprisings and revolutions.

While neoliberalism now dominates global economic activity, what is also clear is that various countries incorporate neoliberal policies at varied levels. For instance, the neoliberal policies one sees in Western European states that embrace tenets of social democracy are less stringent than what one sees in the United States, which in turn has higher levels of inequality. Otherwise noted, the more a country embraces unadulterated neoliberal policies, the more inequality that country is likely to face. In the United States the population that lives in poverty or near poverty is over 30 per cent. Nearly 45 million Americans do not have ready access to healthcare. The country ranks between Senegal and Ghana on the GINI Index (which measures inequality). The continuing relocation of production thanks to globalisation and the basic tenets of neoliberalism are likely to exacerbate America's plight unless drastic changes are made to how its economy is structured. And that will have implications for governance, just as the current inequalities in American society are impacting governance—be it in the form of basic services being curtailed (or eliminated) or individuals and organisations mobilising (a la unions in Ohio and Wisconsin and the so-called Wall Street protestors) demanding more equitable livelihoods.

It appears that one of the issues that have been insufficiently addressed is how neoliberalism affects governance and how especially it may contribute to illiberal governance. This paper attempts to take a stab at that by briefly discussing the crisis of governance in South Asia, especially within the context of corruption and illiberalism, and its possible relationship to the neoliberal policies that hold sway in the region.

The Crisis of Governance in South Asia

Scholars of democracy understandably assumed that the third wave of democratisation that began in the mid-1970s would, like the two waves preceding it, also experience a reverse wave.[10] What transpired instead was a rise in illiberal democracies, some of which have, over time, regressed further in an authoritarian direction.[11] This is especially made clear by the annual country rankings Freedom House has assembled in the past decade.

Illiberal democracies refer to states that maintain the trappings of democracy but whose leaders subscribe to the tenets of constitutional liberalism—i.e. the rule of law; free and fair elections; freedoms of assembly, speech, and religion; and limited government—selectively or in the breach. Political elites in these states undermine good governance to bolster and perpetuate their rule yet mask the attendant democratic deficit by only propagandising aspects of democracy that afford them legitimacy domestically and internationally. Typically in such states the holding of elections are touted even as polls are rigged to favour the ruling party; threats, violence, and crossovers are engineered to ensure the opposition parties and candidates remain weakened; and the media are allowed relative freedom provided they do not overly criticise the ruling party, its leaders and their families, and the venal and predatory practices these elites cultivate when amassing wealth and power.

The longer such regimes stay in place, the more their leaders, family members, and henchmen disregard the rule of law and act with impunity, which in turn makes it more difficult for them to envisage being out of power. Indeed, the desire to consolidate their rule and the fear of being held accountable for their crimes constitute major reasons elites in illiberal regimes veer towards authoritarianism. Numerous authors have analysed the resultant hybrid regimes that combine aspects of democracy with authoritarianism using various nomenclatures, including competitive authoritarianism, electoral authoritarianism, semi-authoritarianism, semi-democracy, electoral democracy, virtual democracy, control democracy, and pseudo democracy.[12] This hodgepodge notwithstanding, the specifics associated with the country being analysed and its evident trajectory may justify a particular designation.

South Asia has its fair share of illiberalism, be it in Pakistan's armoured democracy, Sri Lanka's soft-authoritarianism, and Bangladesh's slander politics. India, the region's most successful democracy, may be the least illiberal especially if the atrocities committed by certain security personnel in Kashmir and the northeast are overlooked, yet widespread corruption combined with dynastic politics, nepotism, cronyism, and impunity sullies India's democratic credentials as well. And irrespective of whether one agrees with the tactics of Anna Hazare and his team, the fact that tens of thousands of Indians (especially belonging to the middle classes) mobilised to support his demands against the Indian state highlights how frustrated people are over India's extant malgovernance.

South Asia has long experienced corruption. Yet one of the issues that have upset especially Indians is the *degree* to which corruption now takes place. Otherwise noted, the issue is less that people connected to government are accepting bribes, because it appears that South Asians have come to expect their representatives, bureaucrats, and business people to take bribes; but the real issue is the types and levels of bribes those connected to government orchestrate.

For instance, those who hoped to accumulate bribes in the hundreds and thousands now expect to accumulate crores. The Indian media, arguably the most free press in South Asia, often sneer at certain individuals of modest means who catapult themselves to crorepatis having merely served a single term in parliament. This partly highlights the strong nexus that has taken root between business people and politicians. Some business persons have figured out that having a relative become a politician avoids having to deal with one layer of corruption, and increasingly one sees businessmen or members of their brood take to politics—not to serve the masses and country, but to feed off the government's trough, sell their own influence, and ensure their family interests progress.

There is a major reason as to why the Indian parliament today meets less frequently than it did in years past and that when it does even important bills hardly get debated: it is because many of those who have sought entry into parliament are less interested in governing and more interested in making money. It is with good reason that India's 2009 elections saw over 8,000 candidates contest for seats in parliament. In Sri Lanka's 2004 parliamentary elections 52 parties and coalitions contested, even though only seven won at least one seat. In the island's 2010 parliamentary elections over 7,620 candidates contested for office. It is a supreme irony that such patriotism only bodes ill for governance.

What India's and South Asia's neoliberal reforms did was create more wealth among certain sectors, leading to higher wages in particular industries that in turn contributed to stratospheric land prices. There are numerous rags to riches stories throughout South Asia but the vast majority of citizens in the subcontinent continue to wallow in poverty and are arguably worse off than they would have been had the reforms never ensued. Indeed, structural adjustment reforms associated with neoliberalism have defenestrated basic protections that the old economic order afforded and thereby only widened the disparity between the haves and have-nots. This is best evidenced when one compares social indicators across South Asia over the past two decades (see Table 1).

One of the striking realisations of the past two decades especially is that countries could experience economic disparity and high gross national income simultaneously, given how neoliberal policies have favoured the wealthy disproportionately even as they have marginalised the lower classes. South Asia proves the point, especially when one looks at the data for India, Bangladesh, and Nepal. For example, while per capita income in India is nearly twice that of Bangladesh, the latter appears to be faring better on many social indicators. Ditto for Nepal, which has a per capita income nearly one-third that of India yet competes with and exceeds India on many social indicators.[13]

Table 1

India's Slipping Social Report Card in the Neighbourhood South Asia: Selected Indicators (1990 and latest)

GNI Per Capita (ppp, current int. $)

	India	Bangla-desh	Bhutan	Nepal	Pakistan	Sri Lanka	China
1990	877	543	1280	513	1210	1420	813
2010	3560	1800	4950	1200	2780	4980	7570

Life Expectancy at Birth (years)

	India	Bangla-desh	Bhutan	Nepal	Pakistan	Sri Lanka	China
1990	58	54	52	54	61	69	68
64	67	67	67	67	67	74	73

Infant Mortality Rate (per 1000 live births)

	India	Bangla-desh	Bhutan	Nepal	Pakistan	Sri Lanka	China
1990	81	99	96	97	96	26	38
2010	48	38	44	41	70	14	16

Under-5 Mortality Rate

	India	Bangla-desh	Bhutan	Nepal	Pakistan	Sri Lanka	China
1990	115	143	139	141	124	32	48
2010	63	48	56	50	87	17	18

Maternal Mortality Ratio

	India	Bangla-desh	Bhutan	Nepal	Pakistan	Sri Lanka	China
1990	570	870	940	870	490	91	110
2008	230	340	200	380	260	39	38

Total Fertility Rate (children per woman)

	India	Bangla-desh	Bhutan	Nepal	Pakistan	Sri Lanka	China
1990	3.9	4.5	5.7	5.2	6.0	2.5	2.3
2009	2.7	2.3	2.5	2.8	3.5	2.3	1.6

Access to Improved Sanitation (%)

	India	Bangla-desh	Bhutan	Nepal	Pakistan	Sri Lanka	China
1990	18	39	-	11	28	70	41
2008	31	53	65	31	45	91	55

Infant Immunisation (DPT %)

	India	Bangla-desh	Bhutan	Nepal	Pakistan	Sri Lanka	China
1990	59	64	88	44	48	86	95
2008	66	94	96	82	80	98	96

Infant Immunisation (Measles %)

	India	Bangla desh	Bhutan	Nepal	Pakistan	Sri Lanka	China
1990	47	62	87	57	50	78	95
2008	71	98	97	80	82	97	94

Mean Years of Schooling

	India	Bangla-desh	Bhutan	Nepal	Pakistan	Sri Lanka	China
1990	3.0	2.9	-	2.0	2.3	6.9	4.9
2010	4.4	4.8	-	3.2	4.9	8.2	7.6

Female Literacy Rate, Age 15-24 Years (%)

	India	Bangla-desh	Bhutan	Nepal	Pakistan	Sri Lanka	China
1991	49	38	-	33	-	93	91
2009	74	77	68	77	61	99	99

Proportion (%) of Underweight Children

	India	Bangla-desh	Bhutan	Nepal	Pakistan	Sri Lanka	China
1990	59.5	61.5	34	-	39	29	13
2007	43.5	41.3	12	38.8	-	21.6	4.5

Source: Jean Dreze and Amartya Sen, "Putting Growth in its Place," *Outlook* (November 14, 2011): 50-9.

Neoliberal policies indisputably create wealth. But they do not promote equity. If anything, they exacerbate economic disparities. And this is where the social justice component of neoliberalism gets discarded. Thus India's burgeoning middle classes clamour for the country to become a superpower while insouciantly disregarding the vast majority of Indians who live in dire poverty and feel disenfranchised by the current economic policies. The country's Naxalite movement is directly related to some of these current policies that focus on the extraction of resources from tribal areas at the expense of those living there.[14] It is most disconcerting to hear privileged Indians and those who have benefited from the post-1991 economic reforms refer to the tribals and India's poor as impediments that stand in the way of India's rise to great power status. This captures well the injustice of neoliberalism and the bases for the illiberalism this theory/ideology promotes. No country in the region, arguably, captures this illiberalism as does Sri Lanka.

The Sri Lankan Case

Sri Lanka was one of the first countries in Asia to embrace parts of the neoliberalism dogma, and it did so in 1977 a year ahead of China. The autarkist and dirigist economy that Prime Minister Sirimavo Bandaranaike and her Sri Lanka Freedom Party (SLFP) oversaw from 1970-77 had led to scarcity, inefficiency, monopolies, and corruption, with cronies associated with political elites benefiting from parastatals and government issued permits and licenses.[15] This allowed the United National Party (UNP), which was headed by the pro-western J.R. Jayewardene and came to power in a massive landslide in July 1977, to collaborate with the IMF and World Bank especially and introduce structural adjustment reforms.

The term structural adjustment is used as a summary description of economic liberalisation and such market reform policies as reducing tariffs, deregulating financial markets, liberalising foreign trade, dismantling food subsidies, privatising government-owned industries, and curtailing the state-employed workforce. Countries pursuing structural adjustment anticipate an increase in their gross domestic product and standards of living, a decrease in unemployment, and, in the long run, further expect free market policies to lead to a stable economic system.[16] This is what the UNP under Jayewardene sought to achieve in Sri Lanka as well.

Overall, structural adjustment policies that were instituted in the island had four immediate effects: first, they generated more foreign investment, foreign aid, and cheap loans from western countries and institutions such as the IMF and World Bank, which led to opportunities for socio-economic upward mobility for certain sectors, which in turn contributed to a widening disparity between the well connected and nouveau riche and those who continued to stay marginalised. The government was initially able to minimise the disenchantment stemming from such disparity by continuing to fund certain social programmes, which the supporters of neoliberalism tolerated because they did not want to see their experiment in Sri Lanka end in failure. Sri Lanka ranked high on numerous social indices when compared to many other Third World countries, and the thinking among the neoliberal fraternity was that if the island failed to institute structural adjustment reforms successfully, then there was no chance of promoting these same reforms in countries that were struggling with even worse social indicators.[17] Notwithstanding this contradictory stance among the promoters of neoliberalism, the economic disparities stemming from the changing economic fortunes in the island hardly altered.

Second, this disparity also cut across ethnic lines in ways that exacerbated the extant tensions between the majority Sinhalese and minority Tamils. The "ethnic outbidding" that accompanied the attempt to make the Sinhala language the country's official language, other anti-Tamil policies that sought to enrich the Sinhalese Buddhists at the expense of the Tamils, and the reactive nationalism and attendant violence that young Tamils resorted to had poisoned relations between the island's two communities starting in the mid-1950s and led to anti-Tamil riots in 1956, 1958, 1977, and 1981.[18] But the 1983 anti-Tamil pogrom that heralded Sri Lanka's civil war was also correlated to a significant extent with the economic changes that ensued from Sri Lanka's post-1977 structural adjustment reforms. The open market reforms allowed a large number of Tamils to use their ethnic and business connections with Indians to become upwardly mobile. Thus, if the pre-1977 era had seen Sinhalese heavy and small industrialists, shopkeepers, and traders using their ethnic identity to procure quotas, licenses, and general access to scarce resources, the open market reforms allowed Tamils to become successful traders and industrialists in their own right. The subsequent prosperity catapulted previously lumpen Tamil groups into the middle- and upper-middle strata, while their Sinhalese counterparts, unable to compete with the cheap and superior imports inundating the marketplace, were stripped of their status as "captains of ... industry."[19]

Economic transitions especially create uncertainty, amid which ethnic cohesion is likely to be strengthened. This is especially the case if one group articulates its grievances and relative deprivation as resulting from the doings of a rival group. Such grievances then lead to chauvinism and the racialisation of politics, which is what partly occurred during the 1983 anti-Tamil riots. Marx may have been right in claiming that the lumpen proletariat lacked class consciousness, but that is not to say that the lumpen proletariat cannot be galvanised along ethnic lines by using such emotive issues as language, religion, and culture. Ethnic rhetoric allows for doing just that, and it is thus not coincidental that the relatively deprived Sinhalese bourgeoisie was able to utilise the destabilising tendencies of the Sinhalese lumpen proletariat in ensuring that the Tamil entrepreneurial classes were more or less wiped out in the 1983 riots. As the *Economist* then reported, "Two weeks ago Tamils owned 60 per cent of the wholesale trade and 80 per cent of the retail trade in the capital. Today that trade is gone."[20] The newspaper further observed that "The majority Sinhalese observed that more than half of 'their' new industries were Tamil-owned—and ... burnt down the Tamil factories."[21] These were factories that were made possible due to the economic reforms unleashed by Sri Lanka's tilt towards neoliberalism, and thus neoliberal reforms unwittingly ended up playing a role in the country's ethnic conflict.

Third, the UNP's political future became inextricably tied to the success of structural adjustment reforms so that the government went on cultivating closer and closer links with Western countries (especially the United States and the United Kingdom) without regard to Indian sensitivities and security concerns—and this at a time when India was exceedingly suspicious of American designs in the Indian Ocean and was, in the main, quite anti-American. For instance, Jayewardene ordered Sri Lanka's UN representative to vote in favour of

Britain's position opposing negations to settle the Falklands dispute; allowed the US nuclear-powered naval carrier Kitty Hawk to dock outside the Colombo harbour; approved of plans for the US to build a powerful Voice of America station that India suspected was designed to eavesdrop on its activities; and similarly permitted an American concern operating out of Singapore to lease the island's oil storage farms in the strategic Trincomalee area. Jayewardene and many of his colleagues in the UNP were admirers of the Indian nationalist movement and fans of Mahatma Gandhi and Jawaharlal Nehru. While Jayewardene and Indira Gandhi did not like each other, he and the UNP were hardly anti-Indian. Jayewardene was pro-Western, but it was the realisation that his government's fortunes were linked to neoliberal reforms that forced the government to repeatedly disregard Indian concerns. The consequences stemming from this inevitably led to tensions with India and exacerbated the separatist conflict between the Sri Lankan government and the Liberation Tigers of Tamil Eelam (LTTE).[22] India ended up sending to Sri Lanka the Indian Peace Keeping Force (IPKF), which fought the LTTE in India's longest war. Most Sri Lankans continue to vilify India for forcibly stationing the IPKF in the island, and some of the current anti-Indian attitudes in the island stem from this episode.

Fourth, with the UNP's legitimacy being directly linked to neoliberalism, J.R. Jayewardene and his government became less and less tolerant of those criticising their economic approach. Anyone perceived to undermine economic reforms were treated as enemies of the state and dealt with violently. The need to institute austere economic reforms justified a more authoritarian style of governance, which Jayewardene embraced with aplomb. For instance, civil society actors, including members of the clergy, who dared protest against the government's economic policies, were assaulted. Supreme Court justices who ruled against the government or in favour of civil society activists were harassed and threatened. Ironically, the UNP used thugs within its labour union to beat up workers in other unions who were protesting against unfair labour practices and the privatisations of certain industries. Neoliberal reforms have often required governments to adopt-ham-handed practices, and both Margaret Thatcher and Ronald Reagan did so especially when dealing with striking workers. Authoritarian leaders can operate against opposing constituencies with much more latitude, and it is no accident that neoliberal reforms have often accompanied authoritarian governance. This was true in Sri Lanka—although this is not to say that neoliberalism caused authoritarianism in the country. There, however, is no gainsaying that the neoliberal reforms helped exacerbate ethnic tensions, compromise good governance, and created authoritarian precedents that have severely harmed the island's democratic credentials.

The upshot is that the new wealth that neoliberal policies created within limited sectors impacted the political process in nefarious ways. For instance, a country that already had a fair share of corruption gradually began wallowing in more and more of it. It is with good reason that former President Chandrika Kumaratunga recently noted that the island's parliament was filled with thieves and murderers who killed each other to enter government in order to steal public funds. With more and more money sloshing around, it was the well-connected and wealthy that promoted the increased rise in corruption, which in turn led a tawdry nexus between politicians and the burgeoning business classes.

With the civil war leading to the increased militarisation of society, these politicians and businessmen soon became bastions that operated with impunity. They were also able to profit from what may be called a "civil war economy" that centred on weapons procurement and industries that supplied the armed forces. The civil war allowed all sorts of malpractices within the government to become veiled since defeating the LTTE and maintaining Sri Lanka's territorial integrity became preeminent goals and the focus of especially the Sinhalese populace. With the election of President Mahinda Rajapaksa and the rise of his brother, Defence Secretary Gotabya Rajapaksa, criticising the military was branded "treasonous" and this has prevented discussion on corruption within the military. Most important, and for the purposes of this paper, the civil war allowed the government to spend so much on the military that this expenditure, which amounted to over 40 per cent of government salaries and over 20 per cent of the national budget, compensated for the state's reduced involvement in ensuring socio-economic safety nets even as it continued to promote the neoliberal agenda.[23] With over 98 per cent of the security forces and over 96 per cent of the government service being Sinhalese (and especially Sinhalese Buddhists), it is the majority community that continues to benefit from increased militarisation and bloated government. Maintaining this ethno-centric arrangement has made the government captive to neoliberalism.

A major way sufficient funds can be channelled into government coffers so a bloated cabinet (where ministers and deputy ministers number nearly 100) can be maintained and cronies kept content is by continuing to promote neoliberal policies; for the wealth creation associated with neoliberalism benefits those closest to the regime and the kickbacks associated with various neoliberal projects also helps bolster the regime. Thus privatisation of industries and leasing out land and other facilities to foreign entities become popular ways through which to raise revenue. This coincides with cutting funding for programmes that fail to generate kickbacks or do not benefit those close to the regime. For example, one ongoing controversy associated with Sri Lankan politics has to do with the government's stealthy attempts to privatise university education even as the education budget has been drastically slashed—so that currently only 1.9 per cent of GDP is allocated towards education (which contrasts with the 2.9 per cent of GDP allocated in 2005 and the 5.2 per cent allocated in 1971). The privatisation attempts and the underfunding have led to faculty and student protests and much turmoil on university campuses. Sri Lanka's high literacy rates and commendable tertiary education was once the envy of developing states. While neoliberalism hardly caused the drop in standards, the politics and funding associated with neoliberal reforms have had much to do with how successive governments over the past three decades have interacted with and slashed funding for the education sector.

Historically, the UNP supported pro-Western policies, including market reforms, while the SLFP promoted leftist economic policies. Chandrika Kumaratunga's own proclivities coupled with the UNP having pursued open market reforms for seventeen years caused her to continue with the structural adjustment policies Jayewardene introduced. Thus today there is hardly much difference between the two parties when it comes to economic policies. The Mahinda Rajapaksa government has continued with open market policies even as the president periodically embraces anti-Western rhetoric and touts autarkist practices. Currently President Mahinda Rajapaksa remains extremely popular thanks to his having overseen the decimation of the LTTE. Yet the increased militarisation that accompanied that effort is now being used to control dissent and undermine opponents, so as to make Sri Lanka increasingly authoritarian.[24] This takes place even as the president and his powerful brothers promote economic development at the expense of ethnic reconciliation and the rule of law. In a real sense, the country appears to have swapped terrorism for authoritarianism. This new dispensation is bound to only further embolden and entrench the forces of neoliberalism—and illiberalism.

Conclusion

Have neoliberalism's fortunes reached their apogee? The manner in which global markets have been affected following the irresponsible practices of banks in the United States and especially Ireland, Greece, Italy, and other countries have put paid to the belief that markets are rational entities that were self-governing, and one might expect that the time has arrived for new regimes that take cognisance of neoliberalism's maladies to be instituted. This, however, is easier said than done. One reason this system is hard to overturn is because political and business elites who have benefited immensely from neoliberalism work hard to ensure that things stay in place. The conspicuous sense of development associated with these individuals and the initial high GDP rates neoliberal policies generate also cultivate a sense that neoliberalism is related to prosperity. From this standpoint, neoliberalism may have more staying power than its opponents care to admit.

NOTES

1. David Harvey, *A Brief History of Neoliberalism* (Oxford: Oxford University Press, 2005); Adam Przeworski, "The Neoliberal Fallacy," *Journal of Democracy*, Vol. 3, No. 3 (July 1992): 45-58.
2. David Harvey, "Neoliberalism as Creative Destruction," *The Annals of the American Academy of Political and Social Science*, No. 610 (March 2007), p. 22.
3. For their important works see Milton Friedman, *Capitalism and Freedom* (Chicago: University of Chicago Press, 1962); Milton Friedman, *Free to Choose* (New York: Harcourt Brace Jovanovich, 1980); Friedrich Hayek, *Law, Legislation and Liberty: A New Statement of the Liberal Principles and Political Economy*, 3 Vols., (London: Routledge, 1973, 1976 and 1979).
4. The claim that political repression and the institutionalisation of pro-market policies are correlated is made by John Sheahan, "Market-Oriented Economic Policies and Political Repression in Latin America," *Economic Development and Cultural Change*, Vol. 28, No. 2 (January 1980): 267-91. The supposed causal link between authoritarianism and dependent development was best made by Guillermo O'Donnell, "Reflections on the Patterns of Change in the Bureaucratic-Authoritarian State," *Latin American Research Review*, Vol. 13, No. 1 (1978): 3-38. The link, however, was effectively refuted in David Collier, ed., *The New Authoritarianism in Latin America* (Princeton: Princeton University Press, 1979).
5. Francis Fukuyama, "The End of History," *The National Interest* 16 (Summer 1989), p. 4.
6. David Harvey, *A Brief History of Neoliberalism*, p. 2.
7. Hugo Radice, "The Crisis of the Global South: From Development to Capitalism," *Economic and Political Weekly*, Vol. XLVI, No. 48 (November 26, 2011), p. 31.
8. Ibid.
9. Quoted in *Economist*, "Unbottled Gini," January 20, 2011, available http://www.economist.com/node/17957381, accessed on November 15, 2011
10. Samuel P. Huntington, *The Third Wave: Democratisation in the Late Twentieth Century* (Norman, OK: University of Oklahoma Press, 1991), 290-94.
11. Fareed Zakaria, "The Rise of Illiberal Democracy," *Foreign Affairs* 76 (November/December 1997): 22-43; Larry Diamond, "The Democratic Rollback: The Resurgence of the Predatory State,"

Foreign Affairs 87 (March/April 2008): 36-48.

12. Steven Levitsky and Lucan A. Way, "The Rise of Competitive Authoritarianism," *Journal of Democracy* 13 (April 2002), 51.
13. Jean Dreze and Amartya Sen, "Putting Growth in its Place," *Outlook* (November 14, 2011): 53.
14. Notwithstanding its polemics, the link between resource extraction and the growing Naxalite threat facing India is well captured in Arundhati Roy, *Walking with the Comrades* (New York: Penguin Books, 2011).
15. The situation was such that designs on locally produced materials would wash off when laundered, restaurants were prevented from serving rice twice a week (with the masses encouraged to eat locally produced yams such as manioc), and people were forced to stand in line for hours to buy a single loaf of bread (which more often than not was half baked by unscrupulous bakers).
16. See Neil DeVotta, "Sri Lanka's Structural Adjustment Program and its Impact on Indo-Lanka Relations," *Asian Survey*, Vol. 38, No. 5 (May 1998), p. 458.
17. Mick Moore, "Economic Liberalisation Versus Political Pluralism in Sri Lanka?" *Modern Asian Studies*, Vol. 24, No. 2 (May 1990), p. 356.
18. Neil DeVotta, *Blowback: Linguistic Nationalism, Institutional Decay, and Ethnic Conflict in Sri Lanka* (Stanford: Stanford University Press, 2004); A. Jeyaratnam Wilson, *Sri Lankan Tamil Nationalism: Its Origin and Development in the Nineteenth and Twentieth Centuries* (Vancouver: University of British Columbia Press, 2000). Also see Alvin Rabushka and Kenneth A. Shepsle, *Politics in Plural Societies: A Theory of Democratic Instability* (Columbus, Oh.: Charles E. Merrill Publishing, 1972); Donald L. Horowits, *Ethnic Groups in Conflict* (Berkeley: University of California Press, 1985), Ch. 8.
19. Newton Gunasinghe, "The Open Market and Its Impact on Ethnic Relations in Sri Lanka," in Committee for Rational Development, *The Ethnic Conflict: Myths, Realities and Perspectives* (New Delhi: Navrang, 1984), p. 199.
20. *Economist*, "Sri Lanka Puts a Torch to its Future," August 6, 1983.
21. *Economist*, "Ergophobia," August 13, 1983, p. 29.
22. DeVotta, "Sri Lanka's Structural Adjustment"; S.D. Muni, *Pangs of Proximity: India's and Sri Lanka's Ethnic Crisis* (New Delhi: Sage Publications, 1993); Maya Chadda, *Ethnicity, Security, and Separatism in India* (New York: Columbia University Press, 1997).

23. Rajesh Venugopal, "The Politics of Market Reform at a Time of Civil War: Military Fiscalism in Sri Lanka," *Economic and Political Weekly*, Vol. XLVI, No. 49 (December 3, 2011): 67-75.
24. For an argument that equates the authoritarian practices in Sri Lanka with those in Russia, see Neil DeVotta, "From Civil War to Soft Authoritarianism: Sri Lanka in Comparative Perspective," *Global Change, Peace, and Security*, Vol. 22, No. 3 (October 2010), pp. 331-43.

PART II

Neoliberalism and The State

2

Developmental State and its Sovereign Gaze

Samir Kumar Das

> The king now sits in his court. The subjects come in a delegation to express their grievances before him. He listens to them—yet does not seem to listen to them. He casts his gaze—yet does not seem to fix it and rarely makes an eye contact with them.
>
> — *Thakurmar Jhuli*

The pronunciation that 'God is dead' is widely believed to have finally rendered sovereignty redundant. It is now widely believed that sovereignty as a practice has suffered at least two—not altogether unrelated moments of crisis in recent times. On the one hand, decolonisation and the subsequent transition to postcolonial statehood in South Asia is believed to have stabilised the order of nation-states and settled such hard issues as reorganisation of interstate borders, internal pacification and establishment of the rule of law—the three key functions of the sovereign. Yet, sovereignty as a practice has its relevance for areas wherever such issues are yet to reach a final settlement—like parts of India's northeast or even the northwest. In other words, sovereignty is unevenly spread across the Indian territory. The transition to the postcolonial is also largely complemented by yet another transformation from the rule by the sovereign into government. Much has already been written on this transition particularly in recent years. As a result, sovereignty as an issue in politics is gradually relegated into the background—if not pushed into oblivion. Partha Chatterjee's famously titled book on *The Politics of the Governed* makes no mention of sovereignty or the sovereign at all while trying to understand democratic politics in 'most of the world'.

On the other hand, the transition to governance and governmentality in a certain sense has been reinforced by the forces and processes of globalisation released particularly in South Asia since the early 1990s. While the impact of globalisation on state sovereignty has been variously assessed in scholarly circles, even a cursory reading of the literature on this suggests that sovereignty in our era of globalisation has substantially reorganised the mix between sovereign rule and government—if not decisively undermined sovereignty. The concept of sovereignty has been engaged predominantly along these two trajectories of literature—albeit at a more theoretical level reflecting on the patently Foucauldian dichotomy between sovereignty and governmentality.

In this paper however, I propose to call this dichotomy into question with the help of a series of case studies on groups of persons displaced by the development projects in postcolonial India in order to show how the introduction of newer technologies of governance implies—not depreciation—but *governmentalisation of sovereignty*. In simple terms, it will be too extravagant to conceptualise sovereignty and governmentality in binary terms. The present paper seeks to drive home this argument only within the limited context of state responses to the internally displaced persons in India, that is to say, their displacement induced by development projects.

Governmentalisation of sovereignty is best understood as an economy of gaze that the sovereign casts with its mission of 'developing' its subjects. The sovereign in our era of globalisation is invested with its developing mission that functions through a complex economy of gaze—by way of fixing, calibrating and controlling it, by distributing and transferring it amongst its different subjects.

What I call the economy of sovereign gaze is to be distinguished from the otherwise widely used concept of governmentality. On the one hand, governmentality, as it is understood, is internal to one who is governed by it. The technologies of governance are deployed in a way that these are in tune with what Foucault calls 'the natural disposition of things' and contributes to what he calls in his *Discipline and Punish* 'positive economy'. In simple terms, governmentality is aimed at achieving the objective of self-governance by way of addressing the dispositions and 'convenience' of the governed and obtaining the perfect identity between the governor and the governed. However, I propose to argue that popular sovereignty pertaining to a given body of people having the potential of being self-governed reaches a threshold beyond which sovereignty no longer remains in the self, but turns as the *other*. The exercise of sovereignty is necessarily pitted against its subjects. This paper seeks to understand the nature and functioning of the threshold beyond which the exercise of power marks the reverse transition from government to rule, from governmentality to sovereignty – reverse of the transition that Partha Chatterjee and others have been referring to.

On the other hand, governmentality, for Foucault, is a ubiquitous concept. The web of governance is cast far and wide so much so that no one—according to him—remains outside its ambit. The 'art of government'—as Foucault famously puts it—is too widespread to leave any space outside it. Foucault defined the concept in maximal terms as one that encompasses everything—the entire web of social relations including relations amongst people, of people with 'things'. The technologies of governance are improvised and deployed—now on a global scale so much so that today one speaks of not local, regional or even national governance—but 'global governance'. By contrast, sovereignty defined as gaze is also likely to be cast through a tunnel producing a tunnel vision that leaves out many objects outside the tunnel. For the sovereign, these *objects simply do not exist* and therefore are deprived of any objective presence. The sovereign gaze is sovereign precisely in this sense—in the sense of having the power of defining its objects over which it is exercised, making them disappear at will, subjecting them to its gaze and thereby subjectifying them, that is say, enabling them as subjects, and most importantly pushing many others out of the tunnel. The sovereign thus deprives many of being objectified in its eye. In a recently published essay, I called them 'people without shadows', for, they remain outside the sovereign gaze and share only a spectral existence. Their existence leaves no shadows behind them.

I will argue that the dilemma inherent in the doctrine of popular sovereignty turned the sovereign as the other—an entity external to the democratic self. Insofar as the sovereign turns into the other, the gaze shapes up its objects by way of making many others 'disappear' from its vision. I call it the *moment of objectification* for it is precisely at this moment that the sovereign produces the object to which it directs itself as its other. Once the gaze is fixed, it turns the objects into the objects of development. I will argue that it is not the sovereign that initiates development—it is the development that becomes the sovereign by way of framing the objects into its scheme of things. As Deleuze and Guattari define it, the sovereign exists by fashioning the whole. I call it the *moment of development*. The third moment is what I call the *moment of configuration*. For, it is the gaze that also configures the space, the locale within which the object is sited—a space that eternally bears the flag of development—development of the nation—sans the people. The locale configures the nation in abstract terms—indeed the nation turns out to be too abstract to be identified with any living body of people so much so that anything and everything can be 'sacrificed' for the nation and not vice versa.

The Economy of Sovereign Gaze

This paper seeks to review not so much the role and mission of the Indian state in developing the country but their implications for the huge population displacement that has been taking place with a renewed vigour since the 1990s particularly in the wake of globalisation and most importantly the gaze that the state casts on the persons displaced by such a role and mission. While at one level it argues that the state's gaze on the displaced persons continues to be shaped by its developmentalist mission ('developmentality' as it is known in theoretical circles) and is actually a corollary to it, at another level it proposes to show

how there operates an economy informing the complexities involved in the state's gaze on the internally displaced persons (IDPs). Accordingly, the first part of the argument dwells on the continuity – if not an identity—between the development policies pursued by the Indian state particularly since independence and its albeit tentative and sporadic policy responses to the developmentally induced IDPs. The second part of the argument concentrates more on the complex functioning of an economy of gaze that—as the epigraph with which we began this paper tells us—calibrates the density, direction and distribution of gaze, manages and controls its impact, fixes its objects and also makes many of the victims 'disappear' from it. Like the king of the popular Bengali fairy tale mentioned above, the state 'casts its gaze—yet does not fix it and rarely makes any eye contact with them'. It is a gaze that is at the same time not a gaze for it retains—if not reinforces—the power asymmetry that exists between the developmentalist state and its hapless victims. The gaze, as we will see, is emblematic of the state's exercise of sovereign power.

India is too large and diverse a country to warrant any simple generalisation. The paper for reasons of convenience draws on select cases distributed across time and regions while driving home its argument. Both Bhakra and Farakka projects showcased by the Indian state as symbols of development in independent India were made fully functional in 1959 and 1975 respectively. The two projects aptly sum up India's continuing nationalist consensus with development and disillusionment started gradually to set in only by the middle of the 1980s. For, while both—Bhakra in particular—were responsible for huge displacement of population, there was hardly any murmur of protest heard during this time. It is only in the mid-1980s that the Bhakra oustees became aware of their rights and established their organisations and it was not till early 2000 that the organisations working with the victims of riverbank erosion reportedly induced by the construction of the Farakka barrage demanded non-engineering solutions to their plight. The demographic landscape of Karnataka's Kuduremukh region has been changing rapidly with the introduction of mining operations in the late-1960s and the establishment of a National Park as recently as 1997. The same nationalist euphoria with development made the problem of displacement 'disappear' from the public eye and the people migrating from outside and employed in such projects have been agitating for fear of any possible loss of jobs due to shutdown of these projects. Orissa today has become the new destination of foreign direct investment. Being the poorest of Indian states, industrialisation is touted in official circles as Orissa's answer to staggering poverty, while the fear of losing land, resources and livelihood encourages the potential victims to agitate and even lay down their lives and successfully hold up work—as in the case of POSCO, the Korean steel giant, for the last three years. Bhakra in the northwest, Kuduremukh in the south, Farakka and Orissa in the east provide incredibly varied experiences with the state's developmentalist gaze falling upon the victims of displacement.

Although varied in their own ways, our case studies point out at one level how the policy responses are shaped by the state's developmentalist gaze. Development—whether by the construction of mega-barrages and dams or by the introduction of large-scale mining operations or by the notification of national parks and forest reserves and setting up of industries with the help of foreign capital—continues to be defined as that of the nation notwithstanding that it displaces millions of people, deprives them of their means of livelihood and tears the family and social ties asunder with disastrous consequences. The nation is always defined by the state in abstract terms—indeed too abstract to be identified with any of its parts or even any of their combination. The gaze of the state is cast on an abstract nation that lies well beyond the world of appearance in which millions of visibly hapless victims exist and does not seem to contain the concrete living persons who have to lose their homestead and cultivable land and pay the price of development. Yet, this loss makes the nation possible. Their loss is constitutive of the nation formation. The gaze is characterised by ambivalence between what they are and what they can potentially become and brings about as it were a certain transformation in their lives from concrete living beings—who have to survive above all else for themselves perhaps more than for others—into beings cloned to make sacrifices for developing the nation. While gazing at them, the king gazes at them not as what they are and appear before his eyes but as what they could become—the nuts and bolts of the nation. He sees them and yet does not quite see them. The gaze is marked by this perennial ambivalence between being and becoming of a nation.

For many a political theorist, the sovereign power of a state circulates through this complex economy of gaze. For, the modern state by 'inscribing, stabilising, and rendering effective a certain figure of the citizen' claims to deploy its sovereign power (Soguk 1999: 39) and abstracts the nation defined as a body of citizens from those who are called upon to pay the price of its development and welfare. Our studies will show how this differentiation is effected, first, by making the victims 'disappear' as in the case of Kuduremukh; second, by restricting the scope of nation to such inanimate assets and objects as port, roads and railway tracks, barrages, embankments and dams and so forth and protecting them[1]—if necessary at the expense of the victims—as in the case of riverbank erosion in Malda; and thirdly, by attempting to 'resettle and rehabilitate' them without in any way compromising with or interrupting the tempo of industrialisation as in the case of Orissa. It seems that the Indian state has exhausted its power of ruling over the people through the development discourse and has been increasingly resorting to violence and coercion in order to effect this differentiation and realise its sovereign power. Despite all the ongoing debates on the imperative of redefining sovereignty in the age of globalisation, the sovereign state in its typically Schmittian form seems to have staged a comeback in India (Schmitt 2007: 39).

While it was successful in forging a nationalist consensus around development during the initial decades of India's independence, disillusionment at another level started to set in by the end of the 1980s. The problem of displacement was 'born' precisely at that time (Das 2005: 120-21). The forces of globalisation and the introduction of the new economic policy in 1991 have only exacerbated the process. The responses of the Indian state—or the policy gaze as we term it—may be considered as a desperate attempt on the state's part to re-build the national consensus and the desperation is clear as we see growing polarisation taking place between the state with all its instruments of violence and baring its tooth and claw and the victims—potential or actual—taking it to the streets and vociferously protesting against it albeit with varying degree of success. Globalisation in other words has invested the state with the responsibility of rebuilding the nation - if necessary through violent means given that the nationalist consensus shows signs of being irretrievably eroded, rather than 'denationalising' it—as Saskia Sassen (2006) would have us believe.

Victims Do Not Exist

Although the number of erosion-affected victims in Malda and Murshidabad is yet to be officially recorded, they—according to Rudra—constitute 'the longest list of displaced persons in West Bengal' (Rudra 2006: 37). The reason cited by the government officials is strange and betrays complete lack of thinking in this regard. While the State Irrigation Department considers that its duty remains confined to the loss of land and other civil structures and assets, the District Relief and Rehabilitation Department can only dish out figures of those who have been provided with relief and rehabilitation. Not all victims are fortunate enough to receive them.

According to an unofficial estimate, the number of victims affected by erosion so far must have crossed the one million mark. In 2005, four villages in Malda disappeared as a result of river erosion rendering at least 1100 families homeless. In the same year—two villages, namely, Paraspur and Tantani were washed away in the district of Murshidabad. Now about 3 million people are facing the threat of losing their homes and agricultural land in these two districts. In course of my field visits, I have witnessed victims who have lost their homes 4-16 times in their lifetime. It is as if the river has been constantly chasing after them. Government assistance is in the nature of providing temporary rations and tarpaulins to the victims for about 20 days and to provide Rs. 5000 as compensation and two cottahs of land. Identification of such land will have to be done by the victims themselves. There is hardly any land within the affordable range of the victims. Only 1956 plots of land could be identified—of which only 850 have been registered till August 2004.[2] In most cases, kickbacks and cut money were paid to the middlemen for expediting the deal.

Where do these victims go? Many of them in Malda live haphazardly on public lands along the highways and roads in slums and makeshift shacks and neighbouring orchards. What struck us in course of our field visit is the community-wise resettlement of the Hindus and Muslims who used to live in the same village cheek by jowl till it was eroded. Though the migrant-native polarisation is becoming stronger, the communal feeling amongst the evicted has not yet taken any alarming turn. About one hundred thousand people of 64 Mouzas spread over three blocks, according to an unofficial estimate, presently live in the river islands or sandbars (*chars*) produced as a result of the shifting course of the river. The settlement of victims in newly emerged *chars* is by no means easy. Although it is done in strict conformity with the already eroded village (a principle of justice that in local parlance is known as *khadir*), money, muscle and power play an important role. They are deprived of all the basic amenities of life including law and order, roads and transport, health centres, primary schools and, most importantly, voting rights. The total length of these *chars* of various shapes and sizes is estimated to be about 200 sq kms in the district. Most of the children remain outside the government's immunisation programmes. The people in these *chars* have to live in virtual anarchy. They become easy victims of river piracy, dacoity and many other sex-related crimes. On January 24, 1992, about a dozen women coming in a country-made boat from Gadai *char* were gang-raped by the ruffians allegedly from the then Bihar—referred to in popular parlance as *thiya* party (*Maldaha Samachar* January 29, 1992: 1). The same *char* witnessed another round of violence on June 25, 2000 when 23 women were again reportedly gang-raped (*Rupantarer Pathe,* August 6, 2000).

There are conflicts of jurisdiction over these *chars* between

India and Bangladesh, between two Indian states of West Bengal and Jharkhand and between two districts of West Bengal. The erosion has in fact washed away many border posts making the demarcation difficult—if not impossible—sometimes triggering off major border disputes with Bangladesh. As Saha points out: "Most of the border clashes arose out of disputes over ownership of *char* land in the border areas"(Saha 2000: 119). Although the Government of India insists that the borders are fixed on the map irrespective of the change in course of the Ganges, Bangladesh refuses to accept this position. If border stands at the mid-channel of an international river, then with the shift of the river the mid-channel too shifts towards India. According to government records, about 356 sq kms of land has been eroded in the district of Murshidabad between 1931 and 1999 resulting in the emergence of *chars* on the other side to which Bangladesh lays its claim. This also results in exchanges of fire between the border police of the two countries. Both India and Bangladesh insist on keeping the water disputes separate from political conflicts over borders as part of their strategy (Nishat and Faisal 2000: 289-310). But, erosion and emergence of *chars* are probably one area where this otherwise successful principle of separation—as they would have us believe—may not be as effective in the long run. The state governments can do very little in this regard as the central government in India's federal structure retains 'the overall management authority' (Giordino et al. 2002: 218).

Similarly, the *char* that has been slowly surfacing in the west bank of the Ganges comprising 191.41 sq kms of land, according to a mass convention organised on September 2, 2001 at Panchanandapur, Malda belongs to West Bengal 'beyond any doubt'—although it is under the jurisdiction of the Jharkhand administration at present. This involves 19 *mouzas* and about 50,000 people. The convention urged the West Bengal Government to take up the issue and settle it without any further delay. Political leaders including ministers of West Bengal have brought the matter to the attention of the central government.[3] The Registrar General of India ordered double census enumeration of Palasgachhi *char* by both the contending states till the dispute is resolved. While underlining the importance of the 'cooperative bargaining framework' in the settlement of water disputes, Alan Richards and Nirvikar Singh of the University of California, Santa Cruz, caution us that any delay in this regard "can encourage inefficient, non-cooperative investments" (Richards and Singh 1996 mimeo). Similarly, as a *char* was surfacing in 2001 along the Malda-Murshidabad border, villagers belonging to Gyamanpara and Ataritola of Malda and Palasipara, Nimtala and Ghoshpara of Murshidabad clashed against each other on December 27, 2001 over its possession (*Jangipur Sambad*, January 3, 2001).

They work mostly as construction workers in booming realities of India, as domestic help and maids, as workers in jewellery workshops, as trafficked women and sex workers and the incidence of AIDS and sexually transmitted diseases is reported to be very high. Those, who are left here, work as *bidi* (country cigarettes) makers, weavers, run tea stalls and cigarette kiosks along the roads, serve as coolies, van rickshaw pullers, petty fruit and fish vendors, etc.[4] While the government still insists on looking for engineering solutions and scientific truths, all this has lost much of its gloss in the eye of the people. Indian Science is no longer a spectacle—a 'Taj Mahal' as Ashis Nandy would have us believe, it is increasingly being viewed as an all-devouring monster. My field visits to different erosion-affected areas of Malda and Murshidabad suggest that people have gradually come to realise the unstoppable nature of erosion and the mockery of anti-erosion measures. Instead, they want government policies to focus on people and the concrete human beings who are affected by it. We have evidences to suggest that even as late as in 1999, the Ganga-Bhangon Pratirodh Nagarik Action Committee was asking for engineering measures that would prevent and manage floods and erosion.[5] It is only in 2007, that it asked for compensation for those who were victimised by erosion between 1965 and 2007.

Strange but true, the Government of West Bengal has as yet no policy regarding the resettlement and rehabilitation for the victims of a slow and protracted process of riverbank erosion. The specialists and voluntary groups working with them have persistently been underlining the importance of a master plan in this regard. Whatever measures have been undertaken is in the nature of providing immediate relief and succour to the victims. The government has done little—if anything—in terms of rehabilitating the victims on a long-term basis. It is yet to formulate any resettlement and rehabilitation policy although the state in recent times is poised up for a major leap for industrialisation. While the Resettlement and Rehabilitation Bill tabled in Parliament of India in 2007 provides for payment of 60 per cent compensation before land acquisition and consequent displacement, government officials in West Bengal have reportedly dismissed it as "impractical". It is true that the government is seriously thinking of formulating a draft; one can well imagine the course that this policy might take in the near future.

Rebuilding the Consensus: The Policy Gaze

As India became independent and took off on the road to industrial development, the installation of massively displacing development projects, barrages and dams did not seem to create even a flutter of resentment. We saw people as in the Bhakra case who were ready to undertake 'little sacrifices' for 'national' development and perhaps eager to pay the price of development of the nation as a whole. The nation was visualised by the state not only as undivided and indivisible but greater than any of its parts or even any of their combination. As this nationalist consensus gradually gets fractured in the wake of globalisation particularly since the late 1980s and the development model of the state faces mounting criticisms, the need for enunciating policies basically meant for reincorporating the fragments into the national body and reestablishing the consensus is more deeply felt. Globalisation therefore coincides with a hitherto unprecedented policy explosion particularly since the 1990s. The Ministry of Rural Development (Government of India) came up with at least half a dozen policy drafts on resettlement and rehabilitation during this period—the latest being the Draft National Policy of Rehabilitation and Resettlement (2006).[6]

Political Theory makes a distinction between the language

of policies and that of rights. Rights are basically defined as claims against the collective, viz. the nation, while policies aim at protecting and securing it against threats. Insofar as the once-vibrant nationalist consensus shows signs of being irretrievably eroded, the collective is also getting vivisected into innumerable fragments. State policies—meant for re-placing and reincorporating these fragments into the national collective—are unlikely to make the latter exactly the same as before. The nation being rebuilt in the age of globalisation will be unrecognisably distinct from what it was in the earlier era. The Indian nation—like most of the nations in today's world—is passing through a great transition. Its scope has incredibly shrunk in recent years (Das 2007 mimeo).

For many, rehabilitation as guaranteed by the latest policy draft is only an adjunct to development—meant basically for assuaging the concerns of the displaced persons produced by it. We have reasons to feel that it is more a development policy than a rehabilitation policy. At no point, is the right against displacement viewed as a value in itself—a reason good enough for scrapping development projects that induce mass displacement and dispensing with the presently followed development strategies—although it talks about compensation in case one is affected by them. While non-displacing or least displacing alternatives need to be explored as per the provisions of the draft, there is absolutely no guarantee that development projects might be scrapped if alternatives could not be found. In short, protection against displacement is never viewed from a rights-based perspective whether by the central government or by the Government of Orissa. More importantly, the land requiring agency is made only partially accountable in the sense that it would get permission under this policy and is to bear the cost of compensation. But it does not make proper rehabilitation a precondition for sanctioning the project in the first place.

Way back in 2000, three of us suggested a typology of internal displacement in the South Asian context and argued in favour of adopting a more nuanced and intricate policy that would take care of the complexities involved in each of these types (Das et al. 2000: 51-52). The present policy draft seems to have rolled all such complexities into one and privileged only one of them—displacement induced by development. We need to ponder why other varieties of displacement particularly the one induced by ethnic and communal conflicts and violence are excluded from its ambit. To borrow Alain Badiou's famous phrase, violence beyond the state's domain constitutes, 'phenomenality without object' (Badiou 2006: 1-8)—for, its recognition as a policy object implies an absurd admission on the state's part of its inability to monopolise the instruments of violence in the society. The government has tabled a Communal Violence Bill in 2007 and this has already sparked off a controversy. The policy draft is also oblivious to population displacement induced by such natural calamities and catastrophes as Tsunamis, cyclones, earthquakes and floods. While development is responsible for displacement, strange but true, displacement in the present era has also become a tool of development. Frequent cycles of communal violence in such cities as Mumbai, Ahmedabad and Vadodara show how population shifts have occurred within and across the cities and how the cities are increasingly being divided into well-garrisoned and planned spaces for the rich and the vast sections of the poor and underprivileged are herded into the unplanned interiors of the walled parts. Such displacement has spawned a new kind of urban development.

As a result, the policy never confers recognition on what we consider as people's inalienable right to home. Although the draft speaks of 'prior informed consent', it makes little room for discussion. The administration is obliged to give the project and the impending displacement its widest publicity. Does this give enough scope for what Chomsky calls, 'manufacturing' of consent (Herman and Chomsky 1988)? There seems to be a standard government lingo that they must go to the people and make them understand the benefits of industrialisation and should wean them away from the 'conspiracy' of those who are putting up 'unprincipled opposition'.[7] Besides, what are the people supposed to deliberate on? This consent is only limited to the question of rehabilitation. The development design is above any kind of democratic auditing and scrutiny.[8] Insofar as dialogues and deliberations as democratic processes are cast off from the development discourse, the state is seen to resort increasingly to violence and coercion in order to get it across the general public. The policy gaze of the state articulates a 'social whole' (cf. Chatterjee 1994: 51-72) and only helps in legitimising the state's exercise of violence and coercion over any of the sections of its population. The message is clear: if the victims refuse or resist, they will be forced to acquiesce to the development consensus. The more they are forced to become part of the prefabricated consensus, the more the development discourse loses its shine and state power acquires its rabidly biopolitical character. The bodies of the IDPs are stamped as it were with the seal of state sovereignty. It seems that the policies of both the Centre and the states in India are only part of the larger developmentalist discourse that has overwhelmed the Indian state particularly in the wake of globalisation. Federal relations do not appear to have any impact on the state responses to developmentally-induced displacement.

The state's gaze, as we argue, speaks of this irresolvable ambivalence—that between the immediate world of particular victims and the imagined social whole that lies at a distance, between being and becoming of our nation. The gaze is also not a gaze for it is cast on objects that are not made but are in the making. Its ambivalence is prompted by the inherent unrealisability of our nationhood. The nation has to develop more in order to exist at present than to flourish in the future and therefore has no end.

REFERENCES

[All translations from original non-English sources are of the author]

Anonymous (2004). 'Maldate Ganga' (in Bengali) [The Ganges in Malda]. *Darpane Muktaman*, August.

Badiou, Alain (2006), *Metapolitics*. London: Verso.

Bandyopadhyay, J. and K. Rudra (2004). 'Jalbaithak' (in Bengali) [Discussion Forum on Water]. *Monchasha*, March.

Bandyopadhyay, K., S. Ghosh and N. Dutta (2006). *Eroded Lives: Riverbank Erosion and Displacement of Women in West Bengal.* Kolkata: Calcutta Research Group.

Chatterjee, P. (1994). 'Development Planning and the Indian State' in: T.J. Byres (ed.), *The State and Development Planning in India*. New Delhi: Oxford University Press.

Chatterjee, Partha (2004). *The Politics of the Governed: Reflections on Popular Politics in Most of the World*. New York: Columbia University Press.

Chaudhuri, A. (2007). 'Banya Bhangon Dushan Pediye' (in Bengali) [Overcoming Floods, Erosion, Contamination]. *Ekak Matra* (Kolkata), 7(5), March.

Das, D.K. and T.K. Chattopadhyay (2007). 'Ganga Erosion: A Non-Technocratic View', Papers on Democratic Governance 11, UGC-DRS (Phase I) Programme. Kolkata: Department of Political Science, University of Calcutta.

Das, S.K. (2005). 'India: Homelessness at Home' in: P. Banerjee, S. Basu Ray Chaudhury and S.K. Das (eds.), *Internal Displacement in South Asia*. New Delhi: Sage.

Das, S.K. (2007). 'What is this Nation that the World is Turning to? Nationalism and Citizenship in the Age of Globalisation', mimeo. Helsinki: Helsinki Collegium of Advanced Studies.

Das, S.K. (2008). 'Introduction' in: S.K. Das (ed.), *Blisters on Their Feet: Tales of Internally Displaced Persons in India's North East*. New Delhi: Sage.

Das, S., S. Basu Ray Chaudhury and T. Bose (2000). 'Forced Migration in South Asia: A Critical Review'. *Refugee Survey Quarterly*, 19(2).

Dey, I. and S. Basu Ray Chaudhuri (eds.) (2007). *The Responsibility to Protect: IDPs and Our National and State Human Rights Commissions*, A Report by Calcutta Research Group. Kolkata: Calcutta Research Group.

Fernandes, W. and M. Asif (2007). *Development Induced Displacement and Rehabilitation in Orissa 1951-1995*, mimeo.

Fernandes, W., M. Kumar, P. Mathur Velath, S. Roohi, I. Dey and S. K. Das (2007). *The Druft National Rehabilitation Policy: A Critique*, Policies and Practices 16. Kolkata: Calcutta Research Group.

Foucault, Michel (1977) *Discipline and Punish: The Birth of Prison*. Translated from the French by Ian Sheridan. New York: Vintage Books.

Giordino, M., M. Giordino and A. Wolf (2002). 'The Geography of Water Conflict and Cooperation: Internal Pressures and International Cooperation'. *The Geographical Journal*, 168(4), December.

Herman, Edward and Noam Chomsky (1988). *Manufacturing Consent: Political Economy of Mass Media*. New York: Pantheon.

Malda CPI (M) District Committee (2004). 'Boundary Disputes between West Bengal and Jharkhand/Bihar with Special Reference to Malda District Due to Shifting of the River Ganga: Correspondences and Comments' (mimeo).

Nandy, A. (1986). 'The Idea of Development: The Experience of Modern Psychology as a Cautionary Tale and as an Allegory' in: Carlos A Hallmann and Oscar Nudler (eds.), *Human Development in its Social Context: A Collective Exploration*. London: Hodder & Stroughton in association with the UN University.

Nandy, A. (2003). 'The Scope and Limits of Dissent: India's First Modern Environmentalist and His Critique of the DVC' in: Ashis Nandy, *The Romance of the State and the Fate of Dissent in the Tropics*. New Delhi: Oxford University Press.

Nishat, A. and I.M. Faisal (2000). 'An Assessment of the Institutional Mechanism for Water Negotiations in the Ganges-Brahmaputra-Meghna System'. *International Negotiation*, 5.

Patel, A. (2007). 'Globalisation, Patriarchal Development, and the Protesting Voices in Orissa' in A. Patel and M. Jha, *Weapons of the Weak: Field Studies on Claims to Social Justice in Bihar and Orissa*, Policies and Practices 13. Kolkata: Calcutta Research Group.

Richards, A. and N. Singh (1996), 'Water and Federalism: Institutions Governing Inter-State River Waters', mimeo.

Rudra, K. (1999). 'Maldahe Gangar Bhangon Pratirodh: Bikalpa Bhavna' (in Bengali) [Resisting Erosion of the Ganges in Malda: Alternative Thoughts]. *Ekahn Bisambad* (Kolkata), 3(2), October.

Rudra, K. (2002). *Ganga-Bhangon Katha* (in Bengali) [The Story of the Ganges Erosion]. Kolkata: Mrittika.

Rudra, K. (2006). 'Charer Manusher Votadhikar Nei' (in Bengali) [The People of River Islands Do Not Have Voting Rights], *Hriday*, Special Annual Collection on 'Eviction and Development', January.

Rudra, K. (n.d.). 'Ganga Ki Farakka Byartha Kare Anya Path Bechhe Nebe?' (in Bengali) [Will the Ganges Take Another Course Bypassing the Farakka?], mimeo.

Saha, Rekha (2000). *India-Bangladesh Relations*. Calcutta: Minerva.

Sassen, S. (2006). *Territory, Authority, Rights: From Medieval to Global Assemblages*. Princeton: Princeton University Press.

Schmitt, C. (2007). *The Concept of the Political*, expanded edition, trans, intro and notes by George Schwab. Chicago: University of Chicago Press.

Soguk, Nevzat (1999). *States and Citizens: Refugees and the Displacements of Statecraft*. Minneapolis: University of Minnesota Press.

Newspapers

Jangipur Sambad (Jangipur)
Maldaha Samachar (Malda)
Rupantarer Pathe (Berhampur)

NOTES

1. For a critique of it, see, Nandy (1986: 257-58).
2. The information has been gathered from 'Maldate Ganga' (2004: 15).
3. The full texts of some of these correspondences are available in a booklet on 'Boundary Disputes between West Bengal and Jharkhand/Bihar with Special Reference to Malda District Due to Shifting of the River Ganga: Correspondences and Comments' (2004).
4. For a detailed account of the socio-economic conditions of the erosion-affected victims particularly the women amongst them, see, Bandyopadhyay et al. (2006).
5. Vide, the Committee's letter to the District Magistrate, Malda dated January 5, 1999.
6. A Rehabilitation and Resettlement Bill prepared in line with the provisions of this policy was tabled in Parliament in 2007.
7. The ruling Left Front Government appreciates the importance of making people understand the virtues of development in the wake of such momentous public protests against land acquisition and displacement as in Singur and Nandigram in 2006-2007.
8. For a more comprehensive critique of the policy drafts in this regard, see Fernandes et al. 2007).

3

Demise of the Developmental State or a Redefinition: Lessons from the State of Andhra Pradesh

Radhika Kumar

Development theory has been witness to numerous shifts in terms of defining development as well as the trajectory best suited to achieve development. While ideological extremes are usually presented in terms of the neo-Marxist and neoliberal school of thought, it is the latter which has come to dominate development debates as also determine the economic policy of most states. However in adopting neoliberalisation, the indigenous context of the state concerned has played as much a role as external compulsions of borrowing from multilateral lending agencies.

In the case of India the latter has often been presented as the fait-accompli justifying adoption of the New Economic Policy by the government in 1991. Indigenous factors have played a multi-pronged role in the policy shift from a mixed economy to a free market economy. While some commentators have seen the industrial classes as the main driving force behind adopting liberalisation others have concentrated on the electoral considerations as having affected the pace and prospect of reforms. Electoral aspirations of marginalised groups have not been easy to reconcile with policies of structural adjustment that demand successive cuts in distribution of state largesse.

Herein it is neoliberal theory itself which comes to the rescue of the political class. Unlike modernisation theory which started with a society-centred analysis, neoliberalism does not posit the relation between the state and market as essentially antagonistic. Rather the state is seen as essential to maintain the policy framework which would keep the reforms going as also ensure recovery of loans. The role of the state is defined in terms of 'good governance' which seen critically is actually a recipe for 'limited governance'. The role of the state thus having been redefined and there being increasing instances of incumbent governments being re-elected one is led to ask the question about the nature of the state in the time of neo-liberalisation.

Through this paper I wish to look at the various ways in which neoliberalisation perceives the state, the extent to which states concerned have imbibed these tenets or otherwise modified the same. Have these played a role in determining their electoral fortunes and in what way? For this purpose I would like to look at the state of Andhra Pradesh which was one of the first to undertake reforms following negotiation of a structural adjustment loan from the World Bank in 1996. The successive victory of the Telugu Desam Party in the 1999 elections was seen as a mandate for liberalisation. The state thus seemed to have found the right fit in terms of conducting economic reforms aggressively as also continuing with populist measures. It is this electoral and economic formula that I wish to interrogate which may be instructive in mapping the contours of the state, i.e. its nature and attributes in the larger context of neoliberalisation.

Forging of a Strategic Partnership: The World Bank and Initiation of Economic Reforms in Andhra Pradesh

The possibility of states in India charting out an independent course of development has been a feature typical of the decade of the 1990s. Following adoption of economic liberalisation by the central government the responsibility of the latter towards the states with respect to the transfer of funds also got diluted. States were expected to maintain greater fiscal discipline

(Rudolph and Rudolph 2001: 154-155) and raise their own resources for purposes of development. This could be seen as an opportunity available to state governments to adopt development strategies that were locally suited. On the other hand, this also translated into the possibility of state governments borrowing funds from foreign multilateral lending agencies such as the World Bank and the IMF. The Bank in turn was also keen that state governments undertake reforms. This was the only way that loan recoveries could be possible. It has been estimated that the state's deficit constituted more than half of the overall deficit. In the case of Andhra Pradesh usual conditionalities imposed by the central government in cases of external borrowing were also waived. While acting as a guarantor in case of external borrowing by a state government, 15 per cent of the loan amount is withheld by the central government. However in the instance of the Andhra Pradesh Economic Restructuring Programme (APERP) this requirement was done away with. Reasons for the Andhra case being treated sympathetically can perhaps be traced to the regionalisation of national politics. The entrenchment of coalition politics at the centre which began in the mid-1990s led to regional parties such as the Telugu Desam Party (TDP) gaining currency at the national level.

Naidu initiated reforms in a two-pronged manner. On the one hand, he released a number of white papers apprising the people of the need to undertake reforms. These concerned state finances as well as restructuring of public sector units including the Andhra Pradesh State Electricity Board (APSEB). A number of committees were also set up for these purposes including rationalising employment in the government sector.

On the other hand, he took a series of steps to showcase to the Bank the creditworthiness of the state for purposes of release of the loan. He initiated the shift in policy by reversing the two main poll promises which were the basis on which N.T.Ramarao had won the 1994 state assembly election. The price of Rs 2 a kg for rice for the poor was now revised upwards to Rs 3.50 and the quantity of rice available in the scheme was reduced from 25 kgs to 20 kgs. The government saving on account of these two measures amounted to Rs 600 crores. Secondly, total prohibition was abolished. Further in 1996 water rates for purposes of irrigation were also upwardly revised while electricity charges were increased across the board.

The Bank on its part was quite appreciative of the measures undertaken by Naidu, in particular passage of the Power Sector Reforms Act which was a precondition for grant of loan. Let us then look at some of the key features of the restructuring programme that formed the basis of economic reforms in Andhra Pradesh. Fiscal discipline was to be established by reduction in fiscal deficit. The same was to be achieved by laying off state government employees, targeting of beneficiaries particularly of the rice subsidy scheme as well as across the board increase in prices of all public utilities. What was interesting to note was the comprehensive nature of reforms. These were not sector specific policies but broad based structural changes marking a clear shift from the welfare state to a limited state. The role of the state according to World Bank terminology was now designed as a 'facilitator' and 'enabler' rather than as a 'provider'. The APERP also included provisions for doubling the expenditure on health and education, however all these services and facilities were to be placed on a 'cost-effective' path. Users of various public services were expected to participate in the working and maintenance of schools, heath centres, irrigation systems, water tanks and all other local infrastructure such as roads, community centres, etc.

The Politics and Economics of Stakeholder Associations: Lessons from the Agrarian Sector

Participation of stakeholders in maintaining and running of various facilities has been another feature of the development strategy favoured by the World Bank. The idea of 'social capital' as a usable resource for purposes of development was first mooted by the World Bank. While the Bank's understanding has been seen as lacking a perspective which includes issues of class and power (Hariss 2001), the idea of 'participation' and promoting local level people's organisations is central to alternative views of development. Discrediting of the idea of participation as promoted by the World Bank has also been from an ideological perspective. Wedded as the Bank is to the neo-liberal view of development the notion of participation is seen as a guise for imposition of user charges and cost-recovery mechanisms. By placing the onus of development on people by talking about people's participation, states can effectively abdicate their responsibility as the primary agent of development.

Andhra Pradesh seems to have internalised most of these policy prescriptions of the World Bank. In consonance with these recommendations, village education committees and water users' committees (WUA) were set up in the state by passing laws regarding the same. Setting up of water users' committees was particularly important as it was a part of agricultural reforms initiated by the government in 1996. Andhra Pradesh in fact set up 10,000 water users' associations. The purpose of the same was to establish local control over use of water as well as promote equity. However, neither of these goals was achieved. The reasons for the same are not just a case of bad economics but also political. As argued by Ratna Reddy (2003), water users' associations in Andhra Pradesh are essentially funded by foreign funds as was provided for under the APERP. These funds have either been spent on rehabilitation and maintenance of existing water works or have act itself which set up the associations only deals with surface irrigation while 2/3rds of the total cropped area is actually covered by ground irrigation. Moreover reduction in public investment in irrigation has resulted in wells becoming the main source of irrigation as opposed to tanks and canals. These are also regionally varied. Rayalseema and Telangana regions of the state have seen an increase in instances of well irrigation as opposed to coastal Andhra which is drained by the Godavari and Krishna rivers. The switch to well irrigation has in fact enhanced inequalities within the Telangana and Rayalseema area. Only the rich are in a position to afford well irrigation.

However the politicisation of these water users' associations has been their main weakness. Elections to these bodies are mostly fought on a partisan basis such that being president of a

WUA is seen as an important way of asserting local influence. Also when contractors get hold of the post of the president of a WUA then the element of equity takes a back seat.

The initiative of setting up WUAs is a part of the larger reform strategy followed by the state government in the agrarian sector. However quite paradoxically it is also this sector that has registered the largest number of farmer suicides in the country. Officially it has been argued that, "Three of every four farmers who committed suicide in India (2000-2002) came from Andhra Pradesh" (Kumar 2003). It has been claimed that the agrarian crisis in Andhra Pradesh became acute particularly after the initiation of economic reforms (Revathi and Galab 2010: 192). The reasons for the same are multipronged. State withdrawal is particularly evident with regard to public investment in agriculture which nosedived from 8.5 per cent in the 1980s to 1.4 per cent. The other state input in terms of extending credit to the agrarian sector has also been declining. The decline is particularly noticed with regard to lending by cooperative banks. These banks are known to extend credit to small and marginal farmers. Overall it is quoted that, "The share of small borrowers in total bank credit declined from 22 per cent in 1991 to 7 per cent in 2001", (Ibid: 197). Besides these factors, closure of various agriculture-related corporations and cooperatives which were engaged in development of seeds, promoting agro-industries and providing support to farmers have removed the safety-net that the state afforded. Farmers have therefore come to be exposed directly to the volatility of the market. While minimum support prices have increased faster in the 1990s as opposed to the 1980s, the input costs have exceeded the output prices which are a clear indicator of the crisis in the agrarian sector. There is also persistence of variations across class and regions with respect to access to institutional credit and dependence on non-food crops. The shift from cereals to raising cash crops such as cotton and oilseeds results in farmers being left with no food crops for personal consumption. This shift has also been attributed to market forces. Apart from the fact that farmers wish to participate in the 'second green revolution' cultivating non-food crops there is aspirational competitiveness between farmers of the backward regions and the more developed regions of the state. The latter factor is rather important as it also explains why farmer suicides are predominant in the more developed states as opposed to the low income states. It has been argued that, "....'high aspirations' or the thrust for upward mobility in the absence of public policy support, as a major causation for suicides in the backward areas of medium growth states"(Ibid: 201).

The question whether stakeholder associations as agents of development at the grassroots level should be promoted as opposed to representative institutions is a question that has no clear answers. Stakeholder associations are usually insulated from partisan politics which dominates in representative institutions. On the other hand, stakeholder associations are often cultivated by governments to maintain their toehold at the local level. If the latter be the case then stakeholder associations cannot be free of the influence of local politics. In the case of Andhra Pradesh membership in these various stakeholder associations is quite politicised. This has been accentuated by existence of habitation level committees of the Telugu Desam Party. These various committees provide opportunities to accommodate aspiring local party leaders. It has been argued that a relatively unimportant appointment such as those of the *anganwadi* (nursery) teacher by the mothers' committee is seen as a show of strength by the concerned parties (Powis 2003: 2617-2622). More importantly these local level networks helped Naidu cultivate a strong party structure which could successfully be mobilised at the time of elections. Local party units also played a pivotal role in disbursing funds awarded to the panchayat for various development purposes. In effect therefore a parallel system of governance came to exist at the local level effectively bypassing the representative institutions. In fact it has been argued that all that the panchayat did was to decide beneficiaries for the centrally sponsored 'food for work' programme (Ibid.).

Reforms and Populism: The Case of Janambhoomi

Janambhoomi was one such programme championed by Naidu which involved mobilising these local level party networks for its implementation. However the purpose of looking at Janambhoomi in this context is to see it as symbolising the populist aspect of Naidu's development strategy in the state. Janambhoomi was launched by the government in 1997 as a people-oriented development programme. The three aspects of the programme included i) Prajala Vaddaku Palana or taking administration to the doorsteps of the people ii) Shramdanam or voluntary labour iii) Micro-planning. The focus areas of the programme were education, health, environment conservation, responsive governance and community works. The programme was conducted once every quarter for a week in what is called a 'campaign mode', i.e. involving intensive activities with Naidu touring the state and large-scale mobilisa-tion of the party, government functionaries and the people.

Micro-planning was initiated by drawing up development plans at the habitation level which would reflect local development requirements, the kind of community participation envisaged and the manner of mobilising resources. For the same a habitation level committee (HLC) was set up which included presidents of various SHGs and user associations apart from elected representatives and members of the bureaucracy. With regard to community works part of the cost was to be borne by the state while the rest was to be contributed by the community either in the form of labour, material or money. To ensure people's participation and ownership, all community works were to be implemented by the people themselves. Therefore contracting out of works was not allowed. Community works were further divided into three categories, i.e. priority, permissible and restricted. In the case of priority works government contribution was 70 per cent while in the case of permissible works the contribution was 50 per cent. The element of public-private partnership is quite evident in the way that the programme was designed. Also the involvement of local level committees was ensured. For instance in case of a community work involving construction of a school building, the village education committee president would be responsible for finalising an agreement with the executing agency. The pivotal role that various committees played in the programme effectively led to sidelining of the panchayat. In fact a kind of party-committee nexus emerged with most of the works being contracted out to private agents who found favour with the ruling party.

The other much celebrated and publicised component of Janambhoomi was 'responsive governance'. This was aimed at redressing both individual and community needs. The three categories included under this were Individual Financial Needs (IFN), Non-Financial Community Needs (NFCN) and Financial Community Needs (FCN). Applications for the same were collected during the Janambhoomi round and were expected to be redressed within a month to three months depending on whether the mandal or district/state administration was involved. The Action Taken Report (ATR) was to be presented at the successive round of Janambhoomi. This aspect of Janambhoomi was most popular because individual needs such as pensions, issuing of 'patadar pass books', house sites, gas connections and ration cards could be demanded and were expected to be fulfilled. On the basis of data collected from Mahbubnagar district, mandal Kondurg in 2004 one found that around 50 per cent of the demands made under the IFN category for the 18 rounds of Janambhoomi had been accepted while the rest were rejected (District Chief Planning Officer).

The success of Janambhoomi is also attested by survey findings conducted for the purpose of mapping citizen and official response to the Janambhoomi programme. The sample for the survey was a random stratified sample including various sections of society while districts were chosen on the basis of a developed and a less developed district. The two districts so chosen were the Rangareddy and Mahbubnagar districts.

A survey was conducted through structured questionnaires and focused group discussions. Some of the interesting observations are that almost all the respondents in both the districts had heard about the programme. In terms of community works construction of roads saw maximum participation by citizens. Also contribution from the people was only in the manner of voluntary labour with no respondent referred to money or material being contributed for community works. As stated earlier petitioning the government for fulfilment of various individual requirements was very popular amongst the respondents. Also almost all the respondents had benefited on an individual basis on account of Janambhoomi. In fact Janambhoomi was rated as a successful development initiative by around 40 per cent of the respondents. The second most popular programme was that of Development of Women and Children in Rural Areas (DWACRA). DWACRA was initiated as a women's self-help group involving micro-financing. Almost all respondents referred to the benefits of DWACRA apart from the fact that most women were also members of a local DWACRA group.

Response of the survey conducted amongst government officials and elected representatives also brought forth some interesting observations. It was largely argued that planning of the programme and defining development priorities was done at the district/ state level. The element of micro-planning therefore remained unfulfilled. With regard to contribution in community works the officials' response matched that of the respondents. People's contribution was mainly in the form of labour and the aspect of responsive government was carried out successfully. The grievance of officials related to the additional administrative responsibilities that Janambhoomi had heaped on them. Frequent and extensive field visits as also constant supervision by senior officials had exhausted the administration. Therefore when asked to list reasons for the party's defeat in the 2004 state assembly elections many said that the bureaucracy did not vote for Naidu. On the other hand, its victory in the 1999 state assembly election is largely attributed to Janambhoomi by the citizens and the officials/political representatives.

In looking for reasons for Naidu's electoral victory in the 1999 assembly elections, Janambhoomi seems to be the most important factor, even more than economic reforms or rather in spite of economic reforms. Reversal of N.T. Ramarao's populist policies would seem like committing electoral hara-kiri. However Naidu managed to perform a perfect balancing act between unpopular economic reforms and populist measures. Janambhoomi by itself did not lead to tangible developmental benefits. It was more in the manner of distribution of token benefits to individuals periodically. However the 'idea of development' that Janambhoomi represented was what seems to have caught the imagination of the electorate. Apart from this, the elaborate public relations exercise that was engaged in during Janambhoomi rounds[1] ensured large-scale public turnouts if not participation in the programme. Also Janambhoomi brought with it enhanced administrative accountability and responsiveness to local community requirements. Many respondents attested to the same during the survey. They said that they were now less fearful of public functionaries as they could question them during various gram sabha meetings. Faceless bureaucrats could now be held accountable. However the whole exercise remained transient in nature invoking people's participation and mobilisation of the government machinery for a short duration of time. Persistent development issues such as irrigation, electricity and others remained unresolved. When the pace of Janambhoomi slackened during Naidu's second term in office it is these development issues which were once again highlighted and neglect of the same was seen as a reason for the TDP'S defeat in the 2004 state assembly elections.

The Politics of Economic Reform

Initiation of economic reforms by Naidu was also influenced to a large extent by the dominant caste community that he belonged to. Andhra politics has for long been dominated by the two non-Brahmin castes, i.e. the Kammas and Reddys. While the Congress equally courted both, it is argued that the Kamma community felt politically under-represented (Kohli 2009: 394-395). However the power equations changed in the 1970s as the Kammas displayed greater entrepreneurial skills. They diversified from their land-related occupations into various other businesses such as sugar and tobacco industries, hotels, newspapers and even in the area of film production (Ibid: 394). Having gained economically they were keen to gain political expression too. The Congress could not have fulfilled these aspirations as it was a house divided. Indira Gandhi's pursuit of populist politics since the 1970s had led to alienation of the dominant castes. Even amongst the poorer sections of society caste cleavages weakened the support for the Congress as the party's focus remained on the Dalits. Frequent changes in state level leadership pointed towards lack of political stability. The upwardly mobile dominant and backward castes were looking for an alternative. NTR therefore stepped into this political vacuum which the Congress had created. His was an opportune entry into Andhra politics. NTR played up the idea of regional nationalism and that the TDP was representative of 'Telugu self-pride', whereas the Congress was essentially a Delhi- directed party. He cultivated the constituency of women and the youth. He promised to provide jobs and educational opportunities to the backward castes. He was in a sense wooing sections of society that the Congress had neglected.

While the entry of the TDP in Andhra politics led to the emergence of a two-party system the developmental policies followed by the two were quite similar except for the element of 'competitive populism' where each party competed to outdo the other in announcing populist measures particularly at the time of elections. The propping up of Naidu was largely the handiwork of regional business entrepreneurs. While the Kamma peasantry had made forays into non-agrarian businesses in the 1970s, they were now keen to forge foreign collaborations for the purpose of expanding and further diversifying their economic assets as also gaining "...leverage over big business" (Baru 2000: 207-253). As stated by Sanjay Baru (2000), "It is therefore not an accident that political dynamics of the state have produced a first generation businessman, Chandrababu Naidu as the new political leader".

At the national level too one of the explanations for shift in the development policy has been "proliferation of the bourgeoisie" (Patnaik, Chandrashekhar and Sen 1994; 119-137).

Proliferation implies emergence of many new business houses 'smaller yet sizeable' which have managed to upstage bigger and older capitalists. While these newer businesses do not support the entire gamut of policy changes recommended by the World Bank and IMF they do support different components as seen relevant to their economic interests.

Conclusion

It would be rather premature to write an obituary for the developmental state in India. The case of Andhra Pradesh is interesting because Chandrababu Naidu attempted to shift the developmental trajectory of the state while continuing to distribute state largesse through various populist policies. In a sense he publicised both the reforms and the populist programmes to appease various sections of the electorate that his party had come to represent. 'Token populism' has come to replace the developmental state commitment of inclusive growth. Moreover as these tokens are delivered through more efficient e-governance initiatives they have been made more palatable to the public. This apparently contradictory policy mix was also well understood and accommodated by the World Bank. For instance, the time frame set by the Bank for power sector reforms which involved upward revision of charges for agricultural users was deferred till the year 2000, i.e. till after the state assembly elections of 1999. In a sense there is collusion between the lending agency and the state to accommodate each others' concerns. This is what has resulted in a winning formula for the political party at the time of elections. That the developmental state has been redefined is the clear conclusion that one can arrive at.

REFERENCES

Baru, Sanjay (2000). 'Economic Policy and the Development of Capitalism in India: The Role of Regional Capitalists and Political Parties' in Z. Hasan, R. Bhargava, B. Arora and F. Frankel (eds.) *Transforming India: The Social and Political Dynamics of Democracy*. New Delhi: Oxford University Press.

District Chief Planning Officer, *Mandal-wise IFN and NFCN Particulars from 1st to 18th Round of Janambhoomi,* Planning Department, District Mahbubnagar.

Hariss, John (2001). *Depoliticising Development: The World Bank and Social Capital.* New Delhi: Leftword Books.

Kohli, Atul (2009). *Democracy and Development in India: From Socialism to Pro-business.* New Delhi: Oxford University Press.

Kumar, Nagesh S. (2003). 'Done in by Cash Crops', *Frontline,* Vol. 19, Issue 26, January 3.

Patnaik, P., C.P. Chandrashekhar and Abhijeet Sen (1994). 'The Proliferation of the Bourgeoisie and Economic Policy', in T.V. Satyamurthy (ed.) *Class Formation and Political Transformation.* New Delhi: Oxford University Press.

Powis, Benjamin (2003). 'Grassroots Politics and the Second Wave of Decentralisation in Andhra Pradesh', *Economic and Political Weekly,* Vol. 38, No. 26, June 28.

Reddy, Ratna P. (2003). 'Irrigation: Development and Reforms', *Economic and Political Weekly,* Vol. 38, Nos. 12 and 13, March 22-29.

Revathi, E. and Shaik Galab (2010). 'Economic Reforms and Regional Disparities' in R.S. Deshpande and Saroj Arora (eds.) *Agrarian Crisis and Farmer Suicides.* New Delhi: Sage.

Rudolph and Rudolph (2001). 'Iconisation of Chandrababu Naidu' *Economic and Political Weekly,* Vol. 36, No. 18, May 5.

NOTES

1. For the purpose of promoting the programme social animators were to be identified and appointed by nodal officers in every habitation. During the programme a Janmbhoomi flag was to be unfurled, a Janmbhoomi song sung at all educational institutions and the logo and slogan of Janambhoomi to be displayed on all government and private institutions.

4

Return of the State: End of Neoliberalism? An Inquiry into the Indian Governmentality

Santanu Rakshit

Are hyperactive days of Neoliberalism over? This paper attempts to find the trace of the hegemonic journey of neo-liberalism and its seemingly fading glamour in the economic, social and political spaces in India. In its continuous hegemonic assertion—Neoliberalism—the expression of International Finance Capital or Global Capital whenever necessary throttled the much acclaimed demand side management of the state. (Keynesianism). The state seemed to be reduced to a mere bystander amidst the high dynamism of International Capital in India. Nevertheless, it was successful in using its establishment to subjugate its own people for extracting resources and surpluses for the Capital (Global)[1]. Rampant land acquisition, illegal mining permissions in forest areas was the order of the day. The state seemed to be very deterministic in these actions and equally ignorant on the plight of the people inhabiting the rural and forest spaces. It conveniently overlooked the turmoil, grievances and conflict arising in these marginalised spaces. For the marginalised section their state (?) seemed to them as an aggressor or exploiter.

However, for some time, amidst such dynamism some reversals are also being observed. In terms of Keynesianism it indicates 'The Return of the State'. In states like West Bengal,

Bihar, Andhra Pradesh, etc. and even in some ministries of the central government (Ministry of Environment, Rural Development, Finance, etc.) we perceive the presence of a benevolent state, the state in an active developmental role — devoid of the naked interference of International Capital. The state seems to be in action, the state that is over-reaching to its people, the state that seems to be in favour of subalterns, the state that is for people. The question arises whether it is really benevolent in nature, can it really be so? Given the structure of the state and the global economic system in which it is embedded. Or that it is a new expression of the hegemony of Capital (Global)? Or just another form of 'Governmentality' in Foucault's sense? The paper intends to deal with the controversy between Neoliberalism and long Keynesianism in terms of pure governmental intervention, which is capable of creating delusory moments, and thus reflect upon its political economy insinuation.

In section I, I will discuss the conflicting orientation of describing the appearances of the market economy, i.e. Keynesianism and Neoliberalism especially in the Indian context, depicting also the basic tenets of Keynes and Keynesianism. In Section II, I will try to locate the foundations of neoliberalism and its controversial expression in less developed regions like India. Section III will deal with the fall out of aggressive implementation of neoliberal policies in the economic, political, societal and cultural spheres and also analyse the seemingly turnaround of the state from its malevolent stance to benevolent one, which appears to be Keynesianism. In the last section, I will interrogate the seemingly benevolent market expression of the Indian state in terms of governmentality or development management.

I

Interesting discussions are already underway in the context of Neoliberalism and Keynesianism after the worldwide financial crisis in 2008. Many arguments and counter-arguments on a diverse theoretical plane are taking place. In this context, I should acknowledge the following contributors, whose papers provoked my thought to present this particular theme. Important among them are Patnaik (2008a, b), Farshad Araghi (2010, 2009), Robert Skidelsky (2009), Paul Davidson (2009), Peter Clarke (2009), Jonathan Kirshner (2010) on the one hand and Ajit Chaudury, et al. (2004) and Kalyan Sanyal (2007) on the other for political economy interpretation.

If we divide the diverse nature of the different debates on the issue of the failure of Neoliberalism and return of Keynesianism after the financial crisis, we can clearly discern the different strains of ideas. The main contention however was that the basic tenets of neoliberalism are inconsistent and have failed to give the world economy a sustaining orientation.

To start with, Araghi (2010), in an interesting article he defined 'Neoliberalism' as negative Keynesianism; and 'Keynesianism' as positive Keynesianism. He is of the view that neoliberalism is actually a moment within long Keynesianism. That is to say that Keynesianism was never abandoned; actually neoliberalism is the Keynesian response to its own contradictions, such as wage inflation and stagflation in developed worlds and unruly developmentalism in developing countries. State and supra-state intervention shifted the basis of demand management from wage contracts and the developmental compromise to micro and macro credit and debt-based globalisation.

Patnaik (2008b), however clearly discerned the two approaches. Neoliberalism according to him is a hegemonic expression of International finance capital, devoid of any substantive intellectual basis and arguments logically inconsistent. To Patnaik, Keynes, favouring capitalist system knew the inconsistencies of the laissez faire capitalism, so he advocated socialisation of investment. Keynes attributed the failure of markets to the intrinsic incapacity of financial markets to distinguish between 'speculation' and 'enterprise', and be dominated by the activities of speculators. Thus, enterprise itself becomes a bubble on a whirlpool of speculation, making output and employment and thus the livelihood of millions of people dependent on the caprices and whims of a bunch of financial speculators. Patnaik's evaluation of the situation is much thorough and very clearly manifests the differences between the basic tenets of Keynesianism and Neoliberalism. Patnaik (2008b) is of the view that neoliberalism is unlikely to persist in the old form of accumulation process. That's why he seems to wait for the return of Keynesianism—that is 'return of the state'.

Davidson (2009) is of the view that embracing rational expectations and the efficient markets hypothesis led the economics profession to make disastrously misguided assumptions about the stability and self-correcting hyper-rationality of financial markets in particular. The government's failure was to embrace these errors of the economics community and run with them. Davidson holds that the origin of the current crisis "lies in the operation of free (unregulated) financial markets." "Liberalised financial markets," he argues, "could not heal the bloodletting that they had caused."

Skidelsky (2009) is of the opinion that Keynes also would have found something troubling about contemporary Western society, or at least the version of it that emerged in the post–Cold War United States. Keynes's economics was rooted, always, in a normative, philosophical vision, in particular that the economic game was not about winning the candle. This was one of Skidelsky's great contributions in his biography, and *Return of the Master* treats us to a chapter on "Keynes and the Ethics of Capitalism," including Keynes's aversion to "the objectless pursuit of wealth." Rather, the purpose of economic activity (and the role of the economist) was to "solve" the economic problem—the provision of adequate needs, opportunities, and comfort—so that the important things in life could be pursued.

Clarke (2009) bemoans the divergence between Keynes and the Keynesians. The score settling continues, as Clarke reminds (or informs) the reader that Keynes's comment "in the long run we are all dead" has been egregiously misinterpreted. Keynes was not devaluing the future, but rather calling attention to the fact that it could take a very long time for markets to restore equilibrium, and there would be much loss and suffering in the waiting. Similarly, Keynes was not "inconsistent," but was admirably flexible, possessing a quality now in painfully short supply. He was open to changing his mind when the evidence suggested that he should, and to changing his policy prescriptions when circumstances demanded. Clarke also reviews Keynes's allergy to Marxism and his "lifelong belief in the unique virtues of the market," clearing away much of the nonsense that has been said about Keynes over the years.

Kirshner(2010) also made an important distinction that Keynes theory and practice in the name of Keynesianism is different. He thinks that "Keynes is back," is a familiar cliché, but also an enigma. Enigmatic, first, because Keynes, the most influential economist of the 20th century, never really left. Like it or not, we live in a macroeconomic world elucidated by Keynes and those who followed in his footsteps. Even Robert Lucas, who won a Nobel Prize for his criticisms of conventional Keynesianism, said in response to the financial crisis: "I guess everyone is a Keynesian in a foxhole."

So, we find an interesting discussion, assertion and debate undergoing in rejuvenating the Keynesianism or disowning its importance theoretically as well as practically. This is founded on the basic belief that neoliberalism in its present form has failed. But what interest us more is actually the practical aspects of Neoliberalism and Keynesianism in less developed countries like India. It is important more to find out what we have experienced in the past and what is undergoing at present in actuality reflects which brand of market economy between the two discussed above.

Fundamentally Araghi's connotation seems to be more dramatic than theoretical in content. He actually stressed the practical aspect of the policy implementation in India. He may be correct to pose Neoliberalism or Keynesianism actually being an expression of market theory, but posing neoliberalism as a moment within Keynesianism actually undermines Keynes's strong theoretical position against speculative activities. However, Araghi's scepticism on the intention of the International finance capital and the developed countries attitude towards the ecology and south seems to be well-placed in humanitarian aspects. He seems to be correct in distinguishing the dichotomised nature of policy intervention in the north and south, intended to pauperise the south. But to relate the present variant of market intervention in developing countries with Keynesianism and equating it on a similar platform seems to be devoid of any valid economic logic. Rather I think neoliberalism is a higher moment compared to Keynesianism in the broad journey of Capital or Capital-non-capital complex.

On the other hand, Patnaik (2008b) clearly demarcates the basic tenets of Keynesianism and shows that neoliberalism in its present form does not seem to be sustaining. He is very optimistic theoretically that developed countries have to fall back on Keynesianism and also needs to propagate the same in the developing countries. He presents ample examples of how the developed countries are already taking recourse to Keynesian policy prescriptions. On the same lines we also find a large section of Western economists, very optimistic of the return of Keynes in the policy and power arena of the developed world. The Signs are already obvious.

Davidson (2009) and Clarke (2009) maintain that Keynes's insights are necessary for understanding today's crisis, overcoming it, and preventing its recurrence. In Skidelsky's *Return of the Master*, this theme is even more explicit, and the arrows from Keynes's theories to today's policies are brightly drawn. Like Clarke, Skidelsky is keen to puncture anti-Keynesian myths ("it may surprise readers to learn that Keynes thought that government budgets should normally be in surplus"); with Davidson, he emphasises disequilibria in the international financial economy. He endorses Davidson's updated Keynesian scheme for an international clearing union. And with the others, Skidelsky emphasises the central role of uncertainty in Keynes's economics, but he gives particular attention to the philosophical foundation of the framework: the purpose of economics is to allow people to live "wisely, agreeably, and well."

However, the political implication in the context of the developing world is missing in the assertions of the Western

Keynesian economists like Skidelsky, Clarke or Davidson. All the others except Patnaik and Araghi seem to be ignorant about the Keynesianism in the developing world perspective. They view the developing world from the perspective of the developed world. They also do not bother to delineate their theoretical positions according to varied perspectives needed to address the respective situations. Patnaik also seems to cling to Keynesianism as a panacea for the third world countries like India. Though, he is scathingly critical on the demonic and diabolical approach of the neoliberal market variety in India. Araghi pointed out that Keynesianism had two faces (chronologically watertight) positive and negative with dual prescription one for the developed world (tackling wage-inflation and stagflation as negative) and another for the developing world (unruly developmentalism as negative).

I feel it is very important to identify the travesty of the neo-liberal approaches which can sometimes appear to be Keynesian and at times even socialist. My contention is that neoliberalism in developing regions can have two faces: one for the market-friendly richer section and the other for the poorer section. The richer section comprises the high income group and upwardly mobile consumption savvy middle class, the poorer section comprising the rest mostly the marginalised section. To elaborate it, in the global periphery neoliberalism has two faces—one for developed economic regions and the other for the rest. Within the rest that is less developed economic regions it pursues different policy initiatives for richer and poorer sections—theoretically Capital, Non-capital and the excluded section, to be discussed in detail in the last section. It should be kept in mind that the theories of the developed world—Keynesianism or Neoliberalism—are totally ignorant of the plight of the less developed regions that results as the consequence of the implementation of policies following them. If chaos and turbulence helps meet their ends they are not at all hesitant to continue with their policy implementation with full vigour. Market expansion and surplus extraction that results in chaos or discipline(?) is not their look out. Though, Keynesianism at the core of the market economy operation till now has proved to be less immiserising and agreeable to the marginalised section in particular.

On the process of accumulation of capital in the neoliberal world we find very important and interesting perspectives. Patnaik (2008a) interprets neoliberal surplus appropriating activities as 'accumulation through encroachment'. Araghi (2010) also holds this view with slightly different connotations—'accumulation through displacement'. Rather Harvey (2003) terms the process to bear both of the meaning—'accumulation through dispossession'. Sanyal (2007) from a different perspective suggests that in India like other less developed regions is experiencing a mix of primitive accumulation of capital and governmentality. Along the same lines, Patnaik (2008c) also argues that the current phase in agriculture in India is undergoing primitive accumulation of capital.

Before substantiating on the issue of the accumulation process and governmentality meant for the Capital-Non Capital-Excluded section of the population, I would try to project the changes and consequences undertaken in the neoliberal regime in India in the following sections.

II

What actually does neoliberalism mean? I have tried to summarise it in the following forms. Neoliberalism is a philosophy in which the existence and operation of a market are valued in themselves, separately from any previous relationship with the production of goods and services, and without any attempt to justify them in terms of their effect on the production of goods and services; and where the operation of a market or market-like structure is seen as an ethic in itself, capable of acting as a guide for all human action, and substituting for all previously existing ethical beliefs. The main goals are generally maximisation[3] of all economic variables.

More appropriately, according to P. Bourdieu (1998), the transition to "liberalism" takes place in an imperceptible manner, like continental drift, thus hiding its effects from view. Its most terrible consequences are those of the long term. These effects themselves are concealed, paradoxically, by the resistance to which this transition is currently giving rise among those who defend the old order by drawing on the resources it contained, on old solidarities, on reserves of social capital that protect an entire portion of the present social order from falling into anomie. This social capital is fated to wither away—although not in the short run—if it is not renewed and reproduced. I have tried to pose Bordieu's expression in the Indian context in the current millennium. Following Bourdieu, I argue that neoliberalism is in reality a higher moment of movement of Capital (global).

We can discern three phases of neoliberalism in India. The infant stage with solid foundation (1991-96), the maturing stage with high aggression (1996-2008), the vulnerable stage (2008-onwards). I will try to explicate the impacts of Capital (global) mainly on the basis of three attributes—economic, philosophical and cultural.

In the growing stages (1991-96) the government of the Congress-led coalition undertook aggressive reforms and liberalised India to get integrated in the circuit of global capital. In this phase only important policies were undertaken and implemented that were irreversible in nature. Irreversible in its destructive impact too! India left its inward looking economic growth path to embrace in totality the neoliberal outward looking strategies. The policies undertaken in this period by successive governments were self-defeating and thoroughly overruled the concept of the nation-state. The state of India acted on the aegis of the cosmopolitan capital and big institutions like IMF, IBRD and WTO. Policies related to demand management were sidelined very carefully and stealthily giving away in full to the Neoliberal logic of market or Capital (Global). The state and its vanguard were fully subjugated in the whirlpool of glamour that neoliberalism carries. The high level of consumption, glittering urbanisation, and speedy spread of the service sector that accompanied the liberalisation process swayed the educated population to the neoliberal wisdom. Theories, policies, plans and implementations were all dictated and pursued according to the norms of maximisation that were propagated by neoliberal advocates. In the 1990s we found heavy turbulence in governance, governments at the centre seemed so volatile and fragile, we observed sudden and unexpected changes in government, we also saw same people as ministers in different opposing governments holding key positions. Those not suited may be to any Indian political party had to be accommodated as suited to the preference of the Global Capital.

During the period 1996 to 2008, we found Neoliberalism in India in a very aggressive posture. By then Indian federalism was totally subjugated to the whims of global capital. Authoritarian uses of different imperial policies were undertaken and speedily implemented to amass wealth and subsequently siphon them into the international circuit. The state itself was used to carry out these diabolic activities under suitable garbs. For example, the 'feel good factor' and 'India shining' slogans of the NDA government were designed to veil their neo-liberal opportunism. This again transcended in the working of the first UPA government and continued unabated, though it got the mandate against the NDA government for its proactive implementation of neoliberal dictates. Alas! The Indian polity had no choice, since they were facing Hobson's choice. Someone has to rule, thus every time a fractured polity constructed with increasingly lesser degree of stability showing the chaotic nature of polity and governance.

However, state power continued to act as an instrument of subjugation of its own people. This was manifested in land grab for SEZ, or selling away of mineral resources, or inviting unscrupulous organisation of dubious character in the insurance, banking, health and education sector, or doing away with the PDS and procurement system to give way to different retail chains in food and food grain sectors. It was a phase of 'go as you like' and 'do as you like' governance. Complete chaos reigned in the minds of rulers, philosophical confusions among the rulers ran so high that otherwise the left government seemed to be running right and so called rightists seemed to be speaking left. Even left-ruled government bowed down to the logic of neoliberalism as if—TINA (there is no alternative). How can a left government at all fight for the establishment of SEZ? Since, to neoliberal advocates SEZ seemed to be the panacea for all ailments! Meanwhile, our core real sector comprising the agriculture and manufacturing sector gradually moved into a hopeless situation. The philosophical confusion and bad economics regarding substitution of a multi-cropped agricultural area into a toy-car manufacturing shed seemed to be the pinnacle of all bewilderment.

I also harp on the philosophical confusions among the literate and educated section of the country, which accelerated the process even more. Patnaik (2008b) points out that 'enterprise becomes the bubble on a whirlpool of speculation' regarding the neoliberal economic activities. This philosophy pursued in the space of economic activities does have its impact on the cultural attributes of the subjects of this type of economic activities. That is to say that this whirlpool of speculative activities in the economic sphere can well get imbued into the general psyche of literate populations. The popular support of the strong middle class of the neoliberal policies is the testimonial to this conjecture. In the Keynesian word 'Casino type' working of the economic system actually lead to the development of 'casino' type culture destroying and distorting the rubric of the benevolent state and the mindset of people. In fact the governance in that case can also be termed as 'casino type'. Thus, the myopic subjects of the state seemed to be obliged to create a strong sentiment towards establishing the hegemonic tenets of neoliberalism. Their ardent followers were those rapidly upwardly mobile middle class having no serious introspection about the cause and effects of such policy implementations. The signs of cultural turbulence with strong interventionism were observable. Even left rulers were seen to embrace and actively prophesied the wisdom of neoliberalism. There was in reality no proper increase in efficiency of the economy or its subjects as a whole, but only an all-round manifestation of superfluous snobbery which was based on the economic and cultural bubbles created. This was sure to get busted and it really did in the financial crisis of 2008. The IT sector in India got the first hit.

It was bad economics altogether when viewed from the Keynesian orientation; and also it was bad politics from the governmentality sense of Foucault (Sanyal, 2007). Still it continued unabated because the global capital as discussed before is little concerned about the plight of the market it dominates. Chaos or no chaos surplus appropriation remains their only objective, unless and until some external brakes are applied. It can be on economic ground, where they fear of getting liquidated as it happened in the 2008 financial crisis or on the political ground, where they face people's resistance.

III

In India a sudden turnaround was noticed by the end of 2008. The Indian government seemed to start applying brakes on its neoliberal vision. I feel primarily on two grounds this happened, first, the economic consequences of the neoliberal policies in the developed world, i.e. the global melt down (financial crisis) and second, the growing people's resistance in developing countries like India. The main source of myth buster was surely the financial crisis of 2008 that originated from the sub-prime lending and associated speculative activities in the developed world. USA was the first to move to Keynesianism by bailing out Lehmann brothers and Morgan Stanley from the government exchequer. Following this path many European nations started dismantling neoliberal policy prescriptions and started looking back to Keynesianism even resorting to nationalisation of public sectors (Patnaik, 2008b). The world economy for the first time seemed to be very vulnerable. The jolt forced the developed world to look back towards Keynesian policy prescriptions, which we have discussed in Section II.

However, the situations in developing regions like India were different. The brakes here were not from the policy makers, but it was from the people. Policy makers conveniently ignored the agitations and resistances and continued with their neo-liberal reforms. Most of the resistances were addressed violently by the state; this made the situation more complicated. Astonishingly a left regime too took recourse to such violent repressive activities on its own people. The people in these cases were the subalterns, the main plank of the left organisation. This is what seems to be a clear induction of the casino type culture in the governance itself. The left generally considered to be more orthodox in their belief and philosophy, completely swayed into the logic of neoliberalism and abdicated the coveted popular crown they earned in their course of pro-people governance. Or else how can a pro-poor regime tend to suppress people's genuine resistance with such virility by bullets in Nandigram and Singur?

Interestingly, the Nandigram movement transmitted the people's defiance to the state neoliberal dictums to other parts of India, wherever state action seemed to be tortuous. For example, POSCO, Kalinganagar, Bhatta Pasoi, Maharashtra's anti-SEZ referendum, clearly disapproved the aggressive neoliberal policies of the state. This defiance also fuelled the anti-state movements of the Maoists mostly in the central mineral-rich region of India. This became possible owing to the popular support on the philosophy of violent reaction against perpetration of state violence. The state-sponsored violence was enacted to evacuate the people settled in these mineral-rich regions. The state acted as a facilitator for smooth functioning of the appropriation process of global capital.

However, the most remarkable part of all these people's reactions was in the different elections that were held from 2008 onwards in West Bengal. The people's mandate became an impressive and effective instrument against the atrocious governance. The left front government were literally drubbed in almost all elections from 2008 onwards and were finally out of power in 2011 after 34 years. The left front government's allegiance to the neoliberal policies and related coercive actions for their implementation made them villains in the psyche of subalterns. To my mind, the way of functioning of the left parties, that is the process of creation of consensus through decentralised structure and its apparent dent among the deprived class were the main attraction for the neoliberal aegis. To their understanding the left government appeared to be capable of creating majority consensus on the neoliberal advents easily due to their enormous popular link existing among all the sections of people, especially the poorer section. But all their speculations busted, as they often do. The end result was more repercussive and unfortunate in the sense that it was not limited only to the denouncing of the left regime, but unfortunately extended to the left ideology as well. This was the most serious consequence of such deviance of the left regime in West Bengal.

The people's resistance and defiance in Indian polity was also observed in the recent trounce of the UPA government and their allies in different state assembly elections; however, West Bengal is the exception, however, for similar reasons discussed above. The symptoms of anger against the neoliberal fallacies redirected to the domestic advocates of greed and casino-type governance, which manifested in the huge chain of corruption in every ministry, notable among them is obviously the telecommunication sector. The anger was also directed towards the denigrating culture of 'do as you like' in the government and among general people.

As stated before the neoliberal praxis continued unabated in India, even after the spiralling people's resistances in these periods, which were contained ruthlessly. That is to say the policy makers were very earnest in the strict enforcement of the neoliberal programmes. However, the worldwide financial crisis of 2008 automatically slowed down the hyperactive global capital. The bursting of the speculative activities in the developed world slowed down the investment inflow to the developing countries, leading to abandonment or arrest of different ongoing or future projects.

These overwhelming impacts forced the Indian state to look the other way. The re-emergence of the nation-state was a necessity in the perspective of governmentality. The Indian government started changing its posture very fast. However when these actions surfaced, we were already amidst severe devastation caused by this casino type ruling initiated by sheer greed. Some symptomatic representations of this re-emergence of the nation-state were positive intervention of the central government's Environment Ministry and Ministry of Finance. The Environment Ministry for the first time rejected the designs of the Monsanto Group in applying genetically modified crops. New land acquisition policy, Forest Policy enactment and MNREGA were the few pro-poor steps undertaken that attracted popular sentiments. Priority to the underprivileged in terms of increasing social sector expenditure also reflects ongoing changes in policy orientations of the government. The federal states of Bihar and West Bengal undertook pro-poor development orientation with the change in regime. It started to appear that the nation-state was slowly coming up into the foreground and the blue eyed Capital (global) going into the background. It seems as if Keynesianism was coming back into action again. However, was it the compulsion of governmentality, or sheer act of benevolence of the central and federal governments in India?

IV

As reiterated before, neoliberalism is actually a higher moment (Hegelian sense) than Keynesianism in the broad journey of Capital (global). Keynesianism in a lower moment had been succeeded by neoliberalism. Structurally we cannot agree with Araghi's position that neoliberalism is a moment within the broad spectrum of Keynesianism, rather Keynesianism and neoliberalism are different moments in the broad movement of Capital globally. Keynesianism and neoliberalism are the different constructs of Capital (or market, in terms of intervention). In the sense of pure governmentality Araghi's contention that Keynesianism having two faces can be justified to some extent. As if the market has some instruments for the governance at its disposal and is fitted according to the requirement of the time. In any case essentially neoliberalism is a higher order which can contain positive and negative aspects of Keynesianism within it, besides the new qualitative aspects that have emanated through the synthesis that gave birth to neoliberalism. It is true that Keynesianism in its hey days comprised different strains of policies for the developed world and the developing countries. Similarly within the developing countries lies broadly two distinct worlds—rich and poor, thanks to the aggressive imposition of neoliberal policies this has become obvious now. Unfettered practice of neo-liberalism uniformly in the developing countries like India has given rise to conflict, tensions and social rifts, which is surely detrimental to the neoliberal causes. One cannot have a single policy prescription for different economic spaces residing in different margins within the developing countries.

Let us try to evaluate the present situation on the perspective of Foucault's governmentality (Sanyal, 2007). To start with I pose the definition of Chatterjee (2004), To quote Chatterjee: "Activities of governmentality requires multiple, cross-cutting and shifting classifications of the population as the targets of multiple policies, producing necessarily a heterogeneous construct of social." However, Sanyal's (2007) definition of governmentality remains more comprehensive "Governmentality… refers to the management of the social body in terms of interventions on the part of the state aimed at promoting the welfare of the society….Foucalt...he calls them pastoral functions of the state. It is different from the other paradigm of power-sovereignty." Sanyal seems to put the very concept of governmentality in a different arena comprising the outcastes of productive activities which he termed as Development Management. He also emphasises the concept of primitive accumulation of capital in the noncapitalist space.

In developing regions like India, neoliberalism as mentioned earlier maintains different approaches for its intervention—for rich and poor—broadly. In my opinion there have been various transformations of the Capital-Non-capital[4] complex in post-colonial India. We can discern three broad economic spaces—Capital (arising)[5], Non-capital and the excluded following Sanyal's (2007) framework.

Specifically the process of capitalist accumulation in case of capital (arising), process of primitive accumulation of surplus in case of non-capital and developmental management (governmentality) for the excluded in the process of surplus appropriation.

Figure 1 below broadly describes the inclusion process of indigenous capitalist development (arising- capital) along with

Non-Capital flourishing in the economic circuit enclosed by the nation-state by the Capital (global) and subsequent transformation of the economic spheres giving rise to the different categories mentioned above. The process refers to all the productive economic activity spheres like industry, agriculture, mining, etc.

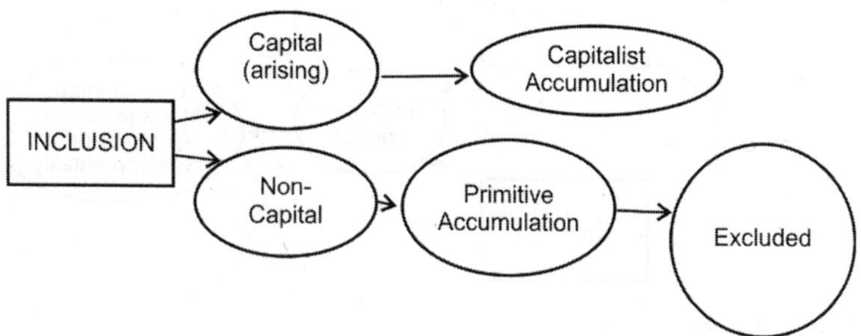

Figure 1: *Inclusion Process of Capital under Neoliberalism*

Figure 2 below describes the different interventions of market (Capital) and state in different economic activity spaces in a less developed economic region. With the intervention of global capitalist accumulation and primitive accumulation, non-capital passes through a phase of distress before getting finally excluded from the productive sphere to get immiserised even more. All these eventually lead to conflict and develops resistances in both the sector against the very process of primitive accumulation of capital Therefore, government needs to intervene and manage it through development management, which Sanyal depicts as governmentality. On the other hand, the part of the Capital (arising) which had been incorporated already into the Capital (global) sphere remains insulated with market and government incentives.

That is we find the following sectors—with the different attributes subsequent to the inclusion process undertaken by the Capital (global) in neoliberal India, which was otherwise closed in a limited form by the government and that helped indigenous capitalist accumulation. The aggressive intervention to open up the circuit led to the following transformation.

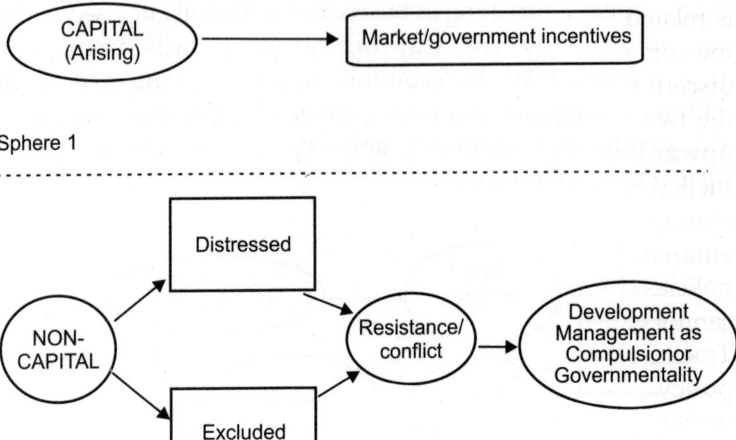

Figure 2: *Intervention of Capital under Neoliberalism*

Capital (arising) that survived and have been included in the global circuit-undergoing capitalist accumulation. Also includes those that have been incorporated in other non-productive forms like lumpen bourgeoisie (Frank, 1978) or comprador. Non-capital: subjected to primitive accumulation of global-capital including those which are structurally transformed from capital (arising) in the neoliberal era.

Excluded: The non-farm space inhabited by labourers transformed from the state of direct producers in non-capital (subjected to Development Management of capital). So, government now withdrawing from productive arena comprising the capital-non-capital complex emphasises more the development management approach directed towards the excluded sector. This management is not directed towards increasing productive capacity of the subjects rather on poverty management of the distressed.

However, I find two very interesting moments residing within the Indian polity mostly related to its governmentality or development management of the excluded and which illusively appears as a resurgence of the nation-state. The first is related to the implementation level and the other related to the composition of polity. On the first moment we can clearly discern that actually government is practising two policies for the two different economies, unfettered neoliberalism for the upwardly mobile section, whose over-consumption is often fuelled by government itself; and the other the development management for the distressed excluded section, which emanated due to the negative repercussions of neoliberal policies enacted. It is the compulsion of governmentality, which cannot be avoided because they are the majority in Indian polity. Tracing the subsequent events since the inception of neoliberal policy adoption shows that practice of neoliberalism gave impetus to high mass consumption and various resource appropriation processes under private capital. These led to many distortions in the normal development of the different sectors. Most importantly as discussed before accumulation through displacement, dispossession or encroachment led to serious crisis of livelihood in all productive sectors, especially agriculture. Agrarian transition got distorted (Rakshit, 2010, 2011) giving rise to involuntary exodus from the farm sector to non-farm sector. On this ground NREGA, and other social development initiatives were taken recourse to mitigate distress, however deliberately overlooking the need for rectification of the basic problems in productive activities that are related to livelihood in agriculture and industry. This brand of intervention is cosmetic in nature and shows how the government is averse to full intervention for the rectification of the negative fallout of neoliberalism, particularly the distortions in the productive activities of its subjects. The government is ready to dole out money for food for the dispossessed but averse to re-instate their livelihood which has been lost during the neoliberal transformation. That is accumulation through displacement would continue unabated and government will carry on its cosmetic help through defining and re-defining the grossly underestimated poverty level and roll out food subsidy for the poor, and also fuel high mass consumption of the other affluent sections through enhancement of dearness allowances and other market incentives.

The other moment is also perceptible and is the only hope in the arena of Indian polity. It is related to the varieties in the composition of Indian polity. The democratic structure of the Indian polity at times put into helms of affair persons, who are critical of the basic tenets of neoliberalism and governmentality along with some who are oblivious to such ideology but work on their own benevolent principles. At present, we find two groups within the ruling government, one fighting for increase in social sector expenditure and the other opposing it on different pretexts, that too openly. This apparent contradiction is too perplexing. The fascinating point is that a section of Indian polity having a pro-poor stance had emerged fighting against the vagaries of neoliberal policies tooth and nail. Their emerging status is indisputable till now, any criticism would be purely hypothetical and should be a query of the future. There is no reason to disbelieve their intentions, their pro-poor stance is visibly honest. The current regime of West Bengal and Bihar seems to be of this variety. Still, can a group of individuals or an individual itself run the government on its own logic overruling the compulsions of governmentality, that too guided by neoliberalism? This moment puts many questions, which can be answered, only in the future, since they are still in their nascent stage.

V

Hegemony of neoliberalism is still continuing in the economic, social and political grounds in India. In its continuous hegemonic assertion—neoliberalism—the expression of International Finance Capital or Global Capital whenever necessary would continue to throttle the much acclaimed demand side management of state (Keynesianism). May be rampant land acquisition, mining permissions in forest areas would be contained to an extent. The states in its compulsion of governmentality has to address the problems of the distressed, specifically the excluded, at least superficially. Return of the state in this context is pure governmentality, guided by the principles of neoliberalism framed particularly for the less developed regions. Only optimism is those moments emerging within this governmentality that seems to be really benevolent in nature. It is to be seen how long they can avoid to get engulfed within the long arms of neoliberal aegis.

REFERENCES

Araghi, Farshad (2010). 'The End of "Cheap Ecology" and the Crisis of "Long Keynesianism" ', *Economic and Political Weekly*, January 23, 2010, Vol. XIV, No. 4.

Araghi, Farshad (2009). "The Invisible Hand and the Visible Foot: Peasants, Dispossession and Globalisation" in A. Haroon Akram-Lodhi and Cristóbal Kay (eds.), *Peasants and Globalisation: Political Economy, Rural Transformation and the Agrarian Question* (New York: Routledge).

Bourdieu, P. (1998). *Le Monde Diplomatique*, 1998 - generacion80.cl.

Chowdhury, Ajit, Das, Dipankar and Chakraborty, Anjan (2000). *Margins of Margins*, Anustup.

Chatterjee, Partha (2004). *The Politics of the Governed: Reflections on Popular Politics in Most of the World*. Bombay: Permanent Black.

Clarke, Peter (2009), *Keynes: The Rise, Fall, and Return of the 20th Century's Most Influential Economist* (New York, Bloomsbury Press).

Davidson, Paul (2009). *The Keynes Solution: The Path to Global Economic Prosperity* (New York: Palgrave Macmillan).

Harvey, David (2003). *The New Imperialism* (Oxford: Oxford University Press).

Harvey, David (2005). *A Brief History of Neoliberalism* (Oxford: Oxford University Press).

Frank, A. Gunder (1978). *Dependent Accumulation and Underdevelopment* (London: Macmillan).

Kirshner, Jonathan (2010). 'Keynes, Recovered', *Real-world Economics Review*, Issue No. 53, June 26, 2010, pp. 144-49.

Marx, Karl (1954). *Capital*, Vol. 1, Part VIII (Moscow: Progress Publishers).

Marx, Karl (1993). *Grundrisse*, Penguin Classics, 1993.

Patnaik, Prabhat (2008a). "The Accumulation Process in the Period of Globalisation", *Economic and Political Weekly*, Vol. 43, No. 26, pp. 108-13.

Patnaik, Prabhat (2008b). "Return of the State" Cover story, *Frontline*, November 7, 2008.

Patnaik, Prabhat (2008c). *The Value of Money* (New Delhi: Tulika Books).

Rakshit, Santanu (2010). 'Agrarian transition'-diversity in nature, notion and observations—A survey of theoretical expositions and empirical studies with reference to India and West Bengal, *Research in Social Stratification and Mobility*, Elsevier, Science Direct, Vol. 28, Issue 4, December 2010, pp. 465-81.

Rakshit, Santanu (2011). 'Capital Intensification, Productivity and Exchange: A Class-Based Analysis of Agriculture in West Bengal in the Current Millennium', *Journal of Agrarian Change*, Vol. 11, No. 4, October 2011 (Wiley-Blackwell).

Sanyal, Kalyan (2007). *Rethinking Capitalist Development* (London: Routledge, Taylor and Francis Group).

Skidelsky, Robert (2009). *Keynes: The Return of the Master* (New York: Perseus).

NOTES

1. Henceforth Capital would mean Global capital. If otherwise it would be indicated as Indigenous Capital. I refuse to incorporate the concept of Nation-Capital and national bourgeoisie which are more fashionable among some sections of academicians.
2. Three interrelated aspects of the process of primitive accumulation of surplus can be identified in Marx (1954), viz.

i) Accumulation of money by merchants.

ii) Conversion of the accumulated money into capital (means of production) and transformation of direct producers into free wage labourers.

iii) Creation of an external market for the product produced under the capitalist mode of production.

Although both the processes actuall entail primitive accumulation of capital, one should be careful that capital here is strictly global in nature. That however does not mean foreign, it can be very Indian in acquaintance too.

3. Transaction maximisation, maximisation of volume of transactions ('global flows'),contract maximisation, supplier/ contractor maximisation, conversion of most social acts into market transactions artificial maximisation of competition and stress; creation of quasi-markets; reduction of inter-transaction interval; maximisation of parties to each transaction; maximisation of reach and effect of each transaction, maximisation of hire/ fire transactions in the labour market (nominal turnover);

maximisation of assessment factors, by which compliance with a contract is measured; reduction of the inter-assessment interval; creation of exaggerated or artificial assessment norms ('audit society').

4. Non-Capital here implies the productive spaces with various modes of production which are not *capitalist* in nature – the productive spaces, which cannot be associated with capital (being) or development of capital (arising). Totally out of the purview of the above incorporating any pre-capitalist mode of production and also incorporates *capitalistic* development as defined in Rakshit (2011), which are primarily subject to primitive accumulation of Capital (global).
5. Capital (arising) here is a category taken from Marx's (1993) idea of "Capital in arising" as explained in Grundrisse and appropriately illustrated in Sanyal (2007). Capital arising here means capital not self-sustaining and needs to depend upon outside support. In the Indian context the government support before the neoliberal advents in 1991 of the Capital (global). That is the indigenous capitals development under the support of the nation-state.

5

Challenges of the Welfare State under Neoliberalism

Asok Kumar Ray

Since the era of classical political economy, the homoeconomicus restricted the role of the state in the public good. The state's public role was only to provide moral justification to accumulative economy and to entrench the private interest against any popular resistance. Adam Smith in his *The Wealth of Nations* pleaded for free market and limited state. He proposed two distinct objects of the political economy: first, to provide a plentiful revenue or subsistence for the people, or, more properly, to enable them to provide such a revenue or subsistence for themselves; and, secondly, to supply the state or commonwealth with revenue sufficient for the public services. The "Sovereign" is responsible for defence of the society and protection of the members of society from the injustice or oppression of other members. Also, government had to provide some public works and institutions in order to make economic growth possible. His explanations of market forces and the role of the state in economics did shape the early capitalist economy. The Utilitarians, in line with this, also pleaded for minimal state and maximum individual liberty. The hedonistic value of any human action was justified on moral grounds and the state power was only to hinder the hindrances of the good life.

In the mid-19th century the first wave of the welfare state

came in England when laissez faire industrialisation was questioned. Liberal thinkers like T.H. Green felt that that state could no longer remain a silent spectator to the sufferings of the people, if the industrial economy had to survive. He therefore made an *alibi* for the proactive role of the state based on moral principles. The second wave of welfare state came with Keynes and Beveridge, the two intellectual founders of the post-war British welfare state and reluctant collectivism. They made a significant theoretical and practical departure from the classical political economy harboured by Adam Smith and Marshal. They held the view that although the market was the best practical mechanism for ensuring individual initiative and hence political freedom, economic efficiency and social justice, a judicious degree of state intervention was necessary to cover up the flaws of the market mechanism. They provided a market-driven approach to the British welfare state that could ensure stability to parliamentary democracy and could protect the system against economic waste and social inequality. In Europe, liberalism promoted individual freedom but it required the state to play an active role in social reform though with limited coverage and in view of the growing unemployment there. Keynes saw the "curse of unemployment" as the root of the evil of market economies. The welfare state therefore demanded a soft state that did not foreground the private sector in the social policy realm, rather it itself took up the major role in economic planning and social development. Both Keynes and Beveridge were concerned with the moral and social problems ensuing from unemployment, but while Beveridge stressed the need to ensure *everybody* against the ill effects of economic activity, Keynes was concerned with *organising material abundance* to yield the fruits of a good life. The welfare state however had no full trust in market forces alone; it relied on government intervention to bring about full employment. This made the case for government intervention.

The Neoliberal Challenge

Neoliberalism made a U turn in the terrain of state-led welfare policy. It reinstated "free market" economy featured by privatisation, deregulation and rolling back of the welfare state. Under neoliberalism, the larger social policy sphere came to be dominated by the market economy that eventually came to influence such policy particularly in the developing and under-developed countries. A major landmark under the neoliberal economy was the Washington Consensus propounded by John Williamson in 1990. This Consensus pleaded for market fundamentalism (Williamson-2000). To remedy poverty, the Consensus insisted on de-regulations, privatisation, abolition of government intervention on prices, labour market flexibility, trade, financial and capital account liberalisation. The Consensus also imposed conditionalities on poor countries facing balance of payments and financial crises. This state of things reduced the role of the state in distributive justice and the Consensus fore-grounded the market economy that claimed to take care of the social needs of the people. This reversed the so-called liberal statist development. Williamson's original version on policy reforms, considered good for the Latin American countries, had 10 propositions including fiscal discipline; Redirection of public expenditure priorities towards fields offering both high economic returns and potential to improve income distribution, such as primary health care, primary education and infrastructure; Trade, interest rate and FDI liberalisation; Privatisation and deregulation; Tax reforms and secure property rights. These propositions caused rolling back of the state and positioning the market against the welfare state. But as Williamson found, "the populist interpretation of the Washington Consensus boiled down to market fundamentalism or neoliberalism" (Williamson, 2000).

The Washington Consensus propounded a universalistic neoliberal ideology based on free market and considered the state as inefficient and corrupt. This ideological stand created the 'failed state syndrome'. This Consensus thus made a significant departure from Beveridge and Keynes and discarded Keynesianism on the plea that it would "under-estimate the ability of the market to be self-adjusting and self-correcting" (Stieglitz-2008). This also brought about a major shift in the concept of the 'soft' state based on welfare principles. The Washington Consensus hypothesised that the post-war peripheral state intervened too much in the social policy sphere. The neoliberal structural adjustment programme put forward the 'failed state syndrome' argument leading to the melt-down of the state. This syndrome was located in the post-colonial welfare states that suffered from weak economy, BoP crisis, debt crisis and eventual reduction of productivity. The Washington Consensus was largely concerned with macro-economic and financial management and required the state to be minimal, allowing the private markets to allocate resources efficiently and to generate robust growth. The Consensus legitimised the policies of opening up of economies, privatising public services, giving priority to profit over social needs, relating the allocation of resources to a market dependent upon private profit criteria and tended to establish total sovereignty of the market over the state. This also implicated supersession of the regulatory regime of the welfare state. Redirection of public spending from subsidies ('especially indiscriminate subsidies') towards broad-based provision of key pro-growth, pro-poor services like primary education, primary healthcare and infrastructure investment, rejected the state's activist role and pleaded for the promotion of a minimalist, non-interventionist state. The most significant impact of the Consensus was the social and political disintegration of the Third World countries and the hegemony of finance capital which was not exclusively tied to any particular national domain but had assumed an international character. This needed a "surrogate global state" (Patnaik-2006). But it decreased the capacity of the state to play its principal role in attaining a just and equitable society. The World Bank's support for informal and market-based social protection arrangements resulted in more interventions of the private sector and its increased role in the social policy realm.

But it took no longer time to face criticisms. Some of these were: a) the notion of a developmental state (the notion of a developmental state was perceived to apply to the successful industrialisations in the East Asian newly industrialised countries, with Japan as the classic precursor, followed by the four 'tigers'—South Korea, Taiwan, Singapore and Hong Kong) in the 1960s and 70s. These were followed, in turn, by Malaysia, Thailand, Indonesia, China and Vietnam. In all these cases, it was found that the state had violated the main tenets of the WC through protectionism, directed finance, and other major departures from the free market; b) notion of 'adjustment with a human face' (human costs of the crisis, rising poverty in the 'adjusting' countries, and the tendency of the adjustment costs to fall on the most vulnerable); c) the growing evidence of the 1980s as a 'lost decade' for development across the portfolio of policies and countries that were subject to adjustment through conditionalities imposed by the World Bank and the IMF (WC policies are not self-correcting, which is a myth, with failure often leading to the *intensification* of the conditionalities under even closer supervision by the IMF, the World Bank, the US Treasury Department and many aid agencies); d) the argument that the problem was not with the policies but with their insufficient implementation, corruption, lack of good governance and the like, invariably shifting the blame to the underperforming countries themselves; e) its antipathy to state intervention (Filho, 2010).

The pathological consequences of the market-based social protection policy were obvious. Samir Amin (1997) found "a sharp increase in unemployment, a fall in the remuneration of work, an increase in food dependency, a grave deterioration of the environment, a deterioration in healthcare systems, a fall in admissions to educational institutions, a decline in the productive capacity of many nations, the sabotage of democratic systems, and the continued growth of external debt" as the result of market-based approach to social policies. The Washington Consensus which was ideologically wedded to the Structural Adjustment programme, came to produce ill effects on the society. Kennett (2004) found that "to a much greater degree in the developing countries global restructuring combined with problems of debt and structural adjustment have resulted in a weakening of what was already inadequate in welfare provision. The provision of services like health and welfare in developing countries has in part come through development aid and development funding of various kinds, which has also seen significant cutbacks since the end of the Cold War. As providers of basic health and social welfare needs, the effects of structural adjustment have fallen disproportionately on women whose labour is expected to stretch in order to compensate for cuts in public services". This scenario created the market failure syndrome parallel to the failed state syndrome. It is this market failure syndrome that led to revisit the fundamentals of the Washington Consensus and to moderate those in order to be more realistic.

Augmented Washington Consensus initiated a brake in the Washington Consensus. Joseph Stieglitz and Dani Roderick stood as the neoliberal critics of the Consensus. Other critiques were Noam Chomsky, Tariq Ali and Susan George. They were of the view that the market alone could not operate adequately without support from the state equipped with strong financial and institutional bases and efficient techno-bureaucracy. The World Bank realised this and reversed the market fundamentalism to make the state a partner in the reforms programme. This revision was also warranted by open or latent armed conflicts in different parts of the world. Stieglitz felt that the state had an important role to play in making appropriate regulation and that social policy could play a great role in economic growth. He thus gave a human face to structural adjustment, talked of sustainability, egalitarianism and democratic development and intended to make the government more effective that could play a complementary role in the market. Stieglitz thus moved towards the Post-Washington Consensus. The attenuating crises arising out of failure of the American financial sector and market failures and the East Asian crisis (only a few months or even weeks before the East Asian crisis erupted, the countries had been praised as models of sound fundamentals to be followed by others. And in 1993 the World Bank had coined the term the East Asian Miracle to describe the now vilified economies. The East Asian Crisis taught the global players to reduce the risks of globalisation and to place limits on its degree of financial liberalisation), led him to proclaim that "we are all Keynesian now" (Stieglitz-2008).

He argued for rolling forward Keynesianism under the market fundamentalism frame and in the context of financial and macroeconomic crises.

The World Bank sided with Stieglitz and evinced adjustment with a human face. Stieglitz envisaged market economy with a combination of political regulations and social intervention. *The World Development Report 1990* on Poverty recognised the importance of safety nets. The World Development Report 1995 took a broader view of labour and it made a groundbreaking study of ageing and pension reform in 1994. The World Bank felt the need to cushion the negative effects of transition on the most vulnerable people. The post-Washington Consensus thus departed from the narrow propositions of the Washington Consensus; it introduced a state-friendly approach; focused on distribution, pleaded for change in social relations and laid importance on community-driven development and social safety net. The ADB, found the instrumental value of such a view in order to ensure social cohesion and to reduce social conflict. But ADB made a clear distinction between the private sector and the state and, much in line with the Commitment 1 of the Copenhagen Summit, it held the view that while high and sustainable growth should be driven by the dynamic private sector, the state should play the enabler role.

The Revised Consensus tended to reverse the exit of the state and made the latter a partner in the larger reforms programme. Thus, democracy-oriented programmes based on proper government appeared once again to the foreground. This made the state under the changed paradigm to be supportive of the market economy while at the same time it needed to obtain political legitimacy through not only popularly mandated government but also through offering social services and social opportunities to the people. The neoliberal critique like Joseph Stieglitz felt that the state had an important role to play in making appropriate regulation, industrial policy, social protection and welfare, providing public education and in creating human capital that could play a great role in economic growth. The hind side of this, as Patnaik (2006) noted, is that "the social legitimacy of the bourgeois state has arisen from this fact, which is why one can say that the position of the bourgeois State as an apparently supra-social entity, acting, not in the ostensible interests of the capitalist class exclusively, but for society as a whole, constitutes a necessary condition for the stability of the system". On the welfare front, the state was always guided by Pareto Optimality and Pareto Efficiency. The neo-classical theory of State Intervention was based on two Fundamental Theorems of Welfare Economics. One, subject to certain assumptions, a general equilibrium, is Pareto efficient. These assumptions are perfect competition, absence of public goods and externalities, absence of non-convexities in production and consumption and perfect information. Two, any Pareto efficient allocation can be achieved as a solution to a general equilibrium system and the State can intervene only by employing lump sum taxes and transfers that relocates individuals on the contract curve and in the process carries out a re-distributive activity. Such a re-distributive activity would be permissible according to the libertarians only if the initial endowments of the better off individuals were acquired illegally. The State could then, invoking the principle of rectification, intervene in order to carry out this limited redistributive activity.

On the other hand, the market failure theory once again justified state intervention to correct such failures. This has much resonance with Adam Smith. The neoclassical theory found presence of public and quasi-public good (like legal system, national defence and efficient government) as an important cause of market failure as this made private provision impossible. Other factors of market failure were presence of externalities (interdependencies that operate outside the market or price mechanism that gave rise to a discrepancy between private and social benefits making the Pareto efficiency difficult), presence of oligopolistic and monopolistic market structures and presence of distributional inequalities. The role of the state in the neo-classical framework is that of piecemeal intervention while the markets are assumed to function efficiently. In case of localised market failures a limited state intervention is called for. On the other hand, state intervention on grounds of equity is justified only via the second Fundamental Theorem of Welfare Economics. The second fundamental theorem also holds that social optimum is achievable in a competitive equilibrium *if accompanied by* appropriate social policy of *initial* distribution of endowments. Dreze and Sen (1995) argued that the agency of government would generally be required for the initial distribution. The state becomes thus relevant only under the second fundamental theorem of social policy that holds that social optimum is achievable in a competitive equilibrium if accompanied by appropriate social policy of *initial* distribution of endowments. This means, the government is not supposed to drag the entire economy towards social optima and after the initial distribution, things could be left to the private and competitive market to find its own way to social optima. Thus though the second fundamental theorem holds that social optima could be reached as a competitive equilibrium, from the utilitarian point of view, such distribution cannot be done (by the state) at the cost of sacrificing efficiency. A recent World Bank document (2006) recognised the "role of public action in equalising opportunities by promoting equality in access to markets and assets and by scaling up efforts to strengthen livelihood strategies through empowerment. Thus even with the best of access to markets and opportunities, there are needs for the government to engage in social protection to assist the poorest and help them in coping with the risks and vulnerabilities that citizens face. Social protection measures are important to combat extreme deprivation, but can have equally important dynamic efficiency effects by allowing people to bear risks and undertake profitable investments". The document also stated that "In contrast to earlier thinking that assumed a tradeoff between equity and growth, recent research indicates that well-designed and well-implemented social protection systems can enhance current and future opportunities by mitigating failures in credit, insurance, and other markets that affect the poor most strongly"(The World Bank 2006). Thus the neoliberal challenge to the welfare state linked together competition and optimality (Feldman and Serrano, 1980). But neither the market fundamentalism nor the

Pareto Optimality could be so promising to the social needs of the people. In the post-liberal era the World Bank and the UN agencies therefore gave serious thought towards the policy approaches of addressing inequality and promoting social inclusion. It was all about gathering social legitimacy to the neoliberal reform. In the Executive Summary of the 'World Social Situation 2010' it was mentioned that "the current global financial and economic crisis threatens to wipe out much of the modest progress in poverty reduction achieved since the 2000 Millennium Summit, while climate change increasingly threatens the lives of people living in poverty. The negative economic and social impacts of these crises highlight vulnerability to poverty and call into question the sustainability of global poverty reduction. This further underscores the need to rethink poverty reduction strategies and, more broadly, the underlying development paradigm".

The worst economic and financial crisis of the recent past has not only affected the poor in the developing world but also has affected a much larger proportion of the lower- and middle-classes in developed economies. And yet, the policy response to address these has been poor. Ali (2007) noted a few factors in this connection. First, there has been relative neglect of the agricultural sector—causing a move from the farm to industry and services and deficiency in public investment in agriculture and rural economy. Second, the interplay between market-oriented reforms, globalisation and technology, dismantling of public-owned enterprises and compressed wage distribution causing unequal growth. Third, increased international integration tended to benefit certain sub-regions within countries over others. Fourth, new technology is biased in favour of skills. All these taken together led the political economists to envisage at least three consequences. First, a visible shift from the Keynesian welfare state to the Schumpeterian workfare state; second, national states have been hollowed out; and third, it led to a paradigm shift from Fordism to post-Fordism[1]. Post-Fordism and neoliberalism affected the developed and the developing countries differently. It is to be noted that neoliberalism did not surrender Keynesianism in the developed states while in the developing countries neoliberalism largely abandoned Keynesianism. It should also be noted that rolling back and rolling forward of the state happened within a short interval of the neoliberal reforms. The role of the state oscillated with the oscillation of the capital and market needs. Once the market was foregrounded as the fulcrum of development and it was instrumental in creating the "failed state syndrome". But as the market economy faced crises, the "failed market syndrome" surfaced which reversed the former.

Welfare State Vis-a-vis Neoliberalism

1. Neoliberalism became coterminous with post-modern politics that abandoned the overarching vision of liberal-modernity based on political parties and trade unions. It also abandoned the emancipatory social policy. "The post-modern political condition is premised on the acceptance of the plurality of cultures and discourses. As a consequence, post-modern politics are the politics of single-issue movements and of single-issue actions, aiming at the strengthening or elimination respectively of a single function of modernity and are wholly incompatible with *redemptive politics of any kind*. Post-modern politics was no longer based on the inclusive and emancipatory political platform of modernity and became therefore functional rather than structural. Macro-politics gave way to multiplicity of short-term micro-politics. The ensuing rise of single-issue movements and single-issue coalitions; reappearance of the 'ethnic component' of politics; prolification of political in all directions, dispersal of power, celebration of plurality, multiplicity, and diversity; open and contextual politics that refuses to privilege any general recipe of social change, were the salience of post-modern politics. The post-modern theory of de-centred power also allowed for the multiplication of possibilities for political struggle, no longer confined simply to the realm of production or the state. The post-modern politics was

also to complete the Gramscian move to extend the political into all spheres, domains and practices of our culture (Bertens, 1995). The neoliberal theory, in tune with the post-modernist view, challenged not modernity per se, but its essentialist, rationalistic and humanistic underpinnings of which social policy is a significant part.

2. The developmental role of the state was stymied under neoliberalism by its increasing reliance on the Public-Private Partnership (PPP) approach to development and increasing cutbacks in social sector expenditure. The PPP was a strong idea of Thatcher as she set up quasi-government institutions to pursue economic development. Under the PPP approach, the business and corporations collaborate intimately with state actors and influence them to make legislations, regulations and public policies to their advantage. PPP also incorporates business and corporate interests into governance through close and secretive consultations. In this approach, the state is to assume maximum political and social risks for the sake of private sector profit. This also makes the state resort to coercive measures against any form of collective opposition to the corporate sector. On the other hand, neoliberal reforms constrained public finance of the welfare state, created dependency relations with foreign finance capital, reduced scope of indigenous capital formation and BoP crisis that led to less share of GDP in social spending. The developing countries also offered maximum policy subsidies to the foreign direct investors, MNCs and corporations; tax subsidies (by waiving tax regulation); service subsidies (like water, electricity costs); and liberally allowed common pool goods and services to squander and exhaust bringing thereby tragedy of the commons). These taken together, caused a serious resource crunch in the welfare states.
3. Privatisation, finance capital, and market economy reconstituted the state powers with minimum intervention in the economy and diminished welfare role of the state. The deepening penetration and dominance

of capital into political, social and cultural realms, centrality to markets, market processes and the interests of capital called for a strong and enabler state. These factors alone justified the power state, opposed to the Keynesian state. Harvey (2007) stated that, "neoliberalisation was from the very beginning a project to achieve the restoration of class power," "a political project to re-establish the conditions for capital accumulation and to restore the power of economic elites". He found the following features of the neoliberal state: strong preference to individual property rights and resource concentration; rule of law; institutions of free market and free trade; non-interventionist state; opposing collective institutions, political party and trade union; strongly limiting democratic governance; reliance upon undemocratic and unaccountable institutions for making key decisions; freedom of the few over freedom of the mass, siding with the good business climate as opposed to collective rights of labour or the capacity of the environment to regenerate itself; subsidising the rich countries at the cost of the Third World states and turning away from government (the state power on its own) to governance (the broader configuration of state and key elements of civil society). The neoliberalism demanded institutional restructuring and policy role of the state that could reshape the whole society in the market model. Once the market model was established, rule of law, protecting of private property (including FDI and corporate assets) and enforcement of property rights became the three core functions of the neoliberal state. On the other hand integration into the global economy also resulted in more transnational terrorism and insurgency. The issues of security and governance became strategically important for trans-territorial market and trade. This required the state to wield power enough to handle terrorism both in a state and in the trans-borders of a state. The issues of terrorist violence however required, apart from strengthening the domestic forces of the state, regional and bilateral cooperation. Thus the Council for Security Cooperation in the Asia Pacific (CSCAP) was established in 1993, as a non-governmental process for dialogue on security issues in Asia Pacific. India became its full member in 2000. Thus for the sake of the neoliberal economy, the scope of the market power well transgressed the sovereign domain of the states. The foreign investors did not rely only on the state-made laws for enforcement mechanisms. They also took recourse to the international law, treaty rules, the WTO rules, etc. for protecting their interest. Also "in pursuit of their economic interest, they have hugely expanded the state. State terrorism in the neoliberal era has been intensified with a view to entrench neoliberalism" (Blakeley, 2009).

4. This scenario led the political economists of structural adjustment to revisit market fundamentalism and to add a human face to it. Although Williamson's original propositions included improvement of income distribution, primary health, primary education and infrastructure, these were not foregrounded as the first reform and were virtually captivated by market fundamentalism. The human face argument tended to legitimise macroeconomic policy of adjustment and was attenuated by two factors: the *risk of losing the economy of mass consumption* as a result of increasing impoverishment and *fear of the mob* against which social policy with a human face could act as a shield. Structural adjustment with a human face became probably the most distinguishing point of intellectual difference between Williamson and Stieglitz who, while sitting on the same saddle of globalisation, stood on two different spatio-temporal situations of the reforms. The paradigm shift from welfare to safety net was another attempt to legitimise the project of economic reforms and to resist the political backlash of the people against economic liberalisation. The first generation political economists of structural adjustment opposed the organised voice of

the people and discouraged associations. The second generation political economists talked of the safety net and social cost of adjustment. The safety net, to them, was a *quid pro quo* for adjustment that solicited the larger role of the state. But safety net measures in both developing and transitional economies yielded varied results owing to inadequate resources and higher reliance on the private sector rather than on the state to run most productive enterprises. State focus on the social costs of reform and on short-term safety net measures diverted attention from necessary reforms in the critical areas. Moreover, Pareto Optimality, as discussed above, created a perennial trade-off between social optima and profit maxima. The Pareto efficiency optimum generated by competitive market economy also did not essentially generate social optimum. Optimum redistribution is in fact decided by social choice and through the non-market forces.

Post-colonial Welfare State Vis-a-vis Neoliberal Governmentality

Neoliberal governmentality posed another challenge to the post-colonial welfare states. The post-colonial scenario in general demanded state intervention for public welfare and state-led welfare measures, although it could not really stand as a serious critique of colonialism and many colonial legacies persisted in the post-colonial states. Neoliberal govermentality added to the problem. Three trends were visible: one, change from hierarchical and sovereignty-based modes of governing to more horizontal, network-based modes; two, diffusion of political authority from the state to other actors and three, the political authority was increasingly dislodged from the sovereign state and went in the direction of transnational policy-networks. These trends invited a crisis of post-colonial welfare-state. The vertical encompassment and of the "local" by the state to establish its superior spatial claims to authority were contested by new forms of transnational connections, local actors and grassroots organisations. This in turn de-essentialised the automatic right of the state claiming the vertical heights of sovereignty. It restructured government techniques, shifted the regulatory competence of the state to 'rational' individuals. Neoliberal governmentality thus also posed a challenge to the power state.

Guided by a competitive market logic, neoliberal governmentality insisted on a smaller government, government-at-a-distance, multiple sites for regulation and domination through the autonomous entities of government with enterprise logic. This government-at-a-distance involves social institutions such as nongovernmental organizations, schools, communities, and even individuals that are not part of any centralised state apparatus and are made responsible for activities formerly carried out by state agencies (Gupta and Sharma, 2006). This is not exactly rolling back of the state but transfer of the operations of government (in Foucault's extended sense) to non-state entities. The logic of the market has been extended to the operation of state functions, so that even the traditionally core institutions of government, such as post offices, schools, and police are—if not actually privatised—at least run according to an "enterprise model". Meanwhile, the social and regulatory operations of the state are increasingly "de-statised," and taken over by a proliferation of "quasi-autonomous non-governmental organisations" (Ferguson and Gupta, 2002). More precisely it is an expression of a changing logic or rationality of government by which civil society is redefined from a passive object of government to be acted upon into an entity that is both an object and a subject of government. The multilayered and polyarchic networks that comprise states, NGOs, IGOs and transnational corporations have become central sites of governance[2]. Neoliberal governmentality, as Foucault perceived, stood as a critique of Keynesianism, juridical model of power, centralised state and rule based on sovereign authority. He brought population to the centre of political analysis that made a transition from rule based on sovereign authority to a governmentalised rule that decentres the state. From this position he made the case for bio-politics and gave stress on body as a productive force, as labour power.

Individuals were not controlled by the society simply by ideological manipulation, but also by and through the body. Bio-politics was a vehicle for subordination to the state that would create solidarity. The new form of the state includes the techniques and tactics surrounding the government of population and if the state continues to exist, it is precisely because it has been govermentalised (Curtis, 2000).

But the criticalities are obvious. The romantic height given to the non-state actors are often contested as these are regulated by the state or international funding agencies. The non-state actors in most cases thus play instrumental roles instead of countervailing the political power of the state. Moreover the non-state actors also include market and corporate entities that however become really powerful in the neoliberal frame. The romantic height to non-state actors is to foreground the market-economy alone that has endangered the concept of bio-politics. What happened on the hind side instead, are the emergence of a larger bourgeois alliance; dominance of "oligopoly-finance capital," which wielded enough power in shaping the markets and in entering into the competitive market.

A governmentalised state created a reasonable amount of discomfort to the post-colonial welfare state. This also caused discomfort to the bureaucratic community that seeks, theoretically speaking, a rule-based state and a top-down hierarchy. Neoliberal governmentality, though opened a new discursive space within the market economy matrix, in fact exposed another 'market failure syndrome' unleashing a central dilemma of the market economy.

REFERENCES

Ali, Ifzal (2007). Inequality and Imperative for Inclusive Growth in Asia, *Asian Development Review*, Vol. 24 (2).

Amin, Samir (1997). *Capitalism in the Age of Globalization*, London: Zed Books.

Bertens, Hans (1995). *The Idea of the Post-modern*, Routledge.

Blakeley, Ruth (2009). *State Terrorism and Neoliberalism: The North in the South*, Routledge.

Cristina Marcuzzo, Maria. 'Keynes and the Welfare State'

(Dipartimento di Scienze Economiche, Università di Roma, "La Sapienza") cristina.marcuzzo@uniroma1.it.

Curtis, Bruice (2006). Foucault on Governmentality and Population: The Impossible Discovery, *Canadian Journal of Sociology*, 27 (4).

Dreze, Jean and Amartya Sen (1995). *India: Economic Development and Social Opportunity*, Delhi: Oxford University Press.

Feldman, Allan M. and Roberto Serrano (1980). *Welfare Economics and Social Choice Theory*, Springer.

Ferguson, James and Akhil Gupta (2002). Spatialising States: Towards an Ethnography of Neoliberal Governmentality, *American Ethnologist* 29(4).

Filho, Alfred Saad (2010). From Washington Consensus to Inclusive Growth: The Continuing Relevance of Pro-Poor Policy Alternatives. Background Paper for the World Economic and Social Survey, University of London, January 4.

Gupta, Akhil and Aradhana Sharma (2006). Globalisation and Postcolonial States, *Current Anthropology*, Vol. 47, No. 2, April.

Harvey, David (2007). A *Brief History of Neoliberalism*, Oxford University Press.

Henry, Nicholas (2010). Public Administration and Public Affairs, New Delhi: PHI Private Limited.

Kennett, P. (ed.) (2004). A *Handbook of Comparative Social Policies*, UK: Edward Elgar.

Patnaik, Prabhat (2006). The State under Neoliberalism, *MacroScan*, October 31.

Stieglitz, Joseph (2008). The Tenth Lakdawala Lecture, Institute of Social Studies, New Delhi, December 20.

The World Bank (2006). Report No. 34580-IN- *India: Inclusive Growth and Service Delivery: Building on India's Success, Development Policy Review* May 29.

Williamson, John (2000). What Should the World Bank Think About the Washington Consensus, *World Bank Research Observer*, Vol. 15 (2), August.

NOTES

1. Fordism was rooted in the scientific management theory of Tailor for maximising production. His time and motion studies wrested control over knowledge of the production process from the workers and placed such knowledge in the hands of management. This was associated with de-skilling and degradation of labour and eroded autonomy of the craft workers. Ford felt the importance of mass production of the Model T Ford

car and mass market. His Assembly Line Approach and division of labour led to introduction of specialised tools and machineries. To keep the show running, Ford introduced the five-dollar-eight hour day to ensure the working class lifestyle that included owning such an automobile. This would ensure workers' compliance. Ford also enlisted support of a small army of social workers who would go from door-to-door to the homes of the workers in order to educate them in the proper habits of consumption. Under Fordism the firms made long-term commitments to workers and wages were tightly linked to productivity growth. Fordism was also associated with trade unionism and collective bargaining. Post-Fordism made a radical departure from Fordism. Post-Fordism is characterised by: flexibility and innovation and maximisation of production to meet the market demand for diverse customised products; decentralisation of work into a non-hierarchical team group; more flexible occupational structure; group production through collaborative work group in place of assembly line approach; acquisition of new skills, increased autonomy; reduction of managerial supervision and growing pride in goods and services that they produce. (Anthony Giddens, *Sociology*, Polity Press, London, Reprint-2008).

2. The discussion on governmentality may be extended to include not only new strategies of discipline and regulation, exemplified by the WTO and the IMF, but also transnational alliances forged by activists and grassroots organisations and the proliferation of voluntary organisations supported by complex networks of international and transnational funding and personnel. The outsourcing of the functions of the state to NGOs and other ostensibly non-state agencies, is a key feature, not only of the operation of national states, but of an emerging system of transnational governmentality.

   The received notions of *verticality and encompassment* have been stretched—often improbably—to adapt to the new realities. Thus, institutions of global governance such as the IMF and the WTO are commonly seen as being simply "above" national states, much as states were discussed vis-a-vis the grassroots. Similarly, the "global" is often spoken of as if it were simply a superordinate scalar level that encompasses nation-states just as nation-states were conceptualised to encompass regions, towns, and villages. (James Ferguson and Akhil Gupta, Spatialising States: Towards an Ethnography of Neoliberal Governmentality, *American Ethnologist* 29(4):2002).

6

Rise of Finance Capital and Decline of the Nation-State

Sudipta Bhattacharyya

The rise and growth of finance capital is inextricably related to the functioning of global capitalism. Lenin in his seminal work 'Imperialism—The Highest Stage of Capitalism' described finance capital as the amalgamation of industrial capital and bank capital to form finance capital during the rise and growth of monopoly capital. Lenin predicted that finance capital only knew how to expand endlessly. However when the home market remains saturated and the investment still goes on following the Marxian two department scheme, scholars have shown that there will be no possibilities of employment rise but only lead to price adjustment process where there will be a forced distribution of factor shares. Particularly under such a situation the workers' share will decline and the share of profit will increase. A negative multiplier will of course take place. The crisis of capitalist commodity production can squarely be blamed on the working class (Kalecki 1971, Bhaduri 1988). The finance capital therefore expanded to the colonies. The rise of imperialism was in effect to jeopardise the concept of the nation -state worldwide. In other words, they were keen to establish an 'integrated world capitalism' that modern Marxists who belonged to the 'Dependency school' tried to establish in a satellite and metropolis (or Centre and the periphery) relationship (Frank 1975, Amin). The imperialism had its objective to develop integrated world capitalism by undermining the nation-state. The export of capital and territorial distribution of the globe attempted to develop two dual worlds within global capitalism. In India British colonialism tried to perpetuate the intermediary system in agriculture through the Permanent Settlement in 1793, which was the pre-British period. The peasantry was subject to a big squeeze. The burden of the peasantry multiplied with the fact that the colonial ruler annihilated the indigenous industries that according to scholars was part of 'de-industrialisation' (Bagchi 1976) that created a big chunk of reserve army of displaced labourers from handicrafts to find no alternative occupation but to join agriculture. The British government attempted forced commercialisation in agriculture in the name of capitalist development in agriculture that caused immiserisation of the vast peasantry of India. Marx in a letter to Vera Zasulich in 1881 wrote, 'the violent abolition of common property in the soil [in India] was only an act of English vandalism which pushed the indigenous people not forward but backward...they [the English] have only succeeded in ruining domestic agriculture and redoubling the number and intensity of famines.' Imperialism therefore created an unresolved problem in the colonies which became a boomerang for them as the colonial population were united in the struggle for national independence. This is the genesis of nationalism in India centring which all classes of Indian population forgetting their conflicting interests participated in the national freedom struggle. This was the foundation of the nation-state in India and other Third World colonies. In other words, the very voyage of global finance capital to create integrated world capitalism landed up in the 20th century formation of many newly independent nation-states. However, these nation-states including India were established on the basis of the social liberalism theory and not on the basis of socialism. Attempts were made by our national leaders and constitution makers to build an otherwise efficient capitalist system and not any socialist state. However the term 'socialist' was introduced in the preamble of the Indian Constitution as the 42nd Amendment of the Indian Constitution in 1976. Though, this term was no more than rhetoric.

The process of neoliberal globalisation in many ways has largely alienated the people from local identity (Huntington 1993). The globalisation as a process intends to introduce a universal capitalism, universal culture and to some extent a uniform language (i.e. English). In other words in the name of globalisation the Western world was trying to impose a culture of their own which is rather homogeneous and monolithic. It is not without the economic motive. The MNCs consciously want to destroy the local culture in order to convert the diversified Third World in race, language and religion into a unified, homogeneous market for their products. For example, drinking water has always been a free good in Indian society. There is a popular proverb in rural India that 'even if your enemy comes to your house for a glass of drinking water, you can't refuse'. With the neoliberal economic liberalisation in India, free water service (maintained by government and voluntary organisations) virtually disappeared from the road. The passersby have no other alternative to purchase Pepsi or Coke produced bottled mineral water from the shops as the World Bank/DFID funded road development projects in the Third World removes all poor coconut sellers from the pavements as conditionality.

At the same time there has been a steady decline in the nation-state and centrist policy in India (Nayyar 1998). Worldwide there has also been a decline in socialist ideology. Therefore when the local identity is being endangered, there were no other positive alternative identities available to absorb the lost identity. Therefore the alienated people in most of the countries reacted in a negative way, which found identity in religion or other ethnic grouping, e.g. caste, tribe, language, etc. This is the context of revival and resurgence of religious/ethnic fundamentalism throughout the world. Secondly, during the Cold War period the United States created and nurtured religious fundamentalism by providing financial and military assistance in most of the fundamentalist countries today. It is now an open secret that Osama Bin Laden or Saddam Hussein are Frankensteins of USA who created them during the 1980s in order to combat bigger enemies like the Soviet Union or Ayatollah Khomeini. Even today USA gives a clean chit to theocratic and military states like Israel, Saudi Arabia or Pakistan. Thirdly, while investing in the Third World, finance capital always find itself comfortable in an anti-working class autocratic regime. In a democratic set up the people's resistance does not let the domestic economic environment come up to the expectation of the finance capital. Particularly, the IMF package of privatisation and the withdrawal of the state are most unpopular in the southern countries. In a country like India with a long-standing democratic tradition, it is not possible to impose autocracy without creation of a fascist culture based on religion or other kind of ethnicity. However, unlike Islamic states the Hindu fascist force in India has cordial relations with the metropolitan capital.

Fractured Liberalism after Indian Independence

'Liberals' according to the Oxford Advanced Learners Dictionary is a view expressed in the 'politics of Great Britain' 'of the party (dominant until the 1920s), favouring the moderate democratic reform and opposed to privilege' (Hornby 1974: p. 486). However, liberalism is not specific to Great Britain, rather it is a widely applicable capitalist development as a whole. Liberalism is the theory and practice of bourgeois reform since the Industrial Revolution in Britain during the 17th century. Liberalism is the driving factor behind the French Revolution and American Independence during the 18th century. Liberalism dominated in the 19th century and suffered a natural death by giving way to socialism or 'allowed itself to be perverted by socialist ideas' (Dahrendorf, Ralf 1988). Liberalism itself is also a subject of transformation from classical liberalism to social liberalism. The classical liberalism gives space to all economic agents to act from their self-interest; but at the aggregative level the operation of Adam Smith's 'invisible hand' would lead to greater welfare. At the same time democracy must prevail at the political sphere. The classical liberalism that promoted the idea of market capitalism transformed into social liberalism that promoted the idea of the welfare state. J.M. Keynes was a self-proclaimed liberal who advocated the idea of state intervention and restrictions of the market. The social liberals revolted against Fascist totalitarianism and emphasised that economic growth should be combined with a growing role of government and with the extension of the social state.

In this section we observe that India emerged as a liberal democratic nation-state after independence. Though it postponed the immediate agrarian agenda of a nascent capitalism, e.g. land reform, it indeed experienced a successful state intervention under the auspicious Five Year Planns. The experience of India since independence is one of the state interventions in a general capitalist framework that runs on the principle of right to private property. A strategy of heavy industrialisation came up since the Second Five-Year Plan. A sizeable public sector was established at the commanding height of the economy. However, the world capitalism that is based on the principle of the free operation of the market was not very happy with such a development. India receives advice from various international organisations that she should not put so much emphasis on any ambitious industrialisation. Rather the agricultural sector should be paid greater attention. It was advised that since the country was on the verge of Malthusian population disaster, its first priority should be to achieve self-sufficiency on the food front rather than a self-sustained industrialisation[1]. However within the national economy, an undercurrent tension prevailed between the state and the domestic monopoly capitalist, on the one hand, and the state and landlords, on the other. The domestic monopoly capital sought free operation of the market that they did not get within the interventionist state. The industrialisation of the first fifteen years after independence was based on gearing up of the public investment and public expenditure. However, for the continual expansion of the industrialisation a land reform was a must that would have created a market for growing industrialisation, particularly a market for mass consumption goods. But in the post-independence period the state made a historical treaty of peaceful coexistence with the landlord class and all the programmes of the land reform were shelved forever[2]. As a result, a phase of industrial stagnation started from the mid-1960s. Moreover, after the mid-1960s when the ruling Congress Party faced an election debacle it was understood that the state had to appear with more populist promises that heavy industrialisation-based strategy with a long gestation period could hardly fulfil. Thus, the Nehru-Mahalanobis strategy of heavy industrialisation was virtually shelved. From then on, there was a decline in public investment and the era of economic stagnation began. Though the initial thrust for industrialisation came from the interventionist state, over time in the absence of sufficient public investment, public expenditure and a sustained industrial growth, the interventionist state turned out to be a tool of red tapism in the hands of bureaucrats and myopic politicians. Thus a phase of fractured liberalism began. Unlike bourgeois liberalism in the West during the early phase of the Industrial Revolution, the ruling capitalist class never fought landlordism. Rather they made an alliance with them to curb the organised power of the working class and poor peasants.

A popular opinion gradually developed against the state interventionist nature of the Indian economy. Thus, when India had to enter into the full-fledged path of liberalisation since the early 1990s as a consequence of structural adjustment programmes of the IMF and the World Bank, it had gained support from domestic monopoly capital, petty bourgeoisie and from the upwardly mobile middle class intelligentsia. The popular support to the liberalised regime was a negative mandate against the stagnant and bureaucratic state. To get rid of the interventionist regime the domestic monopoly capital and petty bourgeoisie swallowed the bitter pill of entry of metropolitan capital. However, for the urban upwardly mobile middle class, the liberalised regime had a cultural appeal of a Western lifestyle and Western consumer goods. The strength of the urban middle class can hardly be undermined since they can influence the popular media to a large extent.

Gangster Neoliberalism and Decline of Nation-State

What happened to the liberal nation-state that developed during the four decades after independence? A discontent gradually developed against the nation-state. The international economic order changed radically during the early 1990s with the collapse of the Soviet Union. As a result with many other LDCs, India also adopted neoliberalism as the *mantra* of the nation-state. Under this system the state was withdrawal in nature. And in the case of intervention it is the other way round. Instead of serving poor people it serves the corporate houses directly. The exemption of the direct tax rate is the example of the same. However, the 1990s also witnessed a steep rise in erosion of centralised politics. Cashing in on the advantage of the local political priorities and the discontents against the liberalisation the Bharatiya Janata Party (BJP) a pro-Hindutva party, came into power. They had a proto-fascist tendency based on religious fundamentalism. However, they failed to obtain a clear majority, for which they had to form an alliance (National Democratic Alliance or NDA) with other regional parties with centrist policy. Even the NDA as a whole were short of a majority in the upper house of the Parliament (Rajya Sabha). This is why for the last few years the BJP could not succeed in implementing its fascist agenda in full swing, at least at the national level. Though BJP could not pass a single bill related to their fundamentalist policy in the parliament, which includes a bill against cow slaughtering, it could build up mobilisation in support of their fascist agenda, the culmination of which was the genocide of the minority in Gujarat. Though the BJP is out of power now, there is a substantial force of religious fundamentalism that still affects the state's secular democratic credentials. In many states the NDA is still in power and in almost all states it remains the major opposition.

The point to be noted is that not only the BJP or Shiv Sena, other centrist parties particularly the All India National Congress followed the identical neoliberal policies. The only difference is that they do not represent organised fundamentalism. But that did not alter the other kind of undemocratic nature of neoliberalism—e.g. to adopt neoliberal policies like FDI in retail or disinvestment not only bypassing the parliament but also without any consultation with the other parties in the alliance.

The question is that why is neoliberalism essentially anti-state and even more anti-state than the classical liberals? The answer lies in the neoliberal belief that the inflow of international finance capital can act as an engine of economic development in a developing country. But the international finance capital has thoroughly changed its character from the era of Lenin's analysis. In Lenin's characterisation the international finance capital was highly productive and highly coercive. However the global finance capital of today may invest in any global market without being concerned about long-term productivity. In other words, finance capital today is highly mobile speculative capital, which follows no consistent tendency of inflow and outflow. The experiences of Mexico, South-East Asia and Argentina have unfolded the 'herd behaviour' of this speculative capital that was withdrawn suddenly and unpredictably leaving those countries in total jeopardy[3]. The contemporary global financial and economic crisis had its root in speculative capital being invested in real estate that created the housing market bubble in the US. The contagion of this bubble spread to all important global financial markets and initiated the most prolonged economic crisis in the world. In India also a big proportion of FDI is being diverted to real estate ($2.12 billion in 2006-07). It actually blocked effective housing space for the poor and middle class with the connivance of corrupt politicians, MNC executives, businessmen and criminals. The finance capital cannot be productive capital since its sole objective is to appropriate the short-term profit (without being concerned about the long run). This is the reason it opposes all sorts of state intervention, which are long-term in nature and not related to the immediate profit motive of any entrepreneur—public or private. Therefore, it was no wonder that the Indian experience of liberalisation started with a 30 per cent cut in a food and fertiliser subsidy. The directed credit to agriculture and the priority sector lending also declined to a great extent. However, since big farmers also became losers for this uniform cut in fertiliser price, government raise the procurement price for paddy and wheat by more than 50 per cent in order to keep the big farmers' lobby in good humour (Nayyar 1996). At the same time the government raised the issue price of foodgrains to a great extent that made the gap between the ration shop price and open market price narrower and virtually the PDS system became almost defunct. The final blow comes with the government announcement of the targeted PDS (TPDS) that should serve only the BPL population (Swaminathan 2002). As different scholars including the High Level Committee on Long Term Grain Policy of the Government of India, 2002 (Abhijit Sen Committee) indicated it is extremely difficult to identify the head count ratio of income poverty and therefore exclude a big proportion of poor people from the BPL list. The Sen Committee Report recommended the re-introduction of the universal PDS. The TPDS instead of serving the poor, aggravated poverty in rural India. It is not surprising that except the NSSO 55th round of data almost all estimates show an increase in poverty in the post-liberalisation period (Sen, 2000). As a consequence, the rural poverty in India marked a steep rise during the liberalised regime (Sen 1996, Tendulkar and Jain 1995, Patnaike 2005, 2009). With the increase in rural poverty, the ratio of consumption on primary food articles to total income registered an increase that reduced rural diversification of the economy and, as a result, rural employment was reduced.

Apart from economic issues the liberalised regime brings out some social deformity that has deep implications. First of all, the prolonged industrial stagnation and poverty creates a reserve army of unemployed youth. It is a matter of fact that the real estate is one of the sectors that attracts the international speculative capital. It is not at all an isolated event that crime based on real estate business suddenly is on an increase in all the big cities in India during the 1990s. In most of these cases the unemployed youths are involved. A reserve army of middle class unemployed young population is organised under the fascist slogan. It might be remembered that this urban unemployed middle class young men had a high representation among *karsevaks* who demolished the Babri Masjid, or among rioters in Bombay, Surat, Kanpur following the demolition. Young people belonging to the majority Hindu community were organised largely by the Shiv Sena and partly by BJP by nurturing a misplaced concept that the minority community grabs the social and economic benefits that would otherwise accrue to the youth belonging to the majority community. The rise of the Shiv Sena in Bombay, the largest financial, trading and industrial centre of the country was directly associated with the decline in trade union power, particularly the murder of renowned and popular trade union leader Datta Samanta. The Shiv Sena gains financial and moral support from corporate capital. In many urban centres riots were conducted by the real estate investors to clear up the slums for the construction of the high-rise buildings. The carnage we witnessed in Gujarat where for the first time the BJP exposed its mission of capturing India by means of genociding the minority. In the past, even after the demolition of the Babri Masjid, BJP were not able to polarise the otherwise highly differentiated Hindu population (mainly by caste). For the first time the BJP has been able to polarise the voters in a religious line.

Towards a Theoretical Understanding

We have discussed before that during the 1990s there was a tendency in India and worldwide that a rise in ethnic and religious fundamentalism grew hand in hand with the advancement of the neoliberal policy. In our view the process of globalisation and ethnic/religious conflict are in a cause and effect relation. In different countries the rise of ethnic and religious fundamentalism is also associated with the process of weakening of democracy and a rise in the proto-fascist autocratic regime. There are several reasons behind such apparently contradictory tendencies. First of all, the goal of the neoliberal globalisation is to establish the rule of capital and property throughout the world. It is rather inappropriate with the democracy in a socio-economic set up where the right to private property is not clearly defined, for example, in a communal way of life where members of a community directly participate in a decision-making process. Secondly, as a post-world war consensus global capitalism adopted the policy of welfare state, as the socialism of the Soviet Union, Eastern Europe and newly socialist China posed a major threat against the inegalitarian nature of capitalism. The neoliberalism in the name of the Washington consensus developed with the demise of the Soviet Union and the socialist Eastern Europe. The time has come again when capitalism has no more need to don the mask of a welfare state. As a concept, capitalism is an anachronism with the concept of the welfare state and as Prabhat Patnaik pointed out that neoliberalism cannot have any human face. However, the transition from welfare state to neo-liberal capitalism cannot be a smooth road without résistance. People in many countries, particularly southern countries raise their voice against the neo-liberal onslaught of selling of the public sector, retrenchment, cut in welfare expenditure, e.g. education, health, rural development, etc., neglect of agriculture, unilateral withdrawal of subsidy. Thus in most countries, which includes India, the neoliberal policies had to be mixed up and messed up with autocratic dictatorship against the will of the people. In other words the neoliberal policies becomes impossible to implement in an environment of liberal democracy. The 'export led development' in Korea and Taiwan in the 1960s was nothing but the imposition of market under dictatorship. The monetarist dictatorial regime of Pinochet in Chile, the dictatorial regime of Suharto in Indonesia, or recent experience Argentina or Bolivia proves the point. As we have discussed before, in India no ruling party had absolute majority in the both houses of the Parliament. In this respect the domain of dictatorship is rather limited. In spite of that respective government was trying to make onslaught of the autocracy. NDA regime tried to sell public sector petroleum industries by passing the Parliament though ultimately the Supreme Court stalled their effort. In several other matters the judicial system supports the ruling classes' efforts to establish anti-working class, autocratic and above all fundamentalist state. For example Supreme Court gave a verdict that public sector workers under no circumstances go for strike. The Supreme Court in another verdict supported the BJP government's efforts to saffronise the education system on the plea that religious education is a good thing. Following the precedence of NDA, the UPA-II government attempted to impose many crucial decisions, e.g. FDI in retail bypassing the Parliament. Apart from organised fundamentalism there is almost no difference between NDA and UPA regarding implementation of onslaught of neoliberalism.

Thus we have seen that the process of globalisation and the tendency towards an autocratic fundamentalist state are complementary to each other. However, so far not enough conditions have developed to describe the Indian state as a fascist one. The Comintern's position on fascism is that it was the 'open terrorist dictatorship of the most reactionary, most chauvinist and most imperialist elements of finance capital'. While this definition was absolutely appropriate to explain fascism in Germany or Italy during the 1930s, it is utterly inappropriate for a developing country like India today. Harriss-White (2003) describes certain characters that fascism practises such as (i) authoritarianism, (ii) nationalism, racism and xenophobia, (iii) statolatory, (iv) unifying ideology and leadership. According to Harriss-White, though some of these tendencies are growing in India, but still now this 'proto-fascist politics' are not dominant enough to describe India as a fascist state. Banaji (2003) also holds the view that the recent developments in India cannot be described as fascist according to the definition given by the Comintern. He preferred to call it the 'political culture of fascism'. He culturally deconstructed fascism at three levels. The first one according to him is nationalism as the rational core of fascist ideology, which borrowed its aspiration from religious myths. At the second level he referred to the culture of authoritarianism and repression, which includes the social repression, family repression or sexual repression. Thirdly organised brutality or violence as common *praxis,* i.e. organised action or 'common action' of organised groups of the majority against the ethnic/religious minority, which includes the campaign of genocide.

Rosa Luxemburg formulated the theory of a military economy that avoids crisis by means of production of military goods on government order. In such an economy a new monopoly capital replaces the old. It replaces scattered uncertain demand from a large number of workers to a concentrated, certain and planned demand from the government. Not only does it ensure the certain source of demand but also a certain source of profit. Though Rosa's theory had its own contradictions, nevertheless it is a historical fact that during the era of late capitalism fascism emerged in almost all countries based on a new monopoly capital backed by the armament lobby. This kind of rule of new monopoly capital is in fact a rule by the gangster capitalist. It is also directly linked with the finance capital. Historically, such gangster capitalism was based on military expenditure and had always been a more conservative, more sectarian and more authoritarian form of government. Particularly Nazism in Germany and contemporary Japanese fascism were in fact based on such new monopoly capital. Even the new monopoly capital of USA based on Texas and California who are interested in oil and armaments had always advocated anti-working class policies and were always backed by the conservative regimes of Nixon and Reagan (Patnaik 1995). However, the counterpart of this new monopoly capital in LDCs does not intend to appear as a new imperialist force in the world market. Rather, they want to survive by wooing the metropolitan capital and, therefore, accommodating them in the domestic market. They generally pursue a fascist anti-working class economic policy at home and liberalised trade policy to keep metropolitan capital in good humour. Suharto's Indonesia, Pinochet's Chile or Fujimori's Peru are examples of that. The first thirteen-month rule of the BJP government had all the fascist tendencies within itself starting from the Pokhran blast to the Kargil war. However, the BJP had to work within its own coalition that was on the verge of collapse from the very beginning. Ultimately they returned to power with a clear mandate. In their second phase the BJP government has dared to take the initiative to privatise key sectors such as power, insurance and major transport like Indian Airlines and Indian Railway. The working class is facing threats of retrenchment and privatisation of all the profit-making public sector undertakings. Above all, they had no hesitation to show a replica of their future rule all over the country in a state-sponsored genocide of the minority in Gujarat. Their responsible ally Shiv Sena showed such a model in Mumbai some years ago, where a large section of the Muslim population were butchered. Ironically except for communal fascism all other economic policies of the Congress Government are identical with BJP. For us the discourse should no longer be confined to a thoughtful seminar that might suggest government for possible omission and commission. The time has come for fierce political battle between the agent of a bunch of gangster neoliberals on the one hand, and all the secular-minded patriotic people, on the other.

REFERENCES

Bagchi, A.K. (1982). *Political Economy of Underdevelopment*, Cambridge: Cambridge University Press.

Bagchi, A.K. (1998). 'Growth Miracle and Its Unravelling in East and South-East Asia: Unregulated Competitiveness and Denouncement of Manipulation by International Financial Community', *Economic and Political Weekly*, May 2-8.

Banaji, Jairus (2002). 'The Political Culture of Fascism', *South Asia Citizens Web*, http://sacw.insaf.net/new/BanajiSept02.html.

Basu, Tapan, et al., (1993). *Khaki Shorts Saffron Flags*, Hyderabad: Orient Longman.

Bhaduri, A. (1986). *Macroeconomics*, London: Macmillan.

Bhaduri, A. and Nayyar, D. (1997). *The Intelligent Person's Guide to Liberalization*, New Delhi: Penguin.

Bhattacharyya, Sudipta (1995). 'Economic Liberalization in India: One Step Forward—Two Steps Back', *Mainstream*, March 18.

Chandrasekhar, C.P. (1995). 'One More Crisis: Some Lessons from Mexico', *Frontline*, January 27.

Chandrasekhar, C.P. (1999). 'A Persisting Obsession', *Frontline*, March 26.

Government of India, *Economic Survey*: Various Issues.

Government of India (1993). *Report of the Expert Group on the Estimation of Proportion and Number of the Poor. 1987-1988*, Perspective Planning Division, Planning Commission.

Dahrendorf, Ralf (1987). 'Liberalism', in John Eatwell, et al. (ed) *The*

New Palgrave Dictionary of Economics, Vol. 3. London: Macmillan.

Frank, A.G. (1967). *Capitalism and Underdevelopment in Latin America,* New York: Monthly Review Press.

Frank, A.G. (1975). *On Capitalist Underdevelopment,* Bombay: Oxford University Press.

Harriss-White, Barbara 2003. *India Working: Essays on Society and Economy,* Cambridge: Cambridge University Press.

Hornby, A.S. (1974). *Oxford Advanced Learner's Dictionary of Current English,* Delhi: Oxford University Press.

Huntington, Samuel P. (1993). 'The Clash of Civilisations?', *Foreign Affairs,* Vol. 72, No. 3.

Kalecki, Michal (1971). *Selected Essays on the Dynamics of the Capitalist Economy,* Cambridge: Cambridge University Press.

Keynes, J.M. (1947). *The General Theory of Employment, Interest and Money,* London: Macmillan.

Luxemburg, Rosa (1951). *Accumulation of Capital,* London: RKP.

MacEwan, Arthur (1999). *Neoliberalism or Democracy? Economic Strategy, Markets and Alternatives for the 21st Century,* London: Zed.

Mehta, Jaya (1995). 'Mexican Crisis: Lessons for India', *Mainstream,* March 18.

Mody, R.J. (1992). 'Fiscal Deficit and Stabilisation Policy', *Economic and Political Weekly,* August 24.

Nayyar, Deepak (1996). *Economic Liberalization in India: Analytics, Experience and Lessons,* Hyderbad: Orient Longman.

Nayyar, Deepak (1998). 'Economic Development and Political Democracy: Interaction of Economics and Politics in Independent India', *Economic and Political Weekly,* December 8.

Patnaik, Prabhat (1995). "Nation-State in the Era of Globalisation", *Economic and Political Weekly,* August 19.

Patnaik, Prabhat (1997). *Whatever Happened to Imperialism and Other Essays,* New Delhi: Tulika.

Patnaik, Prabhat (1999). 'The Finance Minister's Fallacy', *Frontline,* February 26.

Patnaik, Prabhat (1999). 'The Real Face of Financial Liberalization', *Frontline,* February 26.

Patnaik, Utsa (1988). 'Some Aspects of Development in the Agrarian Sector in Independent India', *Social Scientist,* No. 177, February.

Patnaik, Utsa (1996). 'Export-Oriented Agriculture and Food Security in Developing Countries and India', *Economic and Political Weekly,* Special Number, September.

Patnaik, Utsa (2003). 'Ricardo's Fallacy: Mutual Benefit from Trade Based on Comparative Costs and Specialisation?', Mimeo.

Rakshit, Mihir (1991). 'The Macroeconomic Adjustment Programme: A Critique', *Economic and Political Weekly*, August 24.

Reserve Bank of India (1991). *Report of the Committee on the Financial System* (Chairman: M. Narasimham), Bombay.

Ricardo, David (1951). *On the Principles of Political Economy and Taxation*, Sraffa ed., Vol. 1, New York: Cambridge University Press.

Sanyal, Kalyan (1993). 'Paradox of Competitiveness and Globalisation of Underdevelopment', *Economic and Political Weekly*, June 19.

Sen, Sunanda (1998). 'Asia: Myth of a Miracle', *Economic and Political Weekly*, January 17.

Sen, Abhijit (1996). 'Economic Reforms, Employment and Poverty: Terms and Options', *Economic and Political Weekly*, Special Number, September.

Sen, Abhijit (2000). 'Estimates of Consumer Expenditure and its Distribution: Statistical Priorities after NSS 55th Round', *Economic and Political Weekly*, December 16.

Stiglitz, J.E. (2002). *Globalization and its Discontents*, London: Allen Lane: The Penguin Press.

Stiglitz, J.E. and Weiss, A. (1981). 'Credit Rationing in Markets with Imperfect Information', *American Economic Review*, June.

Swaminathan, Madhura (2002). 'Excluding the Needy: Public Provisioning of Food in India,' *Social Scientist*, Vol. 30, No. 3-4, March-April.

Tendulkar, S.D. and Jain, L.R. (1995). 'Economic Reforms and Poverty', *Economic and Political Weekly*, June 10.

Vora, N.N. (ed.) (2003). *Mid Year Review of Indian Economy 2002-2003*, NCAER Report prepared by Suman K. Bery. Delhi: Shipra Publications.

NOTES

1. Ford Foundation team's report in 1959 (Patnaik 1995: 176). Another confidential report of World Bank mentioned by Patnaik (1995).
2. According to Utsa Patnaik (1988), the compromise was made with wishful thinking that the erstwhile landlords would be transformed productively to capitalists even if their landed monopoly would not be seriously challenged. In practice 'it constrains growth by confining investment in productivity raising techniques to an excessively narrow social stratum in the village'.

3. Mexico was the success story of SAP till the early 1990s. Mexico had undergone the same experience of trade liberalisation as India is underway now. Initially, it attracted a huge amount of speculative capital from the international financial market. As a consequence, the higher classes' purchase of US and Canadian goods shot up significantly leading to an unprecedented trade deficit. To tackle the situation the Mexican government declared devaluation of the peso and opening up other markets for speculative activities. At the same time, the US interest rate rose in the international market and there was a heavy depletion of foreign funds from Mexico. In a desperate attempt to stabilise the market, government hiked the interest rate by 30 per cent and allowed the peso to float freely against the dollar. But the results were near complete collapse of stock markets, a bottomless fall in the peso and almost total depletion of forex reserves. [See. C.P. Chandrasekhar (1995), Jaya Mehta (1995)].

   Southeast Asian countries were projected as a model of a fund-bank styled market economic reform for a long time. These countries had been able to attract a huge amount of speculative capital. In a sudden reversal the short-term funds started to move out from these regions in 1997. The governments reacted by a sudden devaluation of the currency along with a hike in the rate of interest. This was the recommended prescription of the IMF to arrest the outflow of finance capital. But it resulted in a loss of confidence and hence a decline in asset price and a near shutdown of the stock market. Particularly the domestic investors who had borrowed foreign funds became the worst victims of the crisis. This resulted in a further outflow of capital and collapse of the domestic economies as a whole. [See. Bagchi (1998), Sen (1998)].

7

Political Economy of Neoliberal Urban Order in India

Joydeep Baruah

Urbanisation, as a demographic phenomenon, especially in the post-Second World War period, has given rise to some serious concerns regarding the overall patterns of population distribution across the world. In 1996, The United Nations Centre for Human Settlement (UNCHS) in its *Global Report on Human Settlement* observed that by the year 2000, almost 50 per cent of the world's total population would be living in urban areas[1]. This was held as the most historic phenomenon since for the first time in history, urban dwellers would outnumber those in traditionally rural areas (UNCHS, 1996). Incessant urbanisation has been more revealing in developing countries. In 1950, 38 per cent of the world's total urban population lived in the Third World cities and towns (UN, 1980). In 1995, the figure rose to around 66 per cent (UN, 1995). The United Nations estimates that by the end of 2025, the figure might well be somewhere near 80 per cent. The discontent over such 'biased' concentrations of people in a few selected areas had generated altogether a newer approach within the development discourse, which was broadly identified as "theories of urban bias". These theories continued to dominate development literature in the 1960s and 70s (Lipton, 2004; Pugh, 1996). It was argued that inequality, in fact, has its roots in the conflict between "rural and urban", and not between "labour and capital" that the stylised Marxist paradigm tended to believe (Lipton, 2004). Many observed and felt that the urbanisation and its attendant social ills are even more severe in the Third World cities than elsewhere (Date, 2006; Karn, Shikura and Harada, 2003; Prakash, 2002; Mishra, 2000).

The first and foremost issue, therefore, consequent on the fast and ever increasing size of these urban agglomerations, is how the Third World cities, given their poor resource-bases, will cope and survive—economically, environmentally and politically—with such heavy concentrations of people. This has, in fact, necessitated newer forms of urban governance involving privatisation, partnership arrangements and promotion of community-based projects for undertaking investments in basic amenities due to the resource crunch in the government. As some would argue, this changed perspective and subsequent decline in public investment, however, are likely to accentuate the disparity in the levels of amenities across the size class of urban settlements (Kundu, Bagchi and Kundu, 1999). While admitting the cost reducing advantages of agglomeration economies, and various forms of economic and social externalities in the urban areas, one must also objectively consider the social and economic costs of such 'congestions'[2], let alone the 'quality amenities' for their resident citizens (Todaro, 2000). The urgency of critically looking at alternatives of sub-national governments, in this context, has been usually stressed and advocated, especially for the developing and transitional economies (Pethe and Lalwani, 2006).

Second, almost twenty years ago, in 1988, the United Nations published the *Report on the Population Policies in the World*. The report revealed that 73 out 158 countries in the world had 'highly unacceptable' geographical distribution of their population. Many blamed the 'misguided policies regarding urban planning' in these countries for such 'unsatisfactory growth' of their urban spheres. It is, therefore, critical to find out to what extent governments can regulate the process of urbanisation so as to keep it within the 'acceptable limit'. In doing so, the urban process, itself, as a particular form of spatial organisation of population, needs careful analysis. For, an urban process not only signifies a particular settlement pattern of population, but also aptly captures the development dynamics of a region, which sometimes influences the urban process and sometimes, gets influenced by the process (Bardhan and Udry, 2000). Equally important is the question whether an intervention in the urban process on the part of the governments is at all desirable. This essentially calls for a thorough review of policy initiatives and options influencing urban systems and processes as a whole, directly or otherwise (Deb, 2006).

Consequently, the third issue that surfaces is the classic debate of rural-urban continuum and dichotomy. Strict physical and pure demographic criteria have gradually been on the wane in differentiating and characterising the rural and urban spaces (Thompson, 2004; Qadeer, 2000; Sharma, 1987). The resultant emphasis on "quality of life" aspects has distinct implications for both theoretical analyses and policy formulations (Rogerson, 1999). It therefore, is appropriate to examine rural-urban cleavages as well as linkages afresh given the present currents and cross-currents of globalisation. The issues of accommodating and managing the so-called 'extra-urbanites' in the global regime are, therefore, very much in order.

Urban "Management" in Global Regime

In the strict literal sense, the term 'regime' primarily connotes 'rule' that is embedded in society; speaking more politically, it is the "rule of government". Although, terms like "global regime" and 'globalisation' are often used interchangeably, there are differences, which are, of course, relative to time and space. James (1999) characterises the "global regime" as a political rule which is fundamentally guided by an economic agenda. Naturally, such a regime is founded on tenets of globalisation. The concept of globalisation, however, makes better sense only in terms of the economic interest of the 'national state', of sovereignty (Harris, 2003). What distinguishes globalisation from the earlier state of affairs is the dichotomy between "political sovereignty" and "economic sovereignty". Earlier, at least at the level of theory, political sovereignty of a state is equated with its economic sovereignty. It is commonly held that economic decisions are in full command of the territorial authority. One amongst most significant changes that the globalisation has brought about is the changes in this perspective of governance by substantively reducing the economic sovereignty of the state. Political decisions, under such circumstances, have to be founded and conditioned by economic interests, which are, in turn, governed by larger global interests. It is in this perspective that James' characterisation of the "global regime" acquires most merits.

The preponderance of the state, in the earlier state of affairs, ensured primacy of politics over economics and of public discretion over markets. Civil society was virtually absorbed into the state; and governments directing the resources at the national interest, assumed responsibility of the housing, health, water supply, sanitation, education and employment. Consequently, the sizeable public sector and publicly protected monopolies were the hallmark of the system. Five Year Plans occupied a central place within such a system, often trying to anticipate the future. The state controlled sector was so sizeable that future results could be predictable and even targeted objectives could be achieved through rational manipulations of resources within the public sector (Shonfiled, 1965)[3]. This was precisely why the planners could think of even master plans for 20 to 25 years.

In this scheme of things, capital (equated with investment, more often than not) emerged as the single most important but relatively scarce resource in economic plans; and attempts and attention were focused mainly on augmenting and allocating it in a manner that would yield best 'national results' (Harris, 2003). In the physical plan, land was treated in a similar fashion, often making judicious arrangements to settle population on it. Control of the location of new housing and industry with zoning, etc. could be rationalised on this ground.

Implications of this approach was that cities were cited as ills and the reason was believed to be the high density of population, rather than failure of public policy. Contingent on such a belief, much of scholarship was devoted to obtain an 'optimal city size' that would minimise the ills associated with increased concentration of people upon space. As a panacea to all ills, at least in theory, "benevolent hierarchy of settlements" was advocated, which was supposed to reduce the so-called "social horror of the primate cities".

Globalisation, however, has brought about a paradigm shift in this whole scheme of thought and approach. At least, three most fundamental changes can be identified in this context in appreciation of such a shift in focus and framework. First, there is a considerable convergence of opinion in the literature that the basic context in which cities are currently perceived is the "heightened mobility of capital" that thrust cities into an entirely new set of city-capital relations (Muhammad, 2006; Kearns and Paddison, 2000; Rogerson, 1999). Contrary to the earlier set of city-capital relations, the newer set of relations tends to weaken the relative position of cities (or urban centres) in relation to capital. This is mainly because of the ability of transnational corporations—and, indeed, smaller and more local organisations—to switch their locations of operation around the globe at a relative ease, which has created a truly global economy—interdependent, integrated and interconnected.

This structural reformulation of original city-capital relations, which were so far discussed, debated and explained within the familiar milieu of "location theories"[4], has some distinctive and substantive spatial implications. Along with the spatial dispersal of economic activities, the changing nature of the activities being undertaken, induced by the changing economic climate, and their organisation, especially the decline in manufacturing activities accompanied by the subsequent rise in services as well as capacity of capital (and labour) to switch locations has enabled a new set of "local place attributes" in capital. The rhetoric of 'local' is, thus, embedded within the process of global accumulation, what has been described as a "fragmented mosaic of uneven development" in which competitive places try to secure a lucrative development niche (Rogerson, 1999)[5]. This, in fact, provides the required setting for discussing the next important issue the global regime ushers in.

The second most important aspect of this paradigm shift incited by waves of globalisation is a reiteration and/or reinterpretation of the concept of 'local' vis-à-vis 'global'. Understanding the relevance and resurgence of 'local' in the context of 'global', seems paradoxical though, is not only academically intriguing, but also necessary for rationalising several attempts at "democratic decentralisations" that many of the developing countries favoured, particularly after the "structural adjustments". This has been viewed as a part of "competitive strategy" to combat with "globalising forces", for two reasons—first, with the reduced economic sovereignty, internal decision-making of a state is no longer independent of exogenous factors. This, in turn, makes anticipation of the future highly irrational and inaccurate. As such, mechanisms like long-term state planning (like five year ones), and master planning are fast losing their significances. Second, as a part of global competition, cities are trying hard to sell themselves for a number of investment and other reasons in what has been termed as "place wars" (Haider, 1992)[6]. As a part of this place war, rooted in efforts of winning capital (and/or investment), apparently homogenising global culture is frequented by simultaneous attempts to develop a city's local, distinctive culture to attract capital investment.

Pervasive, as some would claim, *commodification* driven by the dominant capitalist economies is inextricably bound up with a friction between the local and the global in terms of institutional forms, values, cultures and social priorities. A number of authors have pointed out that 'global' is to varying degrees embedded in 'local' contexts in which specific cultures, policy histories, local institutions and labour markets play a part in creating 'hybridised' rather than necessarily homogeneous and universal forms (Forrest et al, 2004). Although, local variation in benefits, services and amenities is often disparaged as 'inequitable', this is increasingly the case that as long as the minimum standards are protected, variation and innovation in what is provided by the local authority are generally encouraged. Political decentralisation has been championed on the need to be responsive to local requirements and to differences in political demand formulations between localities, outcomes which have ushered in further variations and innovations (Kearns and Paddison, 2000). These trends have been reinforced by recent changes in the political domain such as state fragmentation and agency proliferations, often as a response by local arenas to address simultaneously the agendas of competitiveness and social cohesion. This helps understanding the underlying principles for the reconciliation of 'local' to apparently conflicting notion of 'global'.

In the face of an increasingly competitive world, contingent upon the global regime, local urban body members, both elected members and officials, need to become more entrepreneurial, a role, which potentially conflicts with local welfarism. Short and Kim (1999) describes this as "transformation in urban governance from the welfare state model towards the economic development model". This transition brings forth the third distinctive characteristic of the paradigm shift, i.e. global cities are no longer considered as social evils, but are potent and dynamic nerve centres of all sorts of development activities. The character of these cities has also seen a metamorphosis—as these are turning out to be service cities as against the earlier notion of productive cities (Harris, 2003). The "engine of growth" orientation of cities has resulted in substantial academic efforts in characterising "global cities", "world cities", "mega cities" and "information cities" in the regime of flexible accumulations.

In the early 1970s, Friedman and Wolff (1982) used the concept of "world city", drawing from Patrick Geddes', to initiate a discussion on those cities that have increased in size as they become centres of new global economy. Sassen (1991) calls these cities, such as New York, London and Tokyo, "global cities"[7]. These cities act as command and control centres for the new global economy. Both Friedman, Wolff and Sassen argue that these cities are distinct because they have become nodes for the operation of the global regime and critical foci for a new regime of accumulation. In these cities, one can find trans-national corporations' headquarters, critical business services, such as international finance, other transnational institutions as well as telecommunications and information super high-ways. Their social organisation and spatial forms expand or contract as the latter intervenes in the organisation of economies of scale. To be very precise, global cities (some refer to these as world cities) sit at the top of the hierarchy of control and connectivity within the emerging global economy.

This line of characterisation of global cities bears critical implications. If 'significant' concentration of headquarters and regional offices of most powerful transnational and/or multinational corporations and financial institutions are adopted as the defining attributes of global cities, than global cities does not necessarily imply mega-cities, which are heaving enormous concentration of population. In other words, literatures on global cities distinguish cities, which are nodes of power, control and cultural dominance from those, which have a major concentration of population. Future of a city, thus, depends on recognising this distinction, which presumes cities are a powerful engine of growth, not a necessary evil as they were before.

How can one justify increasing concentration, power and influence of particular cities in a situation in which economic activities are, quite paradoxically, more dispersed? Forrest et al. (2004) explains—"technology enables this simultaneous process of concentration and de-concentration". Castells (1989, 1996) modern urbanisation would assume a pattern, which would be "functionally integrated" but "socially differentiated". This is possible because of revolutionary advancements of telecommunications, which allow both spatial concentration as well as de-centralisation leading to new geographies of networks and nodes within and between the countries in the world, and between and within urban areas (Patel, 2006). The system is, hence, marked by a perceived duality—one that includes those who enter the transnational networks, and excludes others spatially creating extreme inequalities.

There is, however, nothing new about a juxtaposition of affluence and poverty in cities. What is new is the argument that the social divisions and their spatial manifestations evident in these global cities are produced by a distinct and contemporary set of processes associated with the new dynamics of the global economy and, particularly, changes in the nature of employment and opportunity in the labour markets (Castells, 1996; Sassen, 1991).

What essential implications do these three salient features of global regime have on "urban management" per se? Heightened capital mobility and emphasis on its local attributes, which tends to degenerate "centralised statecraft" and gives way to a "new confederal municipalist politics" (Bookchin, 1995), along with the belief that cities and towns are, in fact, the hub of global growth, have shifted the focus from 'governance' to 'management'. In effect, the global regime breeds a more fundamental conflict of local people (voters) against global investors and business houses. Mediating and managing the 'tension' and 'friction', between local democratic conditions and market-guided global 'networks', has become the core of the new municipal agenda. When multinational businesses can relocate themselves with impunity, and thereby undermine a city's economic base, do citizens really have the ability to determine local conditions? In an environment of withering manufacturing sector and increasing low-end service sectors, are citizens and local urban bodies truly able to 'manage' local practices? It is in this context, ideals of "local governance" which ensures "democratic rights of local people" get subverted, and principles of 'management' attains prominence, which seeks to "modifying cost and profit conditions" (Prud'homme and Lee, 1999).

This change in character demands restructuring of the mechanism of municipal finance along with that of urban management. Researchers feel that answer to many of the issues raised above lies in a stronger state-society synergy and social partnerships. As the political system has become increasingly differentiated and fragmented, elected local government may even be more and more marginalised (Pratchett and Wilson, 1996). What it implies is that "local politics" are, in effect, no longer "politics of the local government", and it will tend to be more so in the near future. Since, many of the most important decisions are taken within quite different forums. One of the recent theoretical frameworks developed for discussing the restructuring of the local government is known as "urban regime theories", which advocates a "coalition of political, business and community" members (Stone, 1989). These are perceived, in fact, as parts of the larger coalitions operating on a global scale.

The interesting issue is, in fact, how to ensure such a synergy at the local level. Understanding locality within the global framework brings questions of space-society relations to the fore. In this context, emerging new forms of social space[8] and spatial relations; and its relevance at local levels invites insightful examinations. The pressing question is, therefore, given the existing framework of urban process and forms of local governance in the country, how to respond rationally and intelligently to the global changes and challenges (Stubbs et al; 2000). Is it possible for the local urban systems in the country to gain sustainability? Is it possible for an urban management system to ensure a quality urban life for its urban dwellers still remaining within the necessary 'coalition'? These are some of the questions that emerge as fundamental issues of "urban management" in the "global regime", generating, inevitably of course, both contests and consensus alike, in the contemporary development literature.

Political Economy Perspectives of Policy Framework in India

The approach paper to the Eleventh Five Year Plan of India categorically mentions a definite and distinct "rural-urban divide", which the Planning Commission envisages to bridge through "growth in agriculture" combined with "infrastructural support for non-agricultural activity in rural areas" (Planning Commission, 2007)[9]. The Commission perceives the rural-urban divide in terms of the ever increasing ratio of "urban to rural per capita consumption". Based on the NSS data, the ratio has been found to be 1.91 in 2004-05, which was 1.76 in 1999-00 and 1.62 in 1993-94[10]. Further, the Commission observes, if the comparison is extended to cover "other essential services" than the "chasm is much deeper".

Apart from the distinct rural-urban divide, the Planning Commission also refers to another divide in its approach paper —"a divide within the urban areas, which is also widening"[11].

On consequences of such 'divide(s)', the Commission observes:

> Massive problems have emerged as a result of rapid growth of urban population without a corresponding increase in urban infrastructure and in providing civic amenities. A select few have relatively better access to urban services. Yet even they don't escape the consequences of massive neglect of basic urban services that becomes glaringly apparent in emergencies such as heavy rains, earthquakes, etc. The quality of life of the bulk of our urban people, particularly for the poor, means living with many avoidable hardships. They do not even have access to clean drinking water. Urban renewal is imperative for both efficiency and equity, since cities provide substantial economies of agglomeration and are the growth engines of the economy (p. 82).

Let us now examine carefully the genesis of so-called rural-urban divide. A number of Third World countries attained independence from European colonial rule at the end of the Second World War. An agrarian economy and agrarian population were the legacy of these newly emerged countries. A vast majority of these countries forged constitutions endorsing centralised planning by government to attain modernisation through facilitation of rapid industrialisation in both the public and private sectors. In this context, rural development, quite obviously, tended to be a key element in the national development agenda. Rural development measures adopted in these countries not only aimed at increasing the agricultural production but also tried to redistribute wealth on the grounds of social justice and welfare. The latter provided the legitimacy for government planning, which was seen as the panacea for all ills in countries recently released from colonialism.

The first telling feature of the general approach in addressing the problem of development in rural areas is that many of these countries emulated the American development model. They aimed at increasing and improving the agricultural production through application of the scientific research that was to be developed, disseminated and implemented in the farming practices through the agricultural extension services. This was viewed as the modern way for rural development to support national economic development. The Third World countries intended to use surplus agricultural production to raise capital for industrialisation and development, and the related infrastructure for both rural and urban populations. However, they tempered their desire to increase the agricultural production with the broader objectives of bringing about an improvement in the living standards and quality of life of the economically disadvantaged sections of the countryside. Their emphasis on rural development reflected their recognition that the majority of their people were rural, asset poor, involved in subsistence production and were members of lower echelons of social structures that contained some of the feudalistic elements. In the later stages, these countries have evolved a model for integrated rural development, which was supposed to recognise gender and class differences and attempted to address the social inequalities in access to rural resources—a process differentiated from the earlier production-oriented agricultural development models. The more recent approach to rural development tried to combine and maintain a balance between agriculture and economic development and social welfare and redistributive justice. This, in essence, sums up the two broad approaches adopted by the developing countries, in general, towards rural development.

As has been argued that India's approach to bridge the rural-urban difference by concentrating on improving rural areas (and through containment of urban growth), stems primarily from the theoretical paradigm of "balanced growth". It is important in this context to appreciate that the regional disparity often reduced to the form of disparity in industrialisation and/or development, which sometimes even further reduced the disparity in the rate of urbanisation in the country, like any other country recently emancipated from the colonial rule, is partly a function of resource endowment and allocation, and partly a legacy of colonialism (Chaube, Munsi and Guha, 1975). "Location pattern of productive forces" and "allocation of resources" followed during the colonial period were chiefly "exploitative" (i.e. maximised economic interests of the colonial rulers, not of the colonies) and therefore, "irrational" for an independent country. However, in a country only recently being freed from colonialism with scarcity of resources, the hangover of the colonial form of resource allocation was almost imperative. Chaube et al. (1975, p. 41) argue:

> Colonial economic development in India was meagre and concentrated chiefly on presidency towns to which the rest of the country served as the hinterland. Extreme inter and intra-regional disparity in economic growth was one of the many legacies of British rule in India. Within the framework of colonial backwardness for the whole of India, which grew out of a particular international division of labour imposed on this country by Great Britain, there were huge tracts of even more intense backwardness. The peripheral zones of India were certainly among them.

They further go on to state (Ibid. p. 42) that

> But regional planning by itself may not give the desired result. In its pure form regional planning is aimed at the removal of regional imbalances by maximising the productive capacity of a region. … If, on the other hand, regional planning takes the form of selective promotion of particular sectors of the economy of the region, mainly with a view to serving metropolitan interests, such development must be viewed as a hangover from the colonial era.[12]

The result of such a "colonial hangover" in policy as evidenced in putting emphasis on the "modern way of life" than on "social ability to produce", according to them, "may only enhance the needs for conspicuous consumption" (Ibid. p. 43). This is what has been referred to as the "lopsided way of modernisation", which overtly serves the market for capitalist production taking place in a few urban centres.

The "colonial hangover" referred to regarding public investment in India *until recently*[13] has also been observed by Thavaraj (1972). He posited that the pattern of "public investment in India in the British period" continued to determine, to a large extent, "the locus and course of economic development" in the post-independence period as well. He showed that the British Province of Punjab received most of the public investment during 1860-1947 for irrigation, i.e. about 33 per cent while the Province of Bombay and Sind received most of the public investment, i.e. about 19 per cent for roads.

Investments in irrigation, power and roads, taken together, account for the highest 19.1 per cent in the Province of Bombay and Sind followed by 16.1 per cent in Madras Province. Provinces of Bengal and UP remained at the bottom with 6.1 and 4.4 per cent respectively. He also argued that "under the capitalist path of development, especially in developing countries, the government is assigned the task of developing the economic infrastructure as a necessary prerequisite for stimulating private entrepreneurial activities towards commercial and industrial growth". On the basis of empirical evidences he concluded in the following way (Ibid., p. 19):

> The uneven dispersal of development during this period[14] is partly attributed to the uneven distribution of investment in railways and irrigation as between different regions. This, in turn, was partly because there was no overall planning of public investment during this period. The decisions regarding investments in one line or in one region were taken more or less independently of decisions regarding investments in other lines or other regions. This was particularly true in the initial stages of railway development when immediate commercial advantage and profitability were the two dominant considerations governing the flow of investment into railways. Therefore, the cumulative process of development initiated by the introduction of railways in certain areas *tended to perpetuate the initial imbalance*[15] in the distribution of investment between the different regions even when these railways were taken over by the government... The same was true of investment in irrigation when the large revenues accruing to the state from projects already completed became responsible for attracting more and more investment into irrigation in the regions concerned.

As has been seen, continuing with the alleged "colonial hangover", initial Indian national planning efforts aiming at achieving socio-economic change concentrated on industrialisation at chosen urban spheres on the assumption that the benefits would percolate down to rural areas and permeate through the entire economy. This "urban bias" towards the industrialisation process is understandable as the urban sphere is more conducive for higher capital accumulation than the rural areas given resource constraints at that particular period of time. The initial planners believed that though initially benefits would be concentrated in a few core cities, they would eventually spread to rural areas. Under such an assumption, rural development was viewed as a 'complementary' component in the national development strategy. This serves as a useful basis for appreciating the rural development programmes initiated in the early phases of planning in the country.

Review of the rural development policies of the Government of India in its historical trajectory reveals that in the early phases increasing the agricultural production in the rural areas was the main objective of the rural planning of the country, which continued till the 1970s. Raising the agricultural production was essential on two major counts—ensuring food security within the country newly coming out of the colonial clutch, and helping the process of capital formation required for industrialisation.

The production objective, i.e. increasing production and productivity thus, turned out as a natural political consensus. This consensus was also facilitated by dismal food-grain production in 1946-47 and drastic drop in yield of rice during that period. Substantial increase in food-grain production was therefore, only imperative. Along with this, political debates were engaged in several other important issues, which are aptly summed up by Varshney (1995) as below (p. 28):

> What place agriculture should have in the larger development strategy, what the resource allocation between industry and agriculture should be, what role the government had to play in agriculture, what means were appropriate if government involvement was essential, and whether the land ownership pattern had to be changed in order for agriculture to grow.

The response to these questions came in two forms—technocratic and institutional. The first set of policies included irrigation projects, promotion of scientifically developed cash crops through the provisions of high yielding varieties of seeds, use of modern farm implements and fertilisers (together they were referred to as the green revolution), productive credit for agricultural investment to stimulate production and productivity, and the establishment of a system of extension services to introduce scientific farming techniques at the village level. There were also efforts to regulate the market to boost trade in agricultural commodities, to increase the amount of investment in roads and communications, and to found cooperatives to buy and sell in rural areas. The second set of policies incorporated diverse land reform measures basically aiming at reduction in land scarcity by bringing in more land under cultivation and getting rid of "profound inequalities in land ownership".[16]

The second reason for raising food production in order to support and sustain industrialisation is related to the issue of stability in food prices. The economics of agricultural prices states that food article prices are an important component of wage determination. To accumulate profit in the industries it was essential that the wage cost should remain at minimum and prices remain low and stable. Nehruvian industrialisation thus, required agricultural surpluses for industrialisation. Nehru wrote this on August 1, 1957 saying[17]:

> Next to food production, the question of issue of the price of food-grains is of vital importance. Indeed, the two are intimately connected. If the price of food-grains goes up then the whole fabric of our planning suffers irretrievably.

This Nehruvian model of agricultural development led to enough resentment and factional struggles within the Congress Party and between Nehru himself and his colleagues in the Ministry. The state bosses of the party who were "right of centre" put up opposition to Nehru's "left of centre" approach. Some of the Ministers even resigned from the Cabinet for their resentment over the agricultural policy adopted by Nehru.[18] Varshney (1995, pp. 44-46) writes about why there was a split between the Congress regarding Nehru's agricultural policy:

> The Congress Party was an umbrella party.... The lower wings of the Congress Party—the district and *taluka* (sub-district) levels—came under the control of landlords and substantial land owners. These groups saw the advantages of entering the party in power. Nehru could not displace them ...they were the local "influentials" ... If the Congress Party were to reach far and wide, the local leaders and locally powerful groups had to be used, at least in the short

> run. However, if Nehru's economic model were to succeed, it was precisely these groups which had to be defeated.

Nehru's death in 1964 followed by a drastic drop in food production due to two successive droughts creating a "famine like situation" in the country during 1964-67 paved the way for a fundamental shift in the agriculture policy. Unlike the Nehruvian policy of institutional reorganisation, the new agricultural policy emerged during three years, i.e. 1964-67 accepted the existing institutional arrangements and structure as given but sought to increase production through price incentives and technical change (Varshney, 1995). Political economists have analysed what caused such a shift. They argue that change came from within the State machinery itself and held C. Subramaniam the Food and Agriculture Minister during 1964-67 in the Cabinet responsible for it. His view on agriculture prices was quite a contrast to that of Nehru's as he viewed it from the producers' point of view rather than the consumers'. In the meantime, two important changes were also made with respect to the Planning Commission: first members were given a fixed term, and second the post of Cabinet Secretary, the highest post in the Central Cabinet, was detached from the Planning Commission, which earlier was also the Secretary to the Planning Commission. Also the Prime Minister's Secretariat with economic experts was newly created. All these, obviously had far-reaching implications in the country's economic policy. K.L. Jha, top and senior civil servant and a man more inclined towards market mechanism, became the first Principal Secretary to head the Prime Minister's Secretariat. Evidently therefore, four key players emerged at the policy level—the Planning Commission, Finance Ministry, Food and Agriculture Ministry and Prime Minister's Secretariat along with the Congress Party itself, and political and the economic tussle over policy, especially regarding agriculture, became even more intensified. Also, it needs to be taken into consideration that this was the period when the country's Fourth Five Year Plan was to be implemented for the period of 1966-71 but owing to the developments and changes mentioned above it could only be initiated in 1969 after several rounds of drafting and redrafting accommodating the changes that surfaced at various levels (Varshney, 1995).

The 1970s has been a watershed period in India's political (and economic) history marked by the emergence of an agrarian political class and political mobilisation of the rural masses. Varshney (1995, p. 81) sums up the important dimensions of this "political watershed" in these words:

> Until the late 1960s, the power of dominant agrarian groups was confined to state politics. ...these groups had the capacity to defeat the implementation of agricultural policy but little control over its formulation... a new agrarian force had emerged in national politics. ...On the other hand, new ideologies of rural political mobilization had begun to take root. Agricultural prices increasingly came to replace land reforms...land reform had mobilized only the subaltern rural class against the landlords, never the rural sector as a whole. Agricultural prices ...began to emerge as a sectoral, as opposed to a class issue which, to the great surprise of urban intellectuals, attracted small farmers too. A battle cry of rural-versus urban India, not tenants versus landlords, made its entry into the ideological discourse of Indian politics.

Against this backdrop, generating broad political consensus, therefore, which was relatively easier till the 1960s became increasingly difficult in the 70s. As some writers have pointed out, such consensus was possible through "appeasement of demands" coming from different quarters.

Two important issues need brief comments at this point. First, the process of politicisation of agricultural price policy (1971-1973) as well as 'failure' of nationalisation of food-grain trade (1973-1974); second, as to how mass political mobilisation in the rural areas was possible centring around the agricultural price policy during this period. The first issue has been adequately discussed by Varshney (1995, pp. 90-105). In short, he showed that in the early 70s, the Agricultural Prices Commission (ACP, later known as CACP, i.e. Commission for Agricultural Cost and Pricing) favoured lowering of procurement prices, particularly of wheat, which received vehement contests from farm lobbies within the polity. They demanded a better price and argued that given the various cost conditions across states, the ACP approach of "cost-plus pricing" can not be applied to the states in general. Political articulation of the sentiment took the form of opposition to the insensitive urban-technocratic approach to agricultural pricing denying farmers their due prices. This, in a way, provides the answer to the second issue as to how the politics of agricultural prices helped mass mobilisation in the rural areas irrespective of the class differences[19].

Amidst all these, after Indira Gandhi returned to power in 1971, in 1972, the approach paper to the Fifth Plan (1974-79) appeared. The reflection of the perceived rural-urban gap or, regional disparity per se could become evident in the approach paper, which started to assume more political colour and shapes than ever before during that period. Chaube, Munsi and Guha (1975, p. 40) wrote:

> The Approach Paper to the Fifth Five Year Plan, *for the first time* noted that, in spite of the achievement of an overall growth in the country during the preceding four Five-Year Plans and three annual plans, a considerable portion of the country was deprived of benefits of this growth or had obtained then only marginally. Special emphasis has therefore been laid on *removal of regional imbalances...*[20]

Since then all Five Year Plan documents of the country have been continuously referring to "growing regional imbalances in the country", which no longer remain un-redressed. The political and economic compulsions behind such realisation have been pointed out by K.N. Raj (1990, p. 25):

> The social and political consequences within the country are already beginning to be obvious. Farm lobbies representing the upper level of rural society and propagating its interests have already emerged in several regions, and also been demonstrating their power by organising the masses in the countryside... The most exploited and indigent sections of the rural society are also being organised in certain parts of the country through what are generally described as 'Naxalite' movements. ...the economic consequences can also be serious, particularly when we take note of certain emerging trends in our economic policy. The market

> for the industrial products of the urban sector has not been growing rapidly enough to sustain reasonable rates of industrial growth, and so there has been a growing tendency to adopt policies that stimulate consumer demand...

No doubt that the national policy of investing in industry and commercial agriculture resulted in a gradual increase in the gap between those involved in the corporate formal sectors of the economy both rural and urban, and those involved in the informal and subsistence sectors. Rural landless and rural poor (marginal farmers) squeezed out of the traditional positions in the village society, migrated to the urban spheres leaving major stress in the urban landscape of the country. This has resulted in a huge informal sector, which basically absorbed unskilled rural labourers, and proliferation of urban slums.

Stemming migration to the cities by improving the quality of rural life and diversifying the rural economy emerged as the prime objective in the recent past in rural development strategies of the country. Making rural living more attractive included provisions of safe drinking water and sanitation, better connectivity and communication, rural banking and postal services, healthcare facilities, elementary education to improve skills the poor needed to compete for development benefits, self-employment and alternative employment income generating avenues and electricity in the countryside. As this policy evolved, its objective also expanded to include increasing equity and distributing the benefits of development to the rural poor more explicitly.

The 1990s was a period of transition for the whole economy of the country. The New Economic Policy initiated in 1991 and subsequent 73rd and 74th amendment of the Constitution in 1992 respectively had far-reaching consequences on the rural and national development policies of the country. How this again shifted the political and economic orientation regarding the rural-urban gap and regional imbalances has been discussed in some detail below.

What are then the clearly discernible political economy features of India's approach towards regional equality? When planning started, the perspective on the rural-urban cleavage was seen as more complementary than anything else and, hence, productivity in agriculture was stressed in order to "generate surplus" for "industrialisation". Enhancing agricultural production was tried through technological advancements and institutional reform. The land reform was defeated, inter alia, by the strong farm lobby engaged actively at the local level politics who gradually started to influence the national politics as well. Land reform, thus, pushed aside to the corner and debate over agricultural prices took the centre-stage. Consequently, the rural-urban divide emerged replacing the class contradictions of tenants and landlords, and planning process started thinking accordingly. This was followed by an agricultural policy centring on price incentive in rural areas and policy of industrial dispersal with an objective of bridging the rural-urban gap. At the same time improvement in rural life was targeted for stopping migration to urban areas and providing a market for industrial products in the rural areas was also attempted. It is therefore, important to recognise the "character of regional development policies" rather than "techniques of regional planning". Structural elements of capitalist development and its relation to the peripheral character of Indian urbanisation[21] along with politics surrounding it sum up the political economy perspective of urban and regional policies in India.

Case of Urban Land Ceiling: Characterising Paradigm Shift

Starting with the late 60s and early 70s, "urban congestion" emerged as a central issue in India's urban sphere owing to continuous increase in urban population consequent on, inter alia, sizeable rural to urban migration. This resulted in acute density of population in the limited urban space causing proliferation of slums and huge pressure on urban housing and other amenities. The problem of urban congestion was addressed both directly and indirectly. As has been discussed earlier, several rural development programmes aiming at easing the rural to urban migration coupled with the diversification and dispersal of industrial activities were tried to mitigate the problem. Contrary to this approach, some others viewed this as a problem of scarcity of urban land and distribution of its ownership and suggested that the problem could be remedied by expanding the urban area with most of the ownership belonging to the public sector. There were, basically, two arguments in vogue rationalising public ownership of urban land, one economic and the other political. We will try to elaborate on both.

The economic argument was mostly related to speculative and excessive rise in urban land prices, especially in the urban fringes, which posed "a serious problem for economic planning" (Madhab, 1969). The critical role of urban land price in economic development and planning is evident from the fact that when land acquisition costs for setting up an industry rises, it inflates the overall project cost too and, thereby, adversely affects feasibility of the industry itself. Moreover, the urban land market was characterised by almost monopoly and skewed ownership. According to Srinivas (1991), in most large cities in India, land is owned by a relatively small number of individuals or primordial groups such as kin, caste and sect. For instance, it was revealed that in Mumbai half of the city's population lived in slums and 55 per cent of the city's vacant land was owned by only 91 individuals.

Given the circumstances, public provisioning of housing on the part of the government became extremely difficult. The government needed to acquire large tracts of urban land from the monopoly owners for implementing housing projects in urban areas. As most of the government acquisition of land was governed by the provisions of the Land Acquisition Act of 1894, except in those cases where the State was empowered by special acts, which stipulated that compensation should be provided at the "market price" of the land acquired (plus the solatium). Now that the "market price" of land was on the continuous rise, to acquire sufficient land for housing projects, the government needed large sums of money to be paid as compensation. Moreover, the procedure of the Act of 1894 was such that it required a couple of years from the date of preliminary notification to the date of actual possession.

On the political front, it has been already discussed that in the late 60s and early 70s, the situations were rather compelling at the Centre. The farmer-leaders-cum-politicians were starting to dictate the national politics. Those large land owners (the rural elite) subject to rural land reforms began accusing the government of favouring the urban elite by failing to impose similar ceilings on ownership in urban areas. There was also a concern that wealthy rural land owners would divert their capital into the urban land market, because of the ceilings imposed on the ownership of rural land, and that would further exacerbate shortages, and result in price increase. This was expected to accentuate the rural-urban confrontation that was gradually emerging during the early 70s, which the government was keen to avoid (Srinivas, 1991). All these led to the passing of the Urban Land Ceiling Act of 1976.

The Urban Land Ceiling (and Regulation) Act (ULCA), 1976 came into force on February 17, 1976. Land being a State subject, it was to be adopted by the States. Initially the States of Andhra Pradesh, Haryana, Gujarat, Himachal Pradesh, Karnataka, Maharashtra, Orissa, Punjab, Tripura, Uttar Pradesh and West Bengal adopted the Act. Thereafter, it was adopted by six more States, namely Assam, Bihar, Madhya Pradesh, Manipur, Meghalaya and Rajasthan.

The main purpose of the Act was to prevent hoarding or excessive holding of land in urban agglomerations by a few people so as to facilitate proper distribution and uniform development of all sectors of urban areas. In its preamble it stated its objective as:

> To provide for imposition of a ceiling on vacant land in urban agglomerations, for acquisition of such land in excess of the ceiling limit, to regulate the construction of buildings on such lands and for matters connected therewith, with a view to preventing the concentration of urban land in the hands of a few, and speculation, and profitability therein, and with a view to bringing about an equitable distribution of land in urban agglomerations to subserve the common good.

The Act classified cities into four groups based on population therein with four ceiling limits for each of them. Ceilings for vacant urban land were fixed as 500 sq. metres for four metropolitan cities, viz. Delhi, Bombay, Calcutta and Madras; 1000 sq. metres for cities with over ten lakh population; 1500 for cities with population between three to ten lakhs; and 2000 sq. metres for cities with up to three lakh population. Excess land beyond the stipulated ceilings was to be 'socialised' to "subserve the common good".

It is well-known that under Article 246 (1) of the Constitution, the Parliament has the exclusive power to make laws with respect to matters enumerated in the Union List of the Seventh Schedule. Notwithstanding the Article 246 (1), under the Articles of 249 and 250, the Parliament can legislate with respect to matters enlisted in the State list for "national interest" and during the period when emergency has been declared as per the proviso of the Article 258. Now, land whether agricultural or non- agricultural, falls under entry 18 of the State list in the Seventh Schedule, which is in the purview of the State's jurisdiction. Therefore, if the Centre wants to make a law on the same, then as per Article 252, at least two states have to pass a resolution wanting the Centre to make law on the particular issue for them. Notwithstanding these intricacies involved, it is quite clear from its preamble that the Act was put into force as per the Article 252 (1):

> And whereas Parliament has no power to make laws for the States with respect to the matters aforesaid except as provided in Articles 249 and 250 of the Constitution;
>
> And whereas in pursuance of clause (1) of Article 252 of the Constitution resolutions have been passed by all the Houses of the Legislatures of the States of Andhra Pradesh, Gujarat, Haryana, Himachal Pradesh, Karnataka, Maharashtra, Orissa, Punjab, Tripura, Uttar Pradesh and West Bengal that the matters aforesaid should be regulated in those States by Parliament by law;
>
> Be it enacted by Parliament ...

Although the Act itself was passed with reference to Article 252, one can not, however, ignore the unique political context under which the ULCA was enforced. The ULCA grew out of the particular conditions that existed during the period of emergency, which made "socialisation of urban land" possible only by the "suspension of the democratic process". According to Srinivas (1991, p. 2483):

> ...uring the emergency the right to property was removed from the list of Fundamental Rights so that citizens could not appeal to the courts against state acquisition of their land. Subsequently, the act was protected by a constitutional amendment and therefore, was not subject to judicial review. Though the ULCA may appear to infer Fundamental Rights of a citizen to acquire, hold and dispose of property [Article 19, 31(2)] the 25th amendment provided immunity to laws enacted for securing the principles of Articles 39 (b) and (c) which were concerned with ownership of material resources and concentration of wealth.

It may further be noted that the 44th Amendment to the Constitution omitted Article 19 (f) of the Constitution, which recognised to acquire, hold and dispose of property as one of the fundamental rights. This accorded the Act even greater immunity as Article 13, which, on the contrary, requires that any law that contravenes the provisions of the Fundamental Rights shall "to the extent of such inconsistency, be void". It is also equally important to note that under Article 358, during emergency, Fundamental Rights granted under Article 19 remained suspended.

The ULCA, although enforced under Article 252, had enjoyed the advantage of Article 358, overriding Article 19; and to continue with it after the emergency, several remarkable changes were brought into the Constitution itself by the 44th Amendment in 1978 including removal of right to property under the Article 19.

"Socialising urban land", which the ULCA had attempted, in fact, had been talked about even before in the 60s as well. The Urban Land Policy Committee (Ministry of Health) constituted by the Government of India in 1965 targeted to "achieve optimum social use of urban land" and observed that "there is no escape from large-scale public acquisition if the question of guiding urban development or the provision of adequate housing and other facilities are to be tackled effectively". Further it stated "large-scale advance acquisition of land would really be in the interests of the society as a whole. It is by far the best and perhaps the only way to put an end to speculation in land and to capture subsequent increases in land values. These surpluses, were realised by the public authorities, should benefit the community in more ways than one".

Along with this direct approach of controlling the land prices "for common good" including low cost housing for increasing number of urbanites, indirect approach to tackle urban land price was also in vogue in the late 50s and 60s, which involved enforcement of land use planning, zoning regulations and imposition of taxes on land values, on transfer of assets, and on capital gains realised (Madhab, 1969)[22]. These precisely comprised the elements of town planning.

History of town planning in India dates back to 1960 when Town and Country Planning Acts were enacted by various state governments following the Model Act of 1960 prepared by Town and Country Planning Organisation (TCPO). The TCPO is an organisation of the central government to deal with the subject of planning (regional, urban and rural) and developmental policies. This model act provided the legal framework of urban land use planning and principles of zonation based on the concept of the Master Plan. The model act was subsequently revised by the TCPO in 1985, which still continues to be the basis, more or less, of urban and regional planning in the country. This model was in the nature of a guideline and was the outcome of several reviews and revisions undertaken on the recommendations of the State Ministers' Conference held from time to time. The legality of this model was confirmed to the Ministry of Law. In 1991, the Ministry of Urban Development prepared Urban Development Plans, Formulation and Implementation Guidelines (UDPFI), and on the basis of it, the Model Urban and Regional Planning and Development Law (revised) was also formulated. Today, Master Plan driven and dependent town planning practices in the country are largely guided by enactments of these laws. However, with the 74th Amendment to the Constitution in 1992, urban planning becomes a constituent of overall district planning to be prepared by the District Planning Committee

(DPC) under Article 243 ZD. This has ushered in concrete and very significant changes in attitudes; administrative, planning and financial systems; institutions; and methods of planning. The most significant and core aspect of this amendment (together with the 73rd amendment of 1993 related to rural areas) is that it accorded a constitutional status to institutions of local self-governance, i.e. municipalities and town committees and made them a new, more politically underpinned platform of 'decentralised planning' in urban areas. This has been taken up in some detail separately below.

In any case, two things become obvious from the above discussion: one, compelled by economic and political circumstances a specific legal approach was adopted to maintain a stable and reasonable land price in urban areas both through direct and indirect measures and instruments; and second, as economic and political environs changed, those measures also underwent substantial changes. Consequent upon such changes, in 1999, the Government of India was compelled to revoke the ULCA, 1976. The repeal of the ULCA, nevertheless, qualifies as a good case of new city-capital relation emerging out of the neoliberal policy regime initiated in the country since 1991. The ULCA was repealed on January 11, 1999 through an Ordinance, followed by a repeal act passed in the Parliament in replacement of the Ordinance. Following the repeal act notification on March 22, 1999, States of Haryana, Punjab, Uttar Pradesh, Gujarat, Karnataka, Madhya Pradesh, Rajasthan, Orissa and all Union Territories repealed the act in their own States.

Many authors have illustrated how the ULCA has failed to fulfil the original objectives of the Act (Srinivas, 1991; Mitra, 1990). They showed that the government could take possession of only a meagre percentage of ceiling surplus urban land, land prices continued to remain high, distribution remained as skewed as it was before and, on the contrary, land prices of fringe areas of cities tended to increase. All these issues figured in the Parliament debate when the repeal bill was placed on March 8, 1999 for discussion. While moving the bill, the then Union Minister for Urban Affairs Ram Jethmalani said:[23]

> ...in spite of the existence of the Urban Land Ceiling Act on the Statute Book from 1976 onwards, no land was distributed to the poor people. The slum area people did not get any house. They did not get any allotment of land. The entire land was allotted to the rich people. By repealing this law, I want to annul this sorry state of affairs which have existed because of that Act.

He then went on to argue that

> ...the statute, however good and laudable in its original intentions, was corruptly used, was corruptly exploited and it was used in a manner of hurting the poor and only to satisfy and to fill the pockets of a few selected rich who could pay the monies under the table and earn their exemptions from the provisions of that statute...

As to the queries of the Members of Parliament on how the repeal of the Act was going to help the poor, the Minister offered "simple economics" of this kind:

> I want to tell the hon. Members that the simple economics is that when land gets into the free market, and the land stock becomes available, the prices will fall. The prices skyrocketed because they were in the clutches of the monopolistic hands of the corrupt governments and bureaucrats. As soon as they are released from their clutches, the land stock will improve and the houses will be made available at affordable prices.

Most importantly, it became evident from the Minister's speech that behind the repeal motion moved by him, there was a tacit understanding with private and 'big' real-estate investors for they were to be obliged as privatisation was making gradual and all-pervasive inroads following the liberal policy regime started in 1991 and as a policy government was to make way for them in areas of urban housing, sanitation, infrastructure, water-supply and sewerage, which, of course, was projected as the model way of going ahead with the planning for purposes. The Minister categorically admitted before the Parliament that:

> ...the steel industry is in a bad shape, the cement industry is in a bad shape... there are 289 industries which are connected with housing alone. Revive the housing industry and 289 other ancillary industries will revive... There is no city in which I have not called all the builders of India and some of these builders or those who

> have something to do with the building industry are present in this House. The unanimous advice which I received was to repeal this law and to see how the construction starts. I repealed it by an Ordinance because otherwise the 19th of March would arrive and I would not have been able to give an assurance to the building industry to give a kick start to the economy... I said that I would explain the urgency of it. I explained it throughout my speech why it was urgent. I explained why the Ordinance was necessary because the housing industry may not kick start...

It is, therefore, quite clear that although the pronounced intention of the repeal motion was to end all evils caused by the ULCA, 1976, the actual reason for it was the pressure of the private investors and consequently the government's promise to them. As to how this opening up of urban land market is going to help the poor and low income groups the Minister did not provide a direct answer. This was the major opposition to the repeal motion as well. Opposing the repeal motion, K.S. Rao argued that:

> The rich man, keeping in view his personal benefit and to make more and more money, will go for constructing a five star hotel. He will go for constructing units which can yield better results, like flats which can fetch him crores of rupees. He will not construct units for weaker sections. Then, as usual, the poor man is left to his own fate, which he has criticised. Right from the beginning, he has been left like that, or else, he has to go beyond the urban agglomerate and live away from the society.

Another member Anil Basu criticised the move by saying that

> The basic philosophy of this government is to make everything free. They want free education. The role of the government is continuously being withdrawn from the field of education. In the industrial sector, the government wants to do away with the public sector companies. Prime public sector companies are going in for disinvestment and are handing over companies to the private sector. They are making free all the wealth, all the assets of this country to the richer section of the people while the poor and the middle class people are made to suffer.

Replying to these attacks by the opposition the Minister frankly confessed:

> The Ninth Plan records that we require Rs.150,000 crores for the purpose of being able to wipe out the current deficit apart from the deficit which arises from year to year. That money is just not available and we have to build houses without budgetary support and that can only come with the new policy. *The new policy is that the private sector must be inducted into the construction business*. The private sector has been inducted and hon. Members here even said "Yes. We have no objection to the private sector." But what do you mean by saying that you have no objection to the private sector? If the private sector has to revive the economy, you have to *listen to some of their advice*. The private sector today is unanimous that you must repeal this Act before the private sector will be induced to participate in the construction activity in a big way[24].

It may, therefore, be safely argued that the ULC Repeal Act, 1999 intended primarily to facilitate private participation in the housing sector in cities although it has never been pronounced like that explicitly. This Act objectifies the role of the State as 'facilitator' quite contrary to that of the 'regulator', whose basic aim is to help create a conducive socio-economic and political climate for luring private investors. The repeal of the ULCA, that is why, qualifies as a classic case of new city-capital relation emerging out of the neoliberal policy regime initiated in the country since 1991.

One significant aspect revealed by this whole process of the ULC Repeal Act is that unlike the pre-liberal policy regime when politics and political interests dictated economics, during the post-liberal period, economics and economic interests started determining the course of political actions, the reason being the buttressing role and power of global capital as has been argued in the introductory chapter. It is important here realise that the most elementary difference underlying these marked shifts in the role of the State from regulator to facilitator is that while the first, believed that the free market fails in certain areas the second sees the free market as a panacea of all ills. As a result, the policy thrust of the State was marked by changes from 'equity' and 'social justice' to 'efficiency'. JNNURM is, in fact, characterised by this paradigm shift.

Conclusion

In this paper an attempt has been made to outline and understand India's policy towards urbanisation in particular and overall development policy in general. It can be seen that after independence, and during the initial three Five Year Plans, India's approach towards development relied mostly on industrialisation with a huge investment by the public sector. At the same time, agricultural growth aiming at maintaining a self-sufficient food stock and stable food price was also stressed and deliberately pursued by the government. The institutional and technocratic approach to agricultural growth during this period later on, most particularly, during the 70s, generated intense economic and political confrontations leading to a rural-urban divide in policy and regime. The paper tried to provide a political economy perspective of understanding this rural-urban chasm in India's development policy over the past five decades.

Drawing from diverse evidences and discourses, it was also shown that during the mid-70s, more particularly the Fifth Plan onwards, this rural-urban divide formed the basis for a balanced development approach in the country which continued till the early 1990s. Following the economic liberalisation policy initiated in the country in 1991, India's overall development approach exhibited a shift from principles of "equity" to that of "efficiency", from "public" to "private" sector and from "regulator" state to "facilitator" state. Impact and reflections of such shifts became evident in urban policy initiatives in the country as well with strategy of "dispersal" being gradually replaced by "re-densification" and "renewal".

Since 1991, by emphasising mega-cities and cities with adequate infrastructure and public services (i.e. which are investment-friendly and livable), a selected few cities and urban spaces are made open to global capital, thereby, ensuring India's integration with the "new global order" inherent in which there always is a "new urban order".

This so-called "new urban order" has come to rule with the crises of the Fordist-Keynesian accumulation regime and breakdown of Bretton Woods system coinciding with the period when the world capitalist system became increasingly 'neoliberalised' (Banerjee-Guha, 2009). It has been characterised by, inter alia, universal back-tracking of the welfare state, dismantling of institutional constraints upon marketisation, increased commodification, shrinking of organised jobs and tremendous economic uncertainty. Simultaneously, despite de-regulation and privatisation of state-owned and state-provided services, a new kind of state intervention with a larger entrepreneurial capacity was brought in, to roll forward new forms of governance that ostensibly suited a market-driven globalising economy (Brenner and Theodore, 2002). The specificity of the current neoliberal practices largely lies in the discursive and organisational frameworks that arose out of developments of the above nature (Banerjee-Guha, 2009).

In tune with this, Indian cities of various sizes are being remodelled in recent times as "world class cities" to function as nodes of circulation of global finance and "hi-tech activities of diverse nature". Apparently, the essential objective is to make these cities "sufficiently investment-friendly", acceptable to credit-rating agencies and help them emerge as "geo-strategic points" to further neoliberalism. To accomplish this, a homogenised planning vision is being floated at the behest of global capital, ushering in a new era of remapping the 'urban' by intense gentrification of the urban space and re-casting of the urban form and governance.

The fact that the northeast as a region being increasingly tending to be viewed as a linking point between India and the East and the South East Asia, and Guwahati being recognised as an eligible city under JNNURM, which embodies all the features of so-called "new urban order", urban process in Assam and its stake in the new urban order, thus, makes an interesting case for close scrutiny in the context of overall development scenario of the region at large and the state in particular. Against the backdrop of several international financial institutions like World Bank, International Monetary Fund and Asian Development Bank systematically redirecting investment from 'region' to 'urban' in a big way such scrutiny visibly deserves some merit.

Need for an adequate understanding of the contemporary

neoliberal policy regime based on its politico-economic and ideological framework in understanding urban processes has been well-documented. The extraordinarily renewed metropolitan bias in so-called "new urban policy" has both short and long-term implications. This paper has provided the politico-economic and ideological framework of the new urban policy regime in India. The key issue which the paper tries to raise is whether the homogeneous vision of the new urban order floated by the centre is, in fact, capable of benefiting urban areas characterised by non-economic and non-industrial processes. Our urban future, to a large extent, rests on answer to this question alone. Proposed doctoral work tries to seek an answer to the question.

REFERENCES

Banerjee-Guha, S. (2009). "Neoliberalising the Urban: New Geographies of Power and Injustice in Indian Cities", *Economic and Political Weekly*, Vol. XLIV, No. 22, pp. 75-107.

Bardhan, P. and Udry, C. (2000). *Development Microeconomics*. New Delhi: Oxford University Press, p. 49.

Bookchin, M. (1995). "From Urbanisation to Cities—Towards a New Politics of Citizenship". London: Cassell.

Bose, A. (1973). "Administration of Urban Areas", *(ICSSR) A Survey of Research in Public Administration*, Vol. I, Bombay: Allied Publishers.

Bose, A. (1970). "Urban Development with Social Justice", *Economic and Political Weekly*, Vol. 5, No. 29/31, pp. 1247-1249.

Brenner, N. and Theodore, N. (2002). "From the New Localism to the Space of Neoliberalism", *Antipode*, Vol. 34, No. 3, pp. 341-347.

Castells, M. (1996). *The Rise of the Network Society*, Oxford: Blackwell.

Castells, M. (1989). *The Information City*, Oxford: Blackwell.

Chaube, S.K., Munsi, S. and Guha, A. (1975). "Regional Development and Nationality Question in North-East India", *Social Scientist*, Vol. 4, No. 1, pp. 40-66.

Date, V. (2006). "Travails of an Ordinary Citizen", *Economic and Political Weekly*, Vol. 41, No. 32.

Deb, K. (2006). "Role of the State in City Growth: The Case of Hyderabad City", in *Urban Studies*, Patel. S and Deb, K. (eds.), New Delhi: Oxford.

Forrest, R., Grange, A.L. and Yip, N. (2004). "Hong Kong as Global City? Social Distance and Spatial Differentiation", *Urban Studies*, Vol. 41, No. 1, pp. 207–227.

Friedman, J. and Wolff, W. (1982). "World City Formation: An Agenda for Research and Action", *International Journal of Urban and Regional Research* 6, pp. 309–44.

Haider, D. (1992). "Place Wars: New Realities of the 1990s", *Economic Development Quarterly* 6, pp. 127–34.

Harris, N. (2003), "Globalisation and the Management of Indian Cities", *Economic and Political Weakly*, June 21, pp. 2535–43.

James, C. (1999). "The New World Order: An Economic Global Regime", *Dissertation.com.*

Karn, S.K., Shikura, S. and Harada, H. (2003), "Living Environment and Health of Urban Poor", *Economic and Political Weekly*, Vol. 38, No. 34, pp. 3575–85.

Kearn, A. and Paddison, R. (2000). "New Challenges for Urban Governance", *Urban Studies*, Vol. 37, No. 5-6, pp. 845-50.

Kundu, A., Bagchi, S. and Kundu, D. (1999), "Regional Distribution of Infrastructure and Basic Amenities in Urban India", *Economic and Political Weekly*, Vol. 34, No. 28.

Lipton, M. (2004), "Urban Bias and Inequality" in *Development and Underdevelopment: The Political Economy of Global Inequality*, Seligson, M.A. and Smith, J.T. (eds.), New Delhi: Viva Books.

Madhab, J. (1969). "Controlling Urban Land Value", *Economic and Political Weekly*, Vol. 4, No. 28-29-30, pp. 1197-202.

Mishra, S. (2000). "Forestalling Transport Chaos in Delhi", *Economic and Political Weekly*, Vol. 35, No. 24.

Mitra, A. (1990), "Land Price in Indian Cities: Dimensions and Determinants of Change", *Economic and Political Weekly*, Vol. 25, No. 50, pp. 2723-29.

Muhammad, A. (2006). "Globalisation and Economic Transformation in Peripheral Economy: The Bangladesh Experience", *Economic and Political Weakly*, April 15, pp. 1459-64.

Patel, S. (2006). "Urban Studies: An Exploration in Theories and Practices", *Urban Studies*, Patel, S. and Deb, K. (eds.), New Delhi: Oxford University Press.

Pethe, A. and Lalwani, M. (2006). "Towards Economic Empowerment of Urban Local Bodies in Maharashtra", *Economic and Political Weakly*, February 18, pp. 635–41.

Planning Commission, 2007. Towards Faster and More Inclusive Growth: An Approach to Eleventh Five Year Plan: 2007–2010, Government of India, New Delhi, Available at http://

planningcommission.nic.in (accessed on June 19, 2007).

Prakash, B.A. (2002). "Urban Unemployment in Kerala", *Economic and Political Weekly,* Vol. 37, No. 39, pp. 4073–78.

Pratchett, L. and Wilson, D. (1996). "Local Government Under Siege", *Local Democracy and Local Government,* Pratchett, L. and Wilson, D. (eds.), London: Macmillan.

Prud'homme, R. and Lee, C.W. (1999). "Size, Sprawl, and Speed and Efficiency of Cities", *Urban Studies,* Vol. 36, No. 11, pp. 1849–58.

Pugh, C. (1996). "Urban Bias, the Political Economy of Development and Urban Policies for Developing Countries", *Urban Studies,* Vol. 33, No. 7, pp. 1045–60.

Qadeer, M.A. (2000). "Ruralopolises: The Spatial Organisation and Residential Land Economy of High Density Rural Regions of South Asia", *Urban Studies,* Vol. 37, No. 9, pp. 1583-03.

Raj, K.N. (1990). "Bridging the Urban-Rural Gap", *Economic and Political Weekly,* Vol. 25, No. 1, pp. 25-27.

Rogerson, R.J. (1999). "Quality of Life and City Competitiveness", *Urban Studies,* Vol. 36, No. 5-6, pp. 969–85.

Sassen, S. (1991). *Global Cities: New York,* London, Tokyo, Princeton: Princeton University Press.

Sharma, R.S. (1987). *Urban Decay in India,* New Delhi: Munshiram Manoharlal Publishers.

Shonfiled, A. (1965). *Modern Capitalism: Changing Balance of Public and Private Power,* Oxford University Press/RIIA, London.

Short, J.R. and Kim, Y.H. (1999). *Globalisation and City,* Harlow: Addison Wesley Longman Ltd., p. 118.

Srinivas, L. (1991). "Land and Politics in India: Working of Urban Land Ceiling Act, 1976", *Economic and Political Weekly,* Vol. 26, No. 43, pp. 2482-84.

Stone, C.N. (1989). *Regime Politics,* Kansas: University Press.

Stubbs, M. Lemon, M. Longhurst, P. (2000). "Intelligent Urban Management: Learning to Manage and Managing to Learn Together for a Change", *Urban Studies,* Vol. 31, No. 10, pp. 1801-11.

Thavaraj, M.J.K. (1972). "Regional Imbalances and Public Investment in India (1860-1947)", *Social Scientist,* Vol. 1. No. 4, pp. 3-24.

Thompson, E.C. (2004). "Rural Villages as Socially Urban Spaces in Malaysia", *Urban Studies,* Vol. 41, No. 12, pp. 2357-76.

Todaro, P.M. (2000), *Economic Development,* New Delhi: Addison-Wesley.

UNCHS (1996). *An Urbanising World: Global Report on Human Settlement.*

Oxford: Oxford University Press.

United Nations (1995). *World Urbanisation Prospects: 1994 Revisions*, New York.

United Nations (1980). *Patterns of Urban and Rural Population Growth*, New York.

Varshney, A. (1995). *Democracy, Development and the Countryside*, New York: Cambridge University Press.

NOTES

1. The Human Development Report 2005, however, projects the total urban population of the world as 48.3 per cent. This is indicative of a certain degree of "slowing down" in the urbanisation process, which is also evident in many of the developing countries. Nonetheless, in terms of absolute numbers, the figures still stand tall maintaining the central concern of the argument. *Human Development Report, 2005*, United Nations, Oxford University Press, p. 35.
2. It is important to recognise varied interpretations of the term 'congestion'. The term does not only connote too many people residing in a too small area or in other words density of population over space. A more meaningful interpretation would relate it with the levels of civic services provided. In other words, urban congestion is equivalent to the failure of civic services—water supply, sanitation and swerage, conservancy, healthcare, transportation, housing—to cope with the demands for them generated by the rise in the urban population. See D'Souza, J.B. (1978), Searching for an Urban Policy, *Economic and Political Weekly*, December 2, p. 1976.
3. This point was also discussed by Samuelson, P. as cited in *The Business Cycles Today*, (1972), Zarnowitz (ed.), University of Chicago Press, Chicago.
4. While traditional theories of price, cost and production in economics provides basis for firms' most economics decisions, location theories were offered as the basis for firms' spatial decisions. Amongst many location theories, Central Place Theories offered by geographers and Economic Base Theories offered by economists are worth mentioning.
5. In his article, Robert J. Rogerson (1999), p. 971 also refers to Ashworth, G. and Voogd, H. (1990). *Selling the City*, Belhaven, London while making this point. Market niche and

decentralisation and dispersal of economic activities became the hallmarks of the "new regime", which the post-fordists called the "flexible accumulation regime". Harvey, for instance reflecting upon this form of accumulation and consequent spatial ramifications, sees that in this accumulation regime, the relative advantage of physical infrastructure in core cities are continuously becoming devalued. Cities are now pushed to compete for international division of labour, control and command functions and governmental redistribution. These points are elaborated in Harvey, D. (1990). *The Condition of Postmodernity: An Enquiry into the Origins of Cultural Change*; Blackwell, Cambridge, MA; and his other writings.

6. In 1981, Boyer, R. and Savageau, D. published *Places Rated Almanac: Your Guide to Finding the Best Places to Live in America*, Rand McNally; Chicago. This was a bestseller and has been updated and reprinted several times. Ever since, "city-rankings" in terms of 'livability', have been tried in different countries. These are seen as efforts to *sell* cities in the "financial markets" for they are supposed to attract both capitalists and their capital. World famous *Fortune Magazine* also publishes similar ratings. Interestingly, literature is now developing about the "internal politics" of such ratings and their alternative ratings. This goes to describe the intensity of "place war" in the context of "capital accumulation".
7. Before Sassen (1991), Friedman, J. (1986). *The World City Hypothesis*: *Development and Change*; 17, Blackwell, pp. 69–74 and Trift, N. (1989), The Geography of International Economic Disorder; in Johnson, R. and Taylor, P. (eds.). *A World in Crisis;* Oxford: Blackwell, pp. 15–77 converged on the opinion that New York, London and Tokyo are global cities though both approached differently. Friedman's hierarchy identified primary and secondary centres within core countries and semi-periphery countries, while Thrift distinguishes between global, zonal and regional centres. These are recognised as control points of global trade, however, some consider Beijing's ascendancy as incipient of the process of becoming a part of the global city network (Forrest et al., 2004).
8. Interesting, but more philosophical, issues relating to idealisation and construction or production of "social spaces" are discussed by French philosopher Henry Lefebvre. He says "social space is not a *thing* but rather a set of *relations*". As such, various production of space corresponds to different "social and

productive arrangements". One result of such a position is that a change in culture and a change in the mode of production reveal a change in production of space and vice versa. Many commentators point out some affinity of Lefebvre's social space with the Deleuzean notion of the "event-scene". This social space consists of relations: an assemblage of road, market, estate, suburb, highway or even skyscraper. To apply Lefebvre to contemporary social space, and the notion of "post modern space" would in part entail an examination of the points of "encounter, assembly and continuity"—relations like malls, suburban cluster of homes, public transit system etc.—and ask if there are spaces of resistance enmeshed within these relations. Like Lefebvre, Boudier also tries to capture essentials of social spaces.

9. Imperatives behind bridging rural-urban divide through distinct policy emphasis on rural sphere clearly underline significant elements of political-economy involved in it. This has been discussed in some detail subsequently.
10. The Planning Commission feels that this, however, is an underestimated rural-urban divide since the NSS probably does not fully capture consumption by the rich, particularly in urban areas. It could easily be understood that the gap would increase even more if we consider savings rather than consumption. The articulation of the rural-urban gap in terms of 'consumption' instead of 'savings' serves policy purposes of the neoliberal regime, which we will try to illustrate later.
11. To support this point, The Planning Commission refers to NSS data. According to NSS, the Gini ratio of urban consumption distribution (that ranges from 0 with perfect equality to 1 with perfect inequality) increased from 0.34 in 1993-94 to 0.38 in 2004-05. These too are likely to be underestimated on account of NSSO's underestimation of the urban rich.
12. Elsewhere, I too have argued, although from a different standpoint, in similar line that mere welfare-oriented rural development schemes and programmes do not constitute an efficient regional development strategy and that complete regional development can not be achieved unless we "recognise productive competitiveness of the villages". See Baruah, J. (2004). "Competitive Villages, Rural Enterprises and Rural Development", *Political Economy Journal of India,* Vol. 13, No. 1 and 2, January-June (with I. Dutta); Baruah, J. (2005). "Economic Dualism and Rural Development: The Indian Experiments and

Experiences", in N. Narayan (ed.) *Economic Development: Issues and Policies*, Serial Publications, New Delhi, pp. 479-504 and Baruah, J. (2006). "Transforming the Rural Sphere and Quality of Rural Life: Issue of Employment and Employability in Rural Non-farm Sector" in H.C. Gautam and M.P. Bezbaruah (eds.). *Rural Transformation in North-East India*, Gauhati University, pp. 25-43.

13. Meaning until the early 1970s as the paper was published in 1972.
14. Meaning the British period covering 1860-1947.
15. Emphasis added by italicisation.
16. These inequalities came to light when detailed data on land holdings in India were first collected in 1954 – 55, later published by NSSO, *First Report on Landholding, Rural Sector*, Report No. 10, 1958, Delhi.
17. *Fortnightly Letters to the Chief Ministers*, quoted from Varshney (1995), p. 39.
18. Detail on factional politics over agriculture in the Congress Party is given in Varshney (1995), pp. 44-47.
19. There are several good accounts of political mobilisation of the agrarian class in different parts of the country. For instance, Singh, J. (1992). *Capitalism and Dependence: Agrarian Politics in Western Uttar Pradesh 1951-1991*, Manohar, New Delhi is one of those accounts.
20. Emphasis added by italicisation.
21. The peripheral character of Indian urbanisation implies dominance of a few primate cities over all other urban areas. The history and role of capital in these cities reveals the point made here.
22. The government has also issued a Model State Zone Act in 1970 and supplemented it by the Model Land Use Zoning Regulations in 1971 so as to include mixed land uses as an integrated component of the urban land development process.
23. Text of the entire debate is available in the web-archive of the official website of Parliament of India, i.e. http://www.parliamentofindia.nic.in. Texts are quoted from the archive as found while accessing on June 24, 2010. The static URL for the text is http://164.100.47.132/LssNew/psearch/Result12.aspx?dbsl=1636.
24. Emphasis added by italicisation.

PART III

Neoliberalism, Class and Power Structure

8

Is a Free Market in Land Just?

Indraneel Dasgupta

Suppose a peasant owns one unit of land, from which he earns Rs 10,000 net of input costs, including imputed labour costs. Suppose a factory (township/road/power-plant), if set up, will produce an income of Rs 110,000, over and above the costs of machinery and production, purely because of its advantageous location. Does the peasant have veto right over the transfer price? The answer, according to a currently popular view in India, is yes: the transfer price must be whatever the market decides, including, possibly, infinity (i.e. a unilateral veto against conversion at any price). This view is exemplified by the report of the Land Use Committee of the present government in West Bengal (WB), headed by Debabrata Bandyopadhyay. This committee essentially recommends the following: (a) voluntary sale at a mutually agreed price (and thus an absolute right to private property); (b) a floor price set by the government; (c) continuation of land ceiling laws; and (d) no conversion of multi-cropped land. The government of WB has repeatedly articulated its commitment to these principles.

The recommendations of the Land Use Committee of the WB government are evidently *incoherent*: absolute right to private property, which underpins (a), contradicts (b), (c) and (d). These recommendations are also *inefficient*, in that they are likely to prevent mutually beneficial transfers from occurring, due to well-known factors such as fuzzy property rights, hold-up problems, large negotiation costs, information asymmetry, etc. The purpose of this paper is to argue that (a) is also *unjust*, in that it violates all plausible canons of distributive justice.

I develop my critique of the ethical foundations of the case for a free market in land, from the perspective of distributive justice, through the following steps. In Section 2 below, I begin by examining the evolution of the standard, Lockean, justification for private property in general. Section 3 traces the application of the general argument for private property to private property in land. In Section 4, I show how this justification was progressively qualified and weakened in the writings of David Ricardo, John Stuart Mill, Herbert Spencer and Henry George, and how heavy taxation of income gains from land ownership came to be accepted as a pre-eminent element of the policy agenda, both on the egalitarian left and the competitive individualist right. I conclude in Section 5 by applying the logic of this critique to the current Indian debate about land acquisition for urbanisation and industrialisation. I conclude that an ideological commitment which valorises privatisation of the land market, such as that of the current West Bengal government, suffers from two cardinal errors which can be said to constitute the intellectual landscape of neoliberalism. First, it involves an acceptance of the efficiency claims of the market in precisely that sphere where such claims are, logically and empirically, least warranted. Second, it involves an *a priori* defence of market determination of that form of property income which is ethically least defensible (and least defended). Conversely, other ideological commitments which accept state intervention but valorise landowners' claim to compensation far in excess of any objective measure of their contribution, such as those of the current Haryana government, involve a pre-capitalist privileging of landed property and the consequent imposition of economic inefficiency. The ethics of consistent egalitarianism stand in opposition to both positions, as do those of consistent competitive individualism.

Why Should Anybody Have Private Property?

In liberal *rights-based* theories of property, the justification is typically drawn from John Locke: "Labour being the unquestionable Property of the Labourer, no Man but he can have a right to what that is once joyned to" (Locke, 1988: 288). The basic argument is that of 'self-ownership': since every individual owns herself, she also has ownership of what that self 'creates', or, more broadly, *personal sacrifice deserves reward*. That principle constitutes the ethical core of the Lockean justification for private property: it explains why people have a right to retain the exchange value of their property or labour, to the extent that value represents a fair return on their *actual costs or sacrifice*. John Stuart Mill expressed the matter with admirable clarity: "(P)rivate property, in every defence made of it, is supposed to mean the guarantee to individuals of the fruits of their own labour and abstinence. ... To judge of the final destination of the institution of property, we must suppose everything rectified which causes the institution to work in a manner opposed to that equitable principle, of *proportion between remuneration and exertion*, on which in every vindication of it that will bear the light it is assumed to be grounded" (Mill, 1994: 208-209, italics mine). Locke's case for private property was taken by 19th century conservatives to justify a strong, laissez-faire property rights regime, in which what each person had created from nature or acquired by trade as a free moral agent, she had a right to keep.

Natural rights, of course, as Jeremy Bentham famously put it, may only be 'nonsense on stilts'. Is there an alternative, consequentialist, justification for private property? If returns are not allowed to reflect relative scarcity, individuals will not shift resources to more productive uses. Consequently, some opportunities for mutually beneficial exchange will remain unexploited in society, making at least some individuals worse off, and nobody better off, than they could possible have been. This, consequentialist, justification for private property in mainstream economics is formalised through the well-known First and Second Fundamental Theorems of Welfare Theorem (see, for example, MasCollel et al., 1995, Chapter 16).

Does Locke or Bentham Apply to Land?

Do peasants have a natural (or instrumental) right to the market price of their land, which is simply the capitalised value of the expected rental income stream? It is well-known that some traditional rights can not be justified at all under the Lockean scheme: such rights include land grants, rights of inheritance, and government grants of monopoly privilege. Locke's theory of property rights was, in essence, a theory of sacrifice: that which a person had produced by her own labour became, by virtue of her sacrifice, her own. Rather than supporting an entitlement to whatever price the market might set, Lockean theory, taken seriously, suggests that sellers are entitled only to that portion which compensates them for *cost* of supplying goods or services. To the extent land rights come from inheritance or government grant, it implies no cost whatsoever. The Lockean proviso thus applies only to market purchases of land from labour income, valued at the *original market price*. The market need not ensure Lockean justice: exchange value is limited to return on costs only for marginal producers in competitive markets. For infra-marginal producers in such markets, and for all producers in non-competitive markets, return often far exceeds a return on costs. The excess (rent, unproductive surplus or unearned increment) does not reflect any virtue on the part of the producer; it simply reflects relative scarcity of the goods or services they provide. The seller is able to extract rent from the buyer merely because fortuities of natural and social circumstances have produced a market price in excess of the seller's cost. If anyone has created that surplus value, it is the *community at large*. If, for example, the construction of a highway at public cost leads to a sharp rise in land prices along that highway, as in Singur or Rajarhat in West Bengal, it is the (tax-paying) community at large that is instrumental in the creation of that increment, not the prior individual owners of plots along that highway.

The Lockean theory of property rights can therefore justify giving owners the value of land to the extent of *value added by their own labour and investment*, but it justifies *nothing beyond that*. It does not explain why landlords have a right to rents generated principally by the labour of others, thus, by implication, sanctioning land redistribution. By the same token, it does not explain why those who own and work the land have a right to that portion of its value, realised as higher profit on produce from land or higher resale value of land, which reflects the scarcity of land rather than the labour and investments that are mixed in with it.[1] Thus, the right to retain the full market value extracted in voluntary, unregulated exchange in land not only does not follow from Lockean principles, it is in fact irreconcilable with them.

Nozick (1974) offers an elegant, but ultimately unpersuasive, reformulation of the case for unfettered private property rights in land. He begins with Locke's statement that a person is entitled to an appropriate part of the natural world, which is not yet privately owned, as his own, as long as he leaves "enough and as good in common for others". This proviso clearly denies anyone the right to appropriate scarce natural resources. Nozick therefore amends it to the following: an appropriation of part of the unowned natural world is just so long as it leaves no one *worse off than she would have been had that part remained unowned*. Nozick's appropriation proviso is thus essentially one of first come, first served. Locke's proviso, by contrast, does not permit any individual to appropriate a scarce object, unless all agree to such appropriation. In defining justice in acquisition, the key issue then is that of Nozick's baseline: what the welfare of others would have been, had the resource remained unowned. Is this baseline normatively acceptable? Lockean rights lead to a relationship between persons and the external world that can be thought of as *joint ownership*: no individual can appropriate a part of the external world without the consent of others. Nozick's contra assumption that the external world, before becoming privately owned, was, morally speaking, unowned, is evidently arbitrary. There is no reason why one may not assume instead that the external world was jointly owned by all. This in turn leads one naturally to a case for collective rights, and thus, public control over the disposal of a limited natural resource such as land.

The second step in Nozick's case for unfettered private transfer rights in landed property involves the articulation of his 'principle of justice in transfer': *whatever arises from a just situation as a result of fully voluntary transactions on the part of all the transacting agents is itself just.* The first, obvious, problem that this principle runs into is that of inadequately informed agents. It is by no means intuitively self-evident that the principle carries moral plausibility when agents are ignorant of key aspects of a transaction. In order to address this lacuna, the principle may be amended to the following: *whatever arises from a just situation as a result of fully voluntary transactions on the part of all the transacting agents, which all transacting agents would still have agreed to if they had known what the results of so transacting were to be, is itself just.* The addition of the 'no-regret under full information' clause however implies that actual market transactions need not satisfy the (amended) principle of justice in transfer in general. Thirdly, the outcome of voluntary transactions may threaten third parties: imposing negative externalities of sorts. This is typically so for large-scale land conversion from agriculture to industry. Third party costs/benefits in turn justify third party (or collective) restrictions on private transactions in land. Third party costs/benefits are larger in the case of non-reproducible resources like land in situations of high population density. Nozick's defence of private property rights in land therefore remains unpersuasive.[2] Since the total supply of land is fixed, a higher price does not bring forth more land, unlike the case with labour power and capital. Hence, the instrumental, or consequentialist, case for a free market in land is also non-existent.

In sum, neither Lockean theory nor any other justification for ownership advanced by proponents of laissez-faire offers any plausible justification for why owners of land are entitled to benefit from its pure scarcity value.

Taxing Ground Rent: A Potted Intellectual History

The basic, 'unearned income', justification for taxing ground rent has a long and distinguished lineage in economic theory. David Ricardo developed his case for free trade by pointing out that restriction on imports of agricultural produce only served to increase land rents. Consequently, land-owners benefited at the cost of both workers (who had to pay more for their food) and capitalists (who had to pay workers a higher money wage to compensate for higher food prices). John Stuart Mill put the argument even more incisively: "(S)uppose that there is a kind of income that constantly tends to increase, without any exertion or sacrifice on the part of the owners: those owners constituting a class in the community, whom the natural course of things progressively enriches, consistently with complete passiveness on their own part. In such a case it would be no violation of the principles on which private property is grounded, if the state should appropriate this increase of wealth, or part of it, as it arises. This would not properly be taking anything from anybody; it would merely be applying an accession of wealth, created by circumstances, to the benefit of society, instead of allowing it to become an unearned appendage to the riches of a particular class. Now, this is actually the case with rent" (Mill, 1994: 183-184).

Mill considered returns from owning land as justified only so far as they reflected the landowner's investment in improving land. "These are the reasons which form the justification in an economical point of view, of property in land. It is seen, that they are only valid, in so far as the proprietor of land is its improver. Whenever, in any country, the proprietor, generally speaking, ceases to be the improver, political economy has nothing to say in defence of landed property, as there established. In no sound theory of private property was it ever contemplated that the proprietor of land should be merely a sinecurist quartered on it" (Mill, 1994: 38-39).

Private ownership of land was critiqued by many on the right as well, for being inconsistent with the 'fair field and no favour' precondition for competitive individualism. Herbert Spencer argued that the 'Law of Equal Freedom' requires that if one person shall have right to possess land, then all shall have it. Since scarcity makes that impossible, "(the law of equal freedom) ... does not permit property in land" (see Collini, 1979: 102-107). Furthermore, "(I)n our tender regard for the vested interests of the few, let us not forget that the rights of many are in abeyance, and must remain so, as long as the earth is monopolised by individuals" (quoted in Fried, 1998: 262).

In the United States, Henry George and his Land Tax movement became the most consistent critics of the rights of landowners. They argued that, if surplus returns are morally unjustified in case of private monopolies, they must be so in the case of land. Land rents are a value created by the whole community. The surplus is the fortuitous creation of the market structure, where demand outstrips supply at constant cost. If anyone has a right to this surplus value, it is not any particular factor, but society at large, to do with it as it sees fit to further the common good (see George, 1981). Henry George's Land Tax movement, and the 'Progressivists' of the 1900-1940 era, both argued for a redistributive package that consisted of land tax, monopoly regulation, labour laws and inheritance tax.

By the early 1900s, the economic and ethical argument against economic rents, especially land rents, was translated into practice in the UK as the Liberal Party under Lloyd George's guidance adopted a series of budgets that restructured fiscal policy along rent-theory 'unearned income' lines. *The Nation* (May 8, 1909) characterised Lloyd George's Liberal Party Budget of 1909 thus: "Under it no man can lose any fruit of labour or organisation; the State will merely aim at detecting and applying forms of wealth which cannot be traced to individual efforts at all". In September 1909 Winston Churchill articulated the new attitude of the State towards wealth, as asking not only "How much have you got?" but also "How did you get it?" (Fried, 1998: 296). The true function of taxation was to secure to society that element in wealth that was of social origin, or, more broadly, all that did not owe its origin to efforts of living individuals. The ease with which one can isolate the 'social' component of land values probably accounts for the continued popularity of site value taxation in the UK.

In sum, there is a long-standing general consensus across the political spectrum that land rents constitute ethically the most unacceptable form of income, and land tax the least evil form of taxation. Textbook neo-classical public economics argues that taxation is best when it is least distortionary, i.e. when it affects agents' behaviour the least. This implies land value taxation.

Policy and Politics

Agricultural income tax and land revenue constitute less than one per cent of all tax revenue in India; this proportion has steadily fallen after 1947. Agricultural income is not subject to direct taxation. Consumption taxes also fall more sharply on the urban population. A low cost alternative to direct taxes on land rents and agricultural profits involves high capital gains tax when land is converted from agricultural to non-agricultural use. Administratively, the easiest way to administer this policy is to acquire land at low (pre-corporate entry) prices, sell it to capitalists at high (post-corporate entry competitive) prices, perhaps through open auctions, and redistribute the proceeds among society according to independent (non-Lockean) rules of distributive justice.[3]

Such rules, whether Rawlsian or utilitarian ones, would prioritise the poor *because they are poor*, not because they are the erstwhile landowners. These rules may also permit transfers to capitalists when their investments generate strong positive externalities, or to consumers (e.g. through subsidised housing). This redistribution should emphasise formation of non-land, non-alienable assets: education, skills and health among the poor, on Lockean grounds of self-ownership.

As an administrative rule of thumb, 'low price' implies the current market price for land, though it over-compensates those who bought land at a much earlier point in time, inherited it or received it as a government grant. The current market price for land also provides a rough benchmark for calculating whether land conversion from agricultural to non-agricultural uses would generate a social surplus. On the other hand, high compensation rates for land-losers are inherently regressive: larger land-owners receive more money, leaving less to redistribute among the poor and the landless. The Land Acquisition Act of 1894 incorporated the first part of the policy stance articulated above, but not the second: it entailed the payment of roughly the market price to land-losers, but had no provision for *earmarked* redistribution among the poor, leading to governmental moral hazards. Governments susceptible to corporate pressure acquired an incentive to transfer most of the surplus arising from conversion of agricultural land to non-agricultural uses to the corporate end-users, even when the latter had played no role in the original creation of this surplus.

The land policy of the current WB government is based on an ideological commitment to *privatising* the land market. This ideological commitment is grounded in two cardinal intellectual errors. First, it involves an acceptance of efficiency claims of the market in precisely that sphere where such claims are least warranted. Second, it is predicated on an *a priori* defence of market determination of that form of property income which is, as we have already seen, ethically the least defensible (and the least defended).

This is neoliberalism at its most retrograde. It benefits parasitic large landowners and intermediaries at the cost of every other section of society. Furthermore, by encouraging speculative investment in land and land intermediation, it diverts resources from productive deployment into rent-seeking, creates unstable real estate booms and thereby systemic financial instability and inflation, strengthens the land mafia and consequently encourages forcible eviction of marginal farmers and tenants.

That the land policy of the Trinomool Congress Party would objectively prioritise '*dalal-kulak*' interests, above those of every other section of the population, is not surprising, given the class composition of the core support base of that party in rural areas. Analogously, it is only natural that the political representatives of corporate interests would seek to appropriate the entire gains from land conversion through public enforcement of transfers at low purchase prices, while those of the kulak lobby would seek to inflate purchase prices to the maximum extent possible, whether through governmental agency (as, for example, in Haryana), or through a free sellers' market in a fixed resource (as in West Bengal under the TMC). The ethics of consistent egalitarianism, whether of the radical collectivist or the competitive individualist variety, can only stand in uncompromising opposition to these various articulations of kulak/corporate/intermediary rent-seeking interests, in all their possible permutations, and irrespective of the internal conflicts within this triad. The Left Front government's land acquisition policy in West Bengal under Buddhadeb Bhattacharya, with its core narrative of government acquisition of land at prices relatively close to the prevailing market rates, transfer to non-agricultural end users at significantly higher prices, and the attendant socialisation of the conversion surplus for democratically determined redistributive ends, did indeed reflect this egalitarian opposition to private appropriation of what is, ultimately, a socially generated surplus.

Unfortunately however, significant sections of the Indian Left, especially within academia, have deemed it fit, in effect, to hitch their standards to the 'dalal-kulak' mast, in the name of fighting corporate depredations and 'revisionism in the CPI(M)'. Adopting a mode of rhetorical stridency that I have termed elsewhere 'pidgin agit-prop of the populist kind' (Dasgupta 2009), these sections, through their political valorisation of absolute private property claims in land, have *de facto* become accomplices in the process of socialisation of land improvement costs and privatisation of its conversion benefits, that the land policy of the current WB government entails. They have thereby, wittingly or otherwise, become the little drummer boys and girls of neoliberalism at its most retrograde.

REFERENCES

Cohen, G.A. (1995). *Self-Ownership, Freedom and Equality*, Cambridge: Cambridge University Press.

Collini, S. (1979). *Liberalism and Sociology: L.T. Hobhouse and Political Argument in England 1880-1914*, Cambridge: Cambridge University Press.

Dasgupta, I. (2009). "On Some Left Critiques of the Left", *Economic and Political Weekly*, XLIV (31): 109-111.

Epstein, R.A. (1989). "The Utilitarian Foundations of Natural Law", *Harvard Journal of Law and Public Policy* 12: 713-751.

Fried, B.H. (1998). *The Progressive Assault on Laissez Faire*, Cambridge Mass: Harvard University Press.

George, H. (1981). *Progress and Poverty*, New York: Robert Schalkenbach Foundation.

Locke, J. (1988). *Two Treatises of Government*, Peter Laslett ed., Student edn. Cambridge: Cambridge University Press.

Mack, E. (1983). "Distributive Justice and the Tensions of Lockeanism", *Social Philosophy and Policy* 1: 132-150.

MasCollel, A., Whinston, M.D. and Green, J.R. (1995). *Microeconomic Theory*, Oxford: Oxford University Press.

Mill, J.S. (1994). *Principles of Political Economy*, Oxford: Oxford University Press.

Nozick, R. (1974). *Anarchy, State and Utopia*, New York: Basic Books.

Roemer, J.E. (1996). *Theories of Distributive Justice*, Cambridge, Mass: Harvard University Press.

NOTES

1. See Nozick (1974: 175-176), Mack (1983) and Epstein (1989).
2. For more general and elaborate critiques of Nozick's formulation of distributive justice, see Cohen (1995) and Roemer (1996).
3. Such a policy of 'buy cheap and sell dear' was actually followed by the West Bengal government under Buddhadeb Bhattacharya, especially for large township projects on the outskirts of Kolkata.

9

Investment-Induced Displacement: Analysing the Neoliberal Power Structure

Felix Padel

At least forty million villagers have been displaced by 'development projects' since India's independence. The vast majority have experienced a massive drop in their living standards: for them, these projects were the antithesis of development. It is therefore debatable whether they were displaced by 'development' at all. What is certain is that they were displaced by financial investment, and adivasi villagers in Odisha sometimes say 'we are being flooded out by money'[1]—even when large amounts of this money are earmarked for 'tribal development', a category exposed as exceptionally top-down and corruption-prone in P. Sainath's *Everybody Loves a Good Drought* (1996).

As more investment pours into India for similar projects, based around mining and forced industrialisation, more millions are threatened with displacement, and dozens of high-profile social movements have evolved to resist displacement by companies including Posco, Vedanta, Tata, Jindal, Essar, and Areva, the French company trying to invest in a controversial new nuclear power station at Jaitapur. Behind the companies are foreign and national banks, and other investors such as Hedge Funds and Private Equity Funds, mostly run from

London and New York while registered in tax havens. Warren Buffet's Berkeshire Hathaway Hedge Fund has a 5 per cent stake in Posco for example.[2]

In these ways, analysing the horrors of displacement, and the institutionalised neglect faced by villagers dispossessed of their land and homes, provides a way into analysing the processes of investment, and the globalised social structure of investors. In many ways, the modern power structure is centred around neoliberal ideology and policy—the supremacy of 'market solutions' and deregulation, the retreat of the state as the private sector is allowed to take control of many public domains, and the revolving doors that allow elected politicians and bureaucrats to take up lucrative positions in financial institutions as soon as they leave public office.

Clear lines of responsibility link Indian villagers displaced by a dam or metal factory with high-flying bankers and investors in the City of London and other major cities. Is the investment presently pouring into India creating a bubble? America's 1929 and 2008 financial collapses had 18th century precursors in London, in the South Sea Bubble and the Bengal Bubble—the latter created by massive investment in India following Clive's victories, which led to a crash after gross exploitation and dispossession by the East India Company caused the Bengal Famine of 1770 (Robins 2006).

This investment and crash has been largely forgotten by modern historians. Can it shed light on the present situation by showing fundamental patterns of investment-induced exploitation and dispossession? Does such investment inevitably precede a crash? Charles Ferguson's documentary *Inside Job*, about the Wall Street crash of 2008, and the men and policies that caused it, starts in Iceland, where massive foreign investment in dams and infrastructure for the aluminium industry created a bubble of immense proportions. Credit Rating Agencies were still rating Iceland's banks as a best possible investment, and Iceland's standard of living as the world's highest, until days before the crash. Understanding who made the decisions to promote such investment, and to deregulate derivatives trading, and why, takes us straight to the apex financiers and economists running today's world.

Between what a company or development project promises and what actually happens, a reality gap exists (Padel and Das 2011). Any theory of development needs to grapple with the problem of people displaced by industrial projects legitimised under the rubric of 'public purpose'. Even World Bank statistics show that the vast majority of displaced people experience a huge drop in their living standards, in India as well as worldwide. About half of rural India's displaced people are adivasis. Displacement hits adivasis particularly hard because their social structure binds them to the land. This comes on top of a system of endemic exploitation in tribal areas.

The minerals in the mountains of Central India's tribal belt have become objects of prime desire to the world's mining companies, and behind them, to the banks and speculators who make fortunes out of metals trading. Adivasis have seen all too clearly what happens to displaced communities. Between handsome promises and fine-looking resettlement 'packages' and the endless saga of neglect and injustice, a chasm yawns. As a result, everywhere, resistance is growing, and people are asking what kind of 'development' involves the dispossession and impoverishment of thousands of lives? Do the gods of industrialisation really demand human sacrifice on such a colossal scale?

As the Resettlement & Rehabilitation and Land Acquisition Acts are revised, is there an equitable way to ensure that displaced people are properly compensated? Or is this a clash of cultural values, between those who believe in money, and those who believe in community values and nature? An adivasi perspective often implies that money itself is the problem, along with the commodification of land, water and human relationships. Could these movements against imposed industrialisation represent the cutting edge of a new paradigm of development?

> We have sought an explanation from the government about people who have been displaced in the name of development: how many have been properly rehabilitated? You have not provided them with jobs; you have not rehabilitated them at all. How can you

> again displace more people? Where will you relocate them and what jobs will you give them? (Bhagaban Majhi, for the Kashipur movement in Odisha, in Das and Das 2005)

A total disconnect exists between policy and practice regarding Resettlement & Rehabilitation (R & R, e.g. Padel and Das 2008, 2011). Millions of small-scale farmers have been uprooted from their land and communities without the compensation and improvements in living conditions they were promised. Many families, displaced by 1950s-60s projects such as the Rourkela steel-plant, Mandira, Hirakud, the Damodar valley, Pong, Bhakra Nangal and other dams (to name just a few) are still waiting for proper compensation in terms of land they were promised fifty or more years ago.

> On being displaced people meet the same fate everywhere – buli-buli-buli-buli-bulichhanti [they are on the streets/wander/get lost]..... If they are displaced they will be packed tightly in houses built by Posco, far from the river, getting at most coolie jobs for a few years of construction. (Villagers in Nolia Sahi, quoted in Samadrusti 2009)

The problem is at two levels. On the one hand, new 'generous' R & R policies and packages turn out to be anything but, since they do not offer land for land, and cash compensation soon morphs into debt in the hands of village people not used to handling bank accounts and loan offers. Social Impact Assessments are barely carried out at all, forming at best a very subsidiary component in some Environment Impact Assessments, but without any weight or substance (Mathur ed. 2011: 32-34). And even if the policies were as good as claimed, in practice they have rarely if ever been enforced, due to the yawning gap between policy and practice. Companies' job offers, after an initial labour-intensive phase, become opaque: invariably, local people are left unemployed while outside migrant workers get most jobs, especially those with higher salaries.

Moreover, the shift from agriculture to industry redefines skilled cultivators as 'unskilled', so that even 'training courses' bring people who have been highly skilled cultivators but are now classified as 'unskilled' only one or two rungs at most up the ladder of employability, in a labour system that is degrading, exhausting and dangerous, where market economics is rigged against the labourer, and the price of a human life is often very cheap.

Overall, a rapid drop in people's quality of life characterises the situation for the vast majority of displaced people. Numerous core problems find almost no place in mainstream R & R discourse, such as endemic corruption from top to bottom, the role of goondas, illegal liquor shops, and prostitution. There is a distinct lack of proper analysis or monitoring of people's lives in resettlement colonies. Often, it is up to journalists to record the outrages, since official discourse avoids all mention —e.g. of an estimated 500 prostitutes and numerous illegal liquor shops at Damanjodi, Nalco's prime resettlement colony, often described as exemplary (Perry, 2010). These problems, and other reasons for the disconnect between policy and practice, are systemic, and form part of what has correctly been called a *structural violence* oriented against the interests of small-scale farmers.

Yet instead of first trying to resettle and rehabilitate the millions already displaced without proper compensation, displacement of millions more is imminent and planned—not only by numerous new mega-displacement projects, but also via 'restriction of access' (Cernea 2011), by rivers drying up or becoming polluted, and by the entry of agri-business that favours big farmers and intensive cash crops at the expense of small farmers, whose subsistence-oriented economies are defined as 'unsustainable' by current economic criteria, even though they represent the epitome of long-term sustainability as defined by ecological criteria. Adivasi economies are still rooted in local ecology.

> We are tribal farmers. We are earthworms. Like fish that die when taken out of water, a cultivator dies when his land is taken away from him. So we won't leave our land. We want permanent development. (Bhagaban, in Das and Das 2005)

What is referred to here is something rarely given proper weight in mainstream discourse: the element of community-death or soul-death, often articulated with devastating clarity by displaced people, yet rarely understood by 'educated' people for whom roots in a community tied to a piece of land are barely even a memory. Bringing voices of displaced people thus has value in its own right, since they are so numerous yet so little heard. For example, Subrat Sahu's film *DAM-aged* (2009) features interviews with people in the atrociously neglected communities around the Upper Indravati reservoir in west Odisha. India's tribal areas deserve critical attention as a key resource frontier in today's development wars.

What would constitute real development for people in India's poorest areas? How are people standing up to the corporate invasions and land grabs?

Tens of thousands more are being displaced in cities by 'Slum Redevelopment Projects', with similar injustice to that evident in remote areas and ludicrously inadequate R & R. Here too, the displacing force is that of investor-power—corporate land sharks, backed up by banks, and too often, a nexus of politicians, police and even the law courts.

While in remote tribal areas, thousands more are being displaced by war and communal conflicts. The Maoist/ Operation Greenhunt civil war, and the Kandhamal violence, largely against Christians, may appear as wars coming from a clash of ideologies or religions. In fact, in many ways, these are resource wars, over land and its resources—minerals, forest, water rights—as is also the case in most of the world's wars. From Iraq to Libya, Palestine to Afghanistan, and countless 'small' or 'slow' wars in the world's remotest areas, the 'War on Terror' is a mask that covers takeovers of resources, and conflict between mainstream groups in power against marginalised groups living on increasingly scarce resources.

Mainstream society's disconnect from displaced people operates at many levels. The neglect faced by the displaced represents a fundamental injustice, congruent with the historic injustice towards tribal people which a recent Supreme Court Judgement has drawn attention to as needing to be undone.[3]

But even the subject of displacement is subject to neglect and distortion, with 'R & R', a frequent euphemism for displacement, even though genuine rehabilitation has rarely been achieved.

The disconnect also mirrors a lack of dialogue between the 'two cultures' which Jairam Ramesh drew attention to in an article in *EPW* while he was Environment Minister (October 2010), consisting of very different groups, with extremely different value systems. One is presided over by an elite of economists, bankers, businessmen and financiers—including the IMF/WB economists who orchestrate World Bank loans, and everyone who believes in their system (i.e. a large proportion of the middle classes)—while the other is expressed by a broad alliance of people's movements and social and/or environmental campaigners, based in local communities fighting displacement, as well as professionals in many walks of life.

One of the great ironies, which has to be admitted at the outset of any attempt to bring adivasis and Dalits a better deal, is that projects termed 'development' have caused and are causing millions of people a marked decline in their quality of life. Another is that many of the communities facing displacement have an economy still interwoven with ecology, representing ancient traditions at the core of India's culture of food cultivation—systems that have sustained over centuries, now threatened with enforced extinction as 'uneconomic'.

Displacement of human communities is closely interwoven with a variety of assaults on the fabric of natural life known as the ecosystem. The two are part of the same process, and the disconnect is blatant in a lot of World Bank and corporate literature, promising a reduction in poverty, even as eyewitnesses from the ground report violent tactics used against people resisting displacement, and a huge increase in the poverty of people displaced.

World Bank loans in India and many other countries have funded a history of social and environmental catastrophes. In India alone, tens of thousands of families displaced and impoverished by coal mines and big dams in the Damodar valley, Singrauli, Upper Indravati and Narmada (to name a few well-known names) have World Bank funding to thank for the fate of their communities and the fields and forests they had worked and preserved over many generations. In Indonesia, Philippines, Thailand, Brazil, Columbia, Guatemala, Mexico, and dozens of other countries, millions of families have experienced a similar, planned uprooting that has simultaneously devastated pristine environments.

And who is held responsible for this social and environmental devastation? In the words of women and men in a village to be affected by the Upper Indravati dams, who spoke to a WB consultant, who, unusually, recorded what they said:

> You are a woman and we are women.... You are a literate person from a big country. You understand these things are happening to us. So please, as a woman, help us.... The human society living in America must know what is going on in another human society living in India. And they are responsible because we're all humans, living on earth. They can't escape, you know. If I starve, you also bear a responsibility.[4]

But have WB officials ever taken responsibility for communities who suffer because of WB loans? Have they ever been punished for the 'bad economics', which Josef Stiglitz witnessed as the IMF's top economist, that made him resign?[5]

The reality gap between what R & R is supposed to do—raise people's standard of living—and what displacement actually does—devastate it—reflects the communication gap between the 'two cultures' of banks, economists and corporations on the one hand, and movements resisting the land-grabs on the other. The tendency is for consequences on the greater population, and consequences on the natural environment, to be simply discounted, or treated as unimportant.

How do we weigh the value of huge sums invested by companies taking over land and resources, in relation to the value of communities who have always lived on this land, and managed it for agriculture and forest produce? There is an incommensurability here (Martinez-Alier 2010). On one side, a view where only what can be measured is real, and only what is profitable counts, on the other a long-term vision and practice of cultivating food through respect for the land—the essence, perhaps, of Indian culture, expressed through old and tested methods of cultivation.

Investment banking reports on India's mineral assets have had a considerable impact, emphasising a need for huge-scale construction of infrastructure projects to benefit the mining companies. Particularly influential was McKinsey's report *Building India: Transforming the Nation's Logistics Infrastructure* (2005), which has nothing to say about hundreds of communities inconveniently located in places required for 'development'. It is couched in terms of 'the next big exports opportunity', 'turning the minerals and metals potential of eastern India into a gold mine'—a potential concentrated in 'Jharkhand and Orissa and large tracts of West Bengal', not to mention Chhattisgarh, Andhra Pradesh, Karnataka, Madhya Pradesh and a few other places.

At least it has become increasingly obvious to many people that real profits come only to the controlling elite and those who accommodate them. Yet this does not stop the clearances, and the scale is awesome. In 2005 alone, when the MoU signing spree for mineral projects gathered momentum, Jharkhand's Government under Arjun Munda signed at least 50, and a similar number were signed in Chhattisgarh and Orissa. Tata's and Essar's MoUs for five million tonne steel plants in Bastar and Dantewara districts (whose terms to date remain secret) were signed in June 2005—the same month that Salwa Judum started its anti-Maoist campaign of burning villages and, in effect, the civil war which has displaced at least 200,000 people.

The number of displacement projects is extraordinary. The land-grab/real estate/land speculation aspect has if anything become even more blatant than it was. Mining and other companies frequently try to acquire far more land than they need for a project. The plan for Vedanta University is a classic example of this, and it is a blatant feature of many SEZ projects (Special Economic Zones), such as Reliance's 25,000 acre SEZ in Jhajjar and Gurgaon districts of Haryana, and its 35,000 acre SEZ in Pen-Uran-Penvel taluks of Raigad district, near Mumbai. Over 100 SEZs have been approved and several hundred more are planned—a massive series of takeovers of precious water and electricity, as well as land. Far from benefiting the state economically, SEZs are set to receive huge tax-breaks, special deregulation of labour laws, and draconian power structures to bypass normal democratic forms.

When one starts to enter the world of countless personal stories of upheaval that displacement involves, it is not surprising to find that people's movements of resistance to displacement projects are extremely strong in many places. These movements have begun to enter the popular consciousness in India, and controversies surrounding many major displacement projects are more alive than perhaps ever before, with widespread support for communities fighting displacement by Posco, Vedanta, Polavaram dam, Jaitapur nuclear power plant, to mention a few. In many projects like this, it is not only the direct displacement that people object to, it is also being forced to live close to a dangerously polluting plant. Nuclear plants emit radiation regularly as well as in periodic accidents, while workers there have repeatedly been shown to be at high risk of exposure (Gadekar 1993, Ghanekar 2010 and 2011).

Jairam's clearances as well as refusals represent a historic landmark in India's environmental history—especially coming after several years of A. Raja as environment minister (Krishna 2010). Jairam's clearance of Posco (May 2011) was particularly controversial, since MoEF reports have exposed—in this and other cases—multiple illegalities in procedure (Bidwai, Mittal, Bera, each February 2011). These include shoddy EIAs and absent or highly manipulated Public Hearings.

At least it seems a positive sign that this prevalence of irregularities is coming more clearly to light, since many projects have been cleared on the basis of appallingly sub-standard EIAs, and Public Hearings that were held under extreme pressure or badly misreported. In the Posco case, an independent group has written a report questioning the conventional figures on economic benefits, jobs, etc. (Mining Zone October 2010). This goes into welcome detail on the jobs that the Posco Steel-plant-cum-port would destroy—a very large number in this case, since betel-vine cultivation gives a sizeable income, and an estimated 22,000 people stand to lose their livelihoods if the project goes ahead. Behind non-tribal coastal populations resisting displacement by Posco's port-cum-steel plant stand highland populations in the mountains where Posco plans its iron-ore mines, such as the Pauri Bhuiya (a 'Primitive Tribal Group) in the Kandadhara mountain area of Sundargarh district, north Odisha.

Coal mines have been another particularly controversial issue, with Jairam attempting to classify nine major coal blocks as 'no-go areas' due to extensive stands of primary forest above them. The impact of coal mining is generally less known about than impacts from the higher-grade minerals, though effects on communities and ecosystems are probably just as dire. Uncounted thousands of families are uprooted each year to make way for new coal mines or expanding old ones. Several open-cast coal mines in Jharkhand now occupy as much as 35 sq kms each.

A major reason for the extremely large number of new coal mines and thermal power plants, as well as new nuclear power plants and new big dams being promoted, is that India faces a serious power shortage. But does India need all this electrical power? Or is it a non-sustainable, WB-promoted model of development that is bound to collapse in the not-too-distant future? Does it make sense to clear all the country's easily extractable coal deposits now, when known deposits at present extraction rates can last only another 45 years at most (TERI March 2011). What about the next thousand years?

World Bank-orchestrated loans to India, agreed in January 2011, to finance a huge expansion of roads (Jagota and Gangopadhyaya, January 2011), are causing avenues of old trees to be felled throughout Odisha, Jharkhand and other states. This is another land-grab in itself, and facilitates an 'opening up' of remote areas to many shades of takeover and privatisation. Signposting to the ports in preferance to cities is a prominent feature of these roads. Understanding the linkage with numerous mining and other projects, it is hard not to see this road-building programme, and the new debts taken on to expand the roads, as a rape of the country's resources, that converts fertile fields and long-established villages into a wasteland.

A Financial System Based on Debt

'We are being flooded out with money', expresses an adivasi perception of what is being done to them as well as to the landscape they have always lived in and cared for. Is India's present high growth rate based on a rapid extraction of the country's resources? Isn't foreign investment aimed at making a profit out of looting India? Isn't it therefore above all India's high growth rate, funded through foreign investment and debt, that drives the present escalating scale of displacement?

World Bank loans taken since soon after India's independence for a multitude of development projects, starting with the Damodar dams, have built up a burden of massive debt. As this grew bigger, it quickly became institutionalised into an integral part of the country's economic system, which became dependent on ever larger loans, at the level of both central and state governments. For example, in the financial year 1999-2000, the Government of Orissa, India's most heavily indebted state, made repayments and interest payments totalling Rs 3,068 crores, and received new WB loans totalling Rs 3,609 crores, giving an 'actual' income of Rs 541 crores, and revealing a clear dependency, with 46 per cent of the state's GDP going into interest payments.[6] What is the rationale behind this system? And why was Odisha the most indebted state?

The rationale is that India is officially defined as a 'developing country', and the loans are meant to boost the economy and reduce poverty. After 70 years of this system, has this aim been achieved? The goalposts of poverty indicators have been frequently shifted to make it appear that this goal is getting closer, but in reality, everyone in touch with the situation in this and other states knows that the poor have not got richer. Quite the reverse. The gap between rich and poor has increased, and millions live in hunger and lack basic amenities. Among the worst off are the uncounted numbers of people displaced by development projects funded by the World Bank, including the Upper Indravati and other dams. Every new dam project is able to get officially 70 per cent of funding in the form of loans. The WB, and behind it the IMF, is at the apex of a loan system that includes hundreds of financial institutions that also give loans, including the Asia Development Bank and UN agencies.

Displacement, even according to WB studies, reduces at least 90 per cent of oustees to a desperate poverty, even though, according to WB guidelines, displacement is supposed to raise not lower people's standard of living. Most villagers displaced may have been fairly poor—extremely poor by WB standards, which define poverty almost exclusively in monetary terms—but their standard of living was often quite high, especially in terms of a healthy and varied diet, since the forest guarantees many kinds of food, even in times when areas of intensive farming face famine. India's independence movement built up a sense of *Swaraj* in the sense of local as well as national-level pride in self-government and self-sufficiency. Where has this gone?

President Truman's concept of 'Underdevelopment' has been used in effect to promote dependence on foreign aid—the antithesis of *Swaraj*—by subliminally accentuating people's—and countries'—idea of themselves as 'poor' (Esteva 1992). 'Underdevelopment' sets the tone of prevailing discourse about tribal or 'backward' areas, and has ossified negative stereotyping attitudes towards adivasis. Adivasis facing *investment-induced displacement* often still live in a little-monetised economy, and by cultural values that still emphasise depending on one's own skills and labour for most needs. As one put this, in a letter to the Chief Minister of Madhya Pradesh, appealing against displacement by the Sardar Sarovar dam:

> You take us to be poor, but we're not. We live in harmony and co-operation with each other.... We get good crops from Mother Earth.... Clouds give us water.... We produce many kinds of grains with our own efforts, and we don't need money. We use seeds produced by us.... In the spirit of Laha (communal labour) we produce a house in just one day.... (Baba Mahariya 2001)

'Moneylender Colonialism' is essentially the reason why Odisha was India's most indebted state: it had received most loans from the World Bank and other agencies, financing dam, coal, and other projects in order to create an infrastructure for the mining industry, playing on the state's poverty, but using this debt as leverage to open it up to foreign corporations, starting with a privatisation of electricity (Padel and Das 2010 Ch. 17).

World Bank loans are rarely brought into the political discourse in Indian elections. Jubilee 2000 and other organisations outside India continue to campaign for third world debts to be cancelled, but none of India's main political parties make this an issue. Why not? The key reason seems to be that, as soon as a party is elected to office, it becomes the recipient of loans.

It has been observed that 'capital flight' from developing countries is often similar in amount to new loans coming in, and checks on how loans are spent are not over-rigorous, so the system undoubtedly feeds high-level corruption (Rich 1994). It seems that so long as the ruling party follows policy directives from its funders, in the form of 'conditionalities' on loans, it can be sure that each year's new loans will come to more than the sums owed on repayment and interest payments. Every new annual disbursement of funds from the WB and other institutions raises the burden of unrepaid debts.

Loans from the WB and other sources form a basic part of government income, so dependency is built into the system, with policy directives basically handed down from the IMF and in line with US Treasury Department interests. It is known and has been repeatedly demonstrated that any government making moves to deviate from this policy or to default on repayments, will not get the new loans necessary to keep it afloat. As we shall see, the governments of 'developed countries' are caught in a similar system of spiralling debt themselves, with the US and UK notorious examples.

A basic history of WB loans to India makes the pattern clear:

- At the end of the Second World War in 1945, Britain is near bankruptcy, heavily in debt not just to the USA, but also to the Commonwealth countries, especially India
- By 1956, this situation has turned around. WB loans have

started for the Damodar dams and other projects, the Bombay Plan has started rapid industrialisation, and India is heavily in debt

- By 1962 India is the world's most heavily indebted country to the WB, followed by Ghana (reeling from loans for the Akosombo dam and Master Agreement with Valco, which compounded the debt by guaranteeing all profits from the new aluminium industry go to the US Kaiser corporation)[7]
- During 1964-76 India gets $1.5 billion in 11 fast-disbursing Balance of Payment loans for industrial imports, deferring a Balance of Payment (BoP) crisis through loans funding rapid industrialisation
- In 1980 India's debt stands at $20.58 billion
- By 1990 this has risen to $83.7 billion, and India faces its most acute BoP crisis. After Chandrashekar's government sells off $200 million of the country's gold reserves, Narsimha Rao is elected PM in May 1991. Manmohan Singh as Finance Minister swiftly puts a New Economic Policy in place, and by 1992, the crisis is over, thanks to a massive injection of new fast-disbursing WB loans, given on condition of extensive IMF-dictated liberalising reforms, enshrined in the New Economic Policy (1991)
- In April 1993 the WB withdraws from funding the Sardar Sarovar dam (SSP), under pressure after the Morse report. However, $280 million special low-interest loans have already gone through for SSP, as well as $30 million out of an intended $200 million normal-rate loans
- And in 1994, any lack is more than made up by annual WB loans rising to over $2 billion
- In 2010, from a $3 billion average, the annual WB loan rises to $11 billion
- This is the context of the new $1.5 WB billion loan agreed in January 2011 for expanding 24,000 kms of roads, out of a total $40 billion of loans taken by the GoI from various sources to expand a total 747,000 kms of roads

This new burden of debt, taken on for a new kind of 'modern' road network, should be seen as essentially dictated through economists in the IMF and World Bank. Throughout India, roads are being massively widened, with ancient trees cut and a lot of property encroached on. The loans are coming in fast, and state administrations are giving this work top priority, with no protests allowed to hold up the work. One place where protest has escalated, with several people killed in August 2010 and May 2011, is near Noida in UP, where the Yamuna Expressway is taking fertile land from farmers. Reportedly, farmland bought from farmers at Rs 800 per square metre was sold on to developers, who are selling it as housing plots at Rs 14,000 per metre.[8] Land speculation and the housing market are at the root of India's Black Economy (Arun Kumar 1999).

The WB has retreated from funding some of the worst projects now, leaving this to others, but in May 2011, for example, its International Finance Corporation (IFC), that makes private sector loans, came under investigation from its Ombudsman after complaints about extraordinary levels of pollution and intimidation of displaced communities from a coal-fired power station funded indirectly through IFC's $100 million equity in the India Infrastructure Fund (IIF), a Financial Intermediary, that sub-lent some of this money to the power station, swiftly built and enlarged to 1,400MW by GMR Kamalanga Energy Ltd. This power station is in Dhenkanal, Odisha, in an area where new projects are supposed to be banned, since it ranks 7th among India's 88 most polluted areas. Indirect investment of this kind makes accountability hard to establish.[9]

Debt works in the same way at macro- and micro- levels. The pattern of village moneylenders obtaining adivasi lands through compound interest has been frequently recorded. The modern version of indebtedness to seed companies and microcredit agencies forcing small farmers off the land and often into suicide is now well-recorded too. At the international level, this is the same pattern as the World Bank forcing countries which WB loans have sunk into unrepayable debt to open up and yield their assets to foreign investment. Since the New Economic Order, and new legislation such as the SEZ Act (2005) —all apparently engineered from the IMF, WB and parallel institutions—the pace of takeovers escalates.

This is the substance of the 'bad economics' outlined by Josef Stiglitz in *Globalization and its Discontents* (2002). Bad economics applies standard formulas without regard for effects on people and the ecosystems they live in, or even on a country's overall economy. In one case after another (such as Turkey, Mexico, Argentina, the SE Asian 'tiger economies', except Malaysia that didn't follow IMF advice), countries in crisis that follow IMF prescriptions end up compounding the crisis—and their debt burden.

'Moneylender Colonialism' sums up the power structure and systemic exploitation at work here. In other words, today's power structure is based on debt. Getting countries and people into debt, and using that as leverage to extract whatever the controlling financial interests desire, is a key technique of prevailing power structures.

The problem goes deeper still. Crises of ecocide and resource wars in many parts of the world, and governments' inability to make the emissions cuts necessary to check global warming, have their origin in a financial system based on debt. Frederick Soddy was among those who first drew attention to debt as the basis of the financial system, during the 1920s-30s:

> The productive capital is built up by the creation of a permanent and irrepayable debt owned by the investor and owed to him in perpetuity. (Soddy, *The Role of Money* 1934: 152)

For one thing, a large part of the population of almost every country now lives in debt, to mortgage companies, banks and other entities. The sub-prime mortgage crisis in America that led to the crash in September-October 2008 was caused by a deregulation of derivatives trading that spread 'toxic debts'. This was facilitated by Alan Greenspan as Chairman of the Federal Reserve (1987-2006), Lawrence Summers (US Treasury Secretary 1999-2001 and for many years a key decision-maker in the World Bank), Henry Paulson and Timothy Geithner (Treasury Secretaries 2006-January 2009, and since), top economists running Goldman Sachs, AIG and other leading investment banks, as well as academic economists who got large fees for writing articles supporting policies that inflated the debt-bubble, such as the massive investment in Iceland's banks that precipitated their crash (Fergusson's *Inside Job*, 2008).

Mortgage is medieval French for 'death pledge', *mortuum vadium* in Latin—a type of contract forbidden under Christian law. Indeed, usury (moneylending at interest) was forbidden under Christian law until the Medici got around the restriction in the 14th century by masking it under foreign currency transactions, and it remained forbidden under Islamic law till recent times.[10] Moneylending as a form of foreign investment is actually an ancient phenomenon. Roman historian Tacitus records how the philosopher Seneca, most 'upright' of the Romans, made a loan to the Iceni tribe in Norfolk, Britain, and how recalling it in harsh times led to atrocities by Roman tax collectors and the rebellion of Boudica (Boadicea), Queen of the Iceni, who united the tribes and managed to destroy two legions in 60-61AD, before her Iceni tribe was defeated, facing genocide and extinction as a political entity.

In fact, the history of money has close links with war. The first coins were made around or just before 600 BC by kings of Lydia (in modern Turkey) to pay Greek mercenaries. Within two centuries, the Greeks and Italians had evolved the system of coins made of gold, silver and copper that lasted essentially until the late 20th century, when paper money became ubiquitous and the gold standard was broken—first by inflationary finance used by both sides during the First World War, and then by President Nixon breaking the gold standard as basis of the Bretton Woods system in 1971, impelled by escalating US expenditure on the Vietnam war.

Finance was increasingly deregulated under Reagan and Greenspan, allowing derivatives trading in debt instruments to multiply rapidly. Paper money gave way to electronic money during the years 1980-2000, allowing 'hot money' to move across national boundaries at the click of a mouse. Edward Herman drew attention to the dangers of deregulation of finance, and derivatives trading when the market was emerging during the 1990s:

> Deregulation poses a major danger to overall economic stability. Financial markets, under the impetus of the profit-motive and

> competition, and in environments of prosperity and euphoria, have always tended to take on more and more risks, until the bubble bursts. Weakened regulation, the internationalisation of financial markets, and competition on a global basis have encouraged even greater risk-taking. This has been helped along further by the continuation of deposit insurance in the United States and virtual government guarantees that the largest financial institutions will not be permitted to fail.
>
> The world's financial institutions have moved from one area of high risk and speculative investment to another in their search for fat profit margins, and they have vast holdings of risky debt. The enormous development of the derivatives market in the past decade is the latest new product yet to be tested in a crisis where such instruments might require selling in a falling market. (*Triumph of the Market* 1995: 17)

These dangers were epitomised by the crash of Barings Bank in 1995, the crash of the 'Asian tiger economies' in 1997, the crash of Enron in October 2001—originally an energy company, that spearheaded speculation in the electricity market, remembered in India for prototype financial scams surrounding its Dhabol power plant—as well as the sub-prime-mortgage and Icelandic banks crash in 2008.

Another dimension of the expansion of finance is in funding for mining, metal and energy projects. Since 2000, loans to extractive industry projects arranged in London and the US have multipled by about ten times, and IPO sales by about 100 times. Speculation in metals trading, through 'reputable' mainstream banks as well as hedge funds and private equity funds registered in tax havens but mostly run from the world's top capitals, plays a key role in this finance.[11]

The prototype of an investment bubble using debt as a basis for speculation goes back to the South Sea Company, formed in 1711 in London to capitalise on the slave trade, and to finance Britain's national debt, inflated after a war with Spain. The company took on half the national debt—about £30 million—share prices rose, till the bubble burst, and many investors, big and small, were ruined, as happened again during the Bengal Bubble, when London-based investment in newly conquered Bengal caused the 1770 famine.[12]

In many ways, the East India Company let loose in 1760s Bengal was a prototype of the corporate takeovers taking place all over India now, fuelled by foreign investment and speculation.

Economist Amit Bhaduri shows how today's emphasis on economic growth and a high GDP serves the interests of big corporations and those running the WB/IMF cartel,

> while the ground reality steadily worsens. For the sake of higher growth, the poor in growing numbers will be left out in the cold, undernourished, unskilled and illiterate, totally defenceless against the ruthless logic of a global market dominated by large corporate interests.
>
> This is not merely an iniquitous process. High growth brought about in this manner does not simply ignore the question of income distribution, its reality is far worse. It threatens the poor with a kind of brutal violence in the name of development, a sort of 'developmental terrorism', violence perpetrated on the poor in the name of development by the state primarily in the interests of a corporate aristocracy, approved by the IMF and the World Bank, and a self-serving political class... A massive land grab by large corporations is going on in various guises... ('Growing Wasteland', in Bhaduri 2010: 42)

The Wall Street Crash in 1929, and the 2008 crash have many similar features with the 18th century bubbles, starting with irresponsible encouragement of speculation by those running the financial system, whether from London or the Federal Reserve, Goldman Sachs and the US Treasury Department in the US. But the 2008 crash was caused specifically by using people's homes as a commodity for speculation in America; and American investment promoting the aluminium industry in Iceland was at the root of that country's bubble.

Behind the companies, the banks. To understand 'the outrageous debt which Third World countries have actually paid many times over, but which, due to interest, is now larger than ever before', Michael Rowbotham's *Grip of Death* (1998) starts in the UK, where the national debt in 1997 had risen to £400 billion, in a total money stock of £680 billion, the sum economists call M4. Of this, £25 billion had been created by the government Treasury and circulated in the form of notes and coins; £655 billion had been created by banks and building societies, through loans and mortgages—97 per cent of the money circulating in the UK.

> Every time someone takes a loan or mortgage, the idea is that this sum is gradually returned. This is a false idea, a basic collective illusion: 'There is no physical substance behind the majority of modern money'. In the words of Graham Towers, former Governor, Central Bank of Canada, 'Each and every time a bank makes a loan, new money is created—new deposits—brand new money.' The idea that money loaned is really lent and then paid back is, according to an expert as far back as the 1890s, 'a complete and utter delusion. These deposits are not deposits in cash at all, they are nothing but an enormous superstructure of credit.'[13]

As Rowbotham explains:

> The theory that is supposed to govern banking is all theory and no substance. The rules have all been abolished, or rendered quite invalid.... The suggestion that banks create money was once regarded as pure fantasy and heresy by both bankers and economists.... However, modern economics textbooks are quite open about the process. The ability of banks to multiply the quantity of money beyond the amount originally deposited is even given an accepted title: 'the multiplier effect'. The heresy today is that the wholesale creation and supply of money by banks has any particular relevance to or damaging effect on the wider economy.[14]

This is the system used to force economic growth onto resource rich regions, geared towards extracting their resources, dispossessing their original inhabitants and destroying ecosystems in the process. In Britain and America, the banking system is financialised into an electronic abstraction, no longer based in production—at least, not in their own territories, where industrial production of many items has been phased out, with certain supremely lucrative exceptions, such as the arms industry.

Mining and metal production have been progressively outsourced to other countries, and as resources get scarcer, a frenzy of investment pours into India and other 'developing countries', with the precise aim of 'developing their resources', meaning a free-for-all battle between companies and individuals, Indian and foreign-based, to obtain rights to the country's precious mineral deposits, and the land, water and coal necessary to process them.

If economists and bankers have failed to find any way of checking the spiralling national debt in Britain, America and other rich countries, it's not surprising if India and other 'developing countries' have not even begun to free themselves from their debt burdens. But there are many levels to understanding the system presided over by the WB/IMF. The Bretton Woods system was intended to promote a fairer economic relationship between nations than what had gone before, freeing the world from the whole heritage of colonialism. Instead, as most people see all too clearly now, the IMF-WB regime compounded the colonial power structure, and inverted the original aims of Keynes and others who first conceived the system.

The banking logic described above, creating brand new money with every loan, raises vital questions about the third world debt burden, which now stands at trillions of dollars: who is making a profit from this money? Have the rich countries, and the financial and corporate elite of every country, become dependent on 'new money' created by these loans, for maintaining a high standard of living, at a subsidised, inflated level, at the expense of the displaced populations at the cutting edge of 'development terrorism'?

Isn't it clear now that bankers are doing this by a sleight of hand that dispossesses and impoverishes the poorer populations of the poorer countries, while devastating these countries' ecosystems? Isn't it clear that new loans—much sought-after by politicians as soon as their party is elected to form a government but escalating the burden of debt—create the leverage whereby key policy decisions are in effect being controlled through IMF/WB decision-makers?

Returning to the debt burdens which 'developed' countries are reeling under more visibly, the financial crisis in the US and UK now is multi-level: crippling interest payments to financial creditors, a rising current account deficit, rising unemployment and declining real wages for the greater body of workers, superimposed on a major recession (Prabhat Patnaik 2011: 125).

Similarly in the UK, during 35 years from 1963 to 1998, the cash currency (i.e. money created by the government in distinction to money created by banks and building societies through loans) declined from 21 per cent to 3 per cent of the national economy (Rowbotham 1998: 260).

The US national debt has risen from $5.7 trillion (January 2001) to $10.7 trillion (end 2008) and $14.3 trillion (April 2011), when the debt reached 98 per cent of the US GDP. The vast bank bailout which temporarily ended the credit crash in 2008 reveals the extent of the bubble, of what is increasingly being recognised as phantom money—money that does not exist, having no basis in existing currency. At the time of this bailout,

> The financial assets of the richest 1% of Americans totalled $16.8 trillion.... To put that in perspective, the estimated 2007 gross domestic product was $13.8 trillion, and the total federal government expenditures that fiscal year were $2.7 trillion... These sums all seem trifling however, compared with the $55 trillion in outstanding credit default swaps, which had a central role in the subprime mortgage meltdown... [Even this] pales into insignificance, however, when compared with the $648 trillion that the Bank of International Settlements reports as the total notional value of all outstanding over-the-counter derivatives as of June 2008. (Korten 2009: 67)

Nouriel Roubini, one of the few economists who predicted the 2008 melt-down, calls in *Crisis Economics* for far-reaching reforms of the financial system, along with economic theory, if the increasingly destructive swings between booms and busts are to be regulated (Roubini and Mihn 2010).

People on the streets are calling for fundamental reform of the system of finance along with the economic theory driving the system or used to legitimise it. Between September 17 and October 29, 2011, the 'Occupy Wall Street' movement and its offshoots have spread from New York and San Francisco to 'occupied zones' in at least 2,000 cities worldwide.[15]

Labour and Resources as Sources of Value

Jobs are at the heart of an economy, and when we bring labour into the equation, the picture darkens still further. The World Bank system justifies its hegemony, and further loans, in terms of reducing poverty, when the reality seems to be the precise opposite: the investment, and the burden of debt this is created through, reduces the poor to a more desperate poverty than anything that working men and women faced before.

Labour deregulation plays a key part in this, masked with the mantra of growth. According to the introductory pages of the WB's policy document *India: Sustaining Reform, Reducing Poverty*, 2003:

> Sustained growth is the most powerful driver of poverty reduction.... Health and education are the most important assets of the poor, allowing them to both contribute to and benefit from growth through higher-paying employment.[16]

In practice, the informalisation of labour all over the country means that local populations who grew their own food for generations are first dispossessed, and then ruthlessly exploited as a labour pool, rarely getting promised jobs, and in practice having to compete for even the toughest manual labour, with no job security whatsoever. It is the WB that pushed for labour to be deregulated. In the same policy document:

> Labour market restrictions on the hiring and firing of workers are identified as one of the greatest challenges of doing business in India... These provisions make labour rationalization very difficult.... They are obviously especially burdensome for exporters who have to compete with producers in other exporting countries.[17]

The document then calls for repealing Section 5B of India's Industrial Disputes Act (1947) and Amendments to the Contract Labour Act (1970), so as 'to allow contract labour for all activities —not just for activities of a temporary nature.' In effect, with or without these changes, the system in place now curtails use of industrial action and promotes contract labour. Subcontracting and sub-sub-sub-contracting has become standard practice around the country and allows a ruthless exploitation of people's labour.

So saying that poor people's health and education is their most important asset is a misleading platitude. People's first asset is their land, which has been and is being confiscated in the guise of 'Development-Induced-Displacement'.

Their other vital asset is their labour, on which, till the World Bank came along, they supported themselves self-sufficiently on their own and common land, and which, even without their own land, allowed them to support themselves with dignity, until their bargaining power was taken away by negating the power of unions and promoting contract labour, in which people's bargaining power and labour rights become almost non-existent.

At times there seems to be a collective amnesia about the whole history of Unions, which fought an immensely tough battle to gain recognition in the first place, in Britain and America, as well as in India and most other countries. Part of the erosion of union power may relate to hierarchical tendencies within unions, including frequent underhand deals with management. Undeniably though, a violent erosion of union rights has taken place worldwide since the 1970s-80s under the influence of monetarism (as it was called under Mrs Thatcher) and neoliberalism. In India, Shankar Guha Niyogi, a charismatic trade union leader with the Chhattisgarh Mines Shramik Sangh (CMSS, an exemplary mining and steel workers' union) and Chhattisgarh Mukti Morcha, was murdered in 1991, after confronting oppressive tactics by Simplex and other companies. His murder represents the start of a particularly repressive phase for unions in the country.[18]

Another problem is that, in many people's eyes, the Marxist tradition is seen to have become compromised, betraying workers' rights by following the neoliberal agenda of 'labour rationalisation'/'flexibility' and 'increasing labour productivity', as well as the Chinese model, which has become ruthlessly exploitative of labour, not least in sweatshop factories servicing Western-based as well as Chinese multinationals, making a host of consumer items from clothes to computers. This sense of betrayal is especially acute in West Bengal, where a Marxist government that was expected to uphold workers rights was perceived as often undermining them—a cause, alongside the brutal displacement tactics at Singur and Nandigram, for the CPI(M)'s dramatic election defeat in May 2011.

Marx's Labour Theory of Value, outlined in the opening section of *Das Kapital,* is still of greatest relevance for understanding the modern situation. 'The commodification of labour power constitutes a turning point in the history of mankind' (Ramakumar 2011: 52). Marx's analysis of the ways that labour itself, along with nearly every other domain of life, was commodified, is as relevant now as during the 19th century —indeed, the commodification process he delineated has intensified on every level, in relation to water, land, seeds, electricity, animals, and so on, as well as to labour, under direction from the Chicago school economists, and through the IMF/WB.

'Primitive Accumulation' was behind the eviction of Britain's—and other countries'—rural population, through the enclosures of common land, etc. This applies to India during the present period every bit as intensively as it did to Britain in Marx's time. Neoliberalism has essentially worsened manual workers' conditions almost everywhere, as well as increasing unemployment, often even 'criminalising' sections of the people being dispossessed (Ibid: 56).

Marx essentially overthrew mainstream doctrines of profit by showing how capitalists exploited labour power out of all proportion to what workers get in wages. Primitive Accumulation is Marx's term for the process by which the fruit of workers' labour is a primary source of profit for the owners of factories and heads of corporations. Freed from feudal bonds, workers

> became sellers of themselves only after they had been robbed of all their own means of production, and of all the guarantees of existence afforded by the old feudal arrangements.... The great beauty of capitalist production consists in this—that it not only constantly reproduces the wage-worker as wage-worker, but

> produces always, in proportion to the accumulation of capital, a relative surplus population of wage-workers. (*Das Kapital* Vol. I, pp. 719-20).

Marx finishes Volume I of *Das Kapital* with examples of how this system was being reproduced in Australia, noting that 'the expropriation of the mass of the people from the soil forms the basis of the capitalist mode of production.'

'Commodity Fetishism' refers to a deeply embedded collective illusion based around the tendency to commodify – to separate economic/financial value from any basis in exchange, masking the people's labour that goes into making commodities. This illusion and separation emanates from the central place of private property in capitalism (Ghosh 2011: 40-41).

In Marx's analysis, capitalism (and here mainstream economists would not disagree) is constantly revolutionising its production processes, including technologies, but also the institutions it works through—without however, transforming its basic exploitatitve paradigm.

> Modern industry never looks upon and treats the existing form of a process as final. The technical basis of that industry is therefore revolutionary, while all earlier modes of production were essentially conservative. By means of machinery, technical processes and other methods, it is continually causing changes not only in the technical basis of production, but also in the functions of the labourer, and in the social combinations of the labour-process. At the same time it thereby also revolutionises the division of labour within the society, and incessantly launches masses of capital and of workpeople from one branch of production to another... [causing an] absolute contradiction between the technical necessities of modern industry, and the social character inherent in its capitalistic form... this antagonism vents its rage in the creation of that absolute monstrosity, an industrial reserve army, kept in misery in order to be always at the disposal of capital; in the incessant *human sacrifices* from among the working-class, in the most reckless squandering of labour-power and in the devastation caused by a social anarchy which turns every economic progress into a social calamity. (Marx, *Das Kapital* Vol I, pp. 457-8, emphasis added)

This describes precisely the process going on throughout India now. When tribal villages were displaced at Lanjigarh, they were placed in a resettlement colony right between the new refinery and the mountain, Niyam Dongar, which Vedanta intended to mine, as a labour pool which is kept continually under-employed, due to the system of contract labour. India's rapid, enforced integration into the global market vastly increases the pressures on labour. Pressures on employers to increase *labour productivity* to become more competitive in the world market result in savage reductions of the workforce together with a decrease in wages.

> A high growth in GDP (around 7-8 per cent for India in recent years) but a low growth in employment (slightly over 1 per cent) necessarily implies that most of the GDP growth is accounted for by a growth in labour productivity (about 5-6 per cent), and not by an expansion in employment. Jobless growth in both China and India is driven mostly by relatively high growth in labour productivity rather than in employment. (Bhaduri 2009:104)

So the capitalist model of industrialisation carries a tremendously dynamic power of constant change, but also carries the seeds of periodic stagnation—the boom and bust cycle. Partly this is because workers—whether as labourers in factories, or in terms of whole populations of hugely exploited countries, such as India—are also consumers. The more workers are exploited by keeping wages very low, the less their purchasing power, leading to over-production of commodities and slumps (Bose 2011: 81-3). India's present high GDP is maintained through a relatively large middle class of enthusiastic consumers for new products, co-existing with a much larger working class, whose atrociously low wages do not allow them to consume much of the expanding range of consumer goods—though they are constantly tempted into this world of goods through micro-credit and other forms of debt.

The dynamism of industrial production is also characterised by an inherent instability. Partly this is due to its constant devouring of the raw resources close at hand (productive land, coal deposits, water, etc), and also due to financial fraud, which in Marx's time, as even more perhaps today, seems to be not just an occasional aberration, but an integral part of how the system functions (Ghosh Ibid: 42-3). In the 'three-layered cake' model of industrial society's productive system offered by Hazel Henderson (1988, 1996), the top half consists of

> the monetised, officially measured forms of national production which generate all economic statistics [GNP and GDP], plus an estimated 15% of monetised but illegal 'underground' forms of tax dodging. The bottom half of the cake consists of the non-monetised altruistic 'Counter-Economy' of social co-operation, which itself is founded upon the real wealth of the natural world. The two bottom layers subsidise the monetised layers, providing essential unpaid labour and natural resources. (Hutchinson 2010: 42-44)

Probably 15 per cent is too small an estimate for the illegal, tax-dodging part of the economy. The ubiquitous use of tax havens appears to be a regular part of large corporations' financial organisation, as well as the Hedge Funds and Private Equity Funds that invest in them, which are predominantly registered in tax havens (e.g. Kavaljit Singh 2010). The above formulation also draws attention to the unpaid work of women as mothers and carers—aspects neglected by Marx as also by mainstream economics—and the role of natural resources.

Marx was far ahead of his time in comprehending many ecological impacts, e.g. the overexploitation of soil by synthetic fertilisers:

> Capitalist production.... disturbs the circulation of matter between man and the soil, i.e. prevents the return to the soil of its elements consumed by man in the form of food and clothing; it therefore violates the conditions necessary to lasting fertility of the soil. (Marx, *Das Kapital* Vol. I, p. 474)

He also drew attention to the destructive role of debt.

> The credit system appears as the main lever of over-production and over-speculation in commerce.... The credit system accelerates the material development of the productive forces and the development of the world market.... At the same time credit accelerates the violent eruptions of this contradiction [inherent in the financial system].... (*Das Kapital* Vol. III, p. 441)

Interest-Bearing Capital, Marx often stresses, holds the key to rapid accumulation, but is also at the heart of the system's periodic crises and inherent instability, through over-accumulation, and ballooning debt. In the words of Jayati Ghosh (2011: 47):

> Economic neoliberalism does not actually imply a withdrawal of the state from economic activity, as many tend to assume; rather it implies a shift in the nature of state involvement, away from attempting to provide social and economic rights of citizens, to ensuring conditions of profitability for large capital and in particular finance.

In other words, the state is shifting its role to become a facilitator for mining and other corporations, 'generating a planetary scale set of ecological contradictions, imperilling the entire biosphere' (Bose 2011: 47-8).

Since Marx's time, the vast intensification of extractive industries technologies (in mining, as well as oil and gas drilling), and the exponential rise in industrial pollution, has increased the 'real costs' of production, in a way that was barely conceivable in Marx's time. The externality costs of extracting minerals and processing them were already massively exploitative, but had not begun to be properly analysed, while the technology of capitalist extraction of raw materials had not progressed close to today's scale and speed.

Today, the externality costs of industrialisation pose a multi-dimensional threat to human society, from scarcity, by depleting water especially, as well as the remaining deposits of oil, gas, coal, bauxite, iron, etc; from global heating; and also from escalating resource wars. Even if we had 200 more years of all these extractable/non-renewable resources at present rates of extraction (which we certainly don't) do we wish to escalate these resource wars? How long can the growth models that have dictated industrialisation from Marx's time to the start of the 21st century continue?

Our planners have apparently given up on the idea of a steady state economy (Daly 2008)—an economy that doesn't grow but aims to maintain a steady level. And as yet, we have not come close to solving the problem of distribution through a more equitable sharing of resources. Some communist countries, for a while, came close to this, but owing to the corruption of their own hierarchies, and failure to formulate a strong ecological counterpart to official Marxist doctrine, most did not handle environmental issues much better than capitalist countries, and failed to create a lasting theoretical counterpoise to capitalist economics' mantra of growth.

For mining companies, their 'starting point of value creation' is getting ores as cheap as possible, and that they club together as a cartel, alongside financial institutions and powerful, if hidden, government interests, in order to enforce the cheapest possible prices for ores. We see that sections of governments are often complicit with mining companies in mining India's iron ore and other minerals for far too little return in terms of government revenue, let alone benefit for the local population of mining areas, who are hideously exploited on a regular basis.

Current systems of valuation are at the heart of the ecological unsustainability built into present-day capitalism (Burkett 2009). How prices are set, and relative values placed on natural resources, consumer goods, and people's labour, needs profound adjustment if economic imperatives are to be brought into balance with the long-term health of ecosystems and human communities.

Natural resources are clearly a prime source of value alongside labour. In holistic understanding of the momentous impacts of capitalist economics over the life of labourers and the natural resources embedded in ecosystems, the work of Marx and Engels laid the foundation for the tools of Ecological Economics (Foster and Burkett 2004). Frederick Soddy first showed how the 'entropy' law—the Second Law of Thermodynamics—applies to 'real wealth' (i.e. natural resources of all kinds), while money and debt are subject to the laws of mathematics, bringing in an incommensurability at the heart of 'virtual' or 'phantom wealth'. Marx and Engels understood how the laws of capitalism systematically over-exploit labour as well as natural resources—the 'loss of heat' implicit in the entropy law (Foster and Burkett 2008).

With a proliferation of new power projects and metal factories springing up in India, battles are escalating everywhere over land itself, as well as over water, mountains, forests, and rights to the commons, telescoping the whole history that Marx described so poignantly in terms of the expropriation of working people from the soil.

In this process, the conflict over coal and minerals becomes especially intense, between numerous different companies on the one hand—essentially a surface conflict, since it makes relatively little difference to either displaced communities or to the banks and other investors which companies win, so long as the latter can invest in them—and between local people and environmentalists against the expropriators on the other.

Lado Sikoka spoke for many adivasis when he said (in Odia, in the Belamba Public Hearing, recorded on Youtube) 'Niyamgiri is not just a pile of money—it's our Maa-Baap, who has always nourished us!'[19] For J.P.Morgan and the other banks who supported Vedanta's entry to the London Stock Market, for McKinsey and similar entities, for the *Financial Times* and London-based investors, and for a large section of Odisha's middle classes who feel no loyalty to the life-giving properties of this mountain, and don't recognise this aspect, a pile of money is precisely what it is: a pile of money 'lying unutilised', till the ore can be extracted and sold, while people's movements represent an annoying 'anti-development' barrier to that agenda. For the banks perhaps, the delay doesn't matter much, since the conflict serves to push prices up even further. But what do banks understand about ecosystems?

From a Power Structure Based on Debt to a New Economics?

In many ways, the situation that has been engineered in India and other countries by World Bank/IMF/WTO policies is one that has aptly been described as *Mortgaging the Earth* (Rich 1994), or mortgaging our grandchildren's future. For example, through much of 2010-11, the coal ministry, backed by strong economic-financial interests, was lobbying the Prime Minister's Office against Jairam Ramesh's attempt (which has the backing of the conservation lobby) to declare about 30 per cent of India's coal reserves as No-Go zones for the moment. What kind of madness have we come to that *all* the country's mineable deposits of coal—and the same applies to its bauxite reserves, iron ore deposits, and other minerals—should be granted clearance for mining now?

We saw that TERI's report (March 2011) gives India's coal deposits another 45 years at most, while gas reserves have just 20-30 years. How long for bauxite and iron? Even if it was 200 years (and the reality at present extraction rates is far less), this is not a long time in terms of the historical traditions we inherit. Why do financial planners presume that we should be planning for only as long as our children and grandchildren may live out their lives? Our intellectual ancestors who left us a heritage that includes Kautilya's *Arthashastra*, Aristotle's and Plato's extensive writings on philosophy, science, maths and politics, Confucian and Taoist writings in China—all written over 2,000 years ago—would have found it absurd that our planners' decisions cover such a short time-frame.

Aristotle drew a distinction between *oikonomia* as laws of housekeeping, and *chremistiki*—the art of acquisition. In many ways, it is the latter that has come to dominate both the financial world and the discipline of economics—spinning us into a vortex of debt, without any solution in sight. Is this a death grip (*mort-gage*) for our civilisation?

Economist Susan Feiner, approaching 'economic man' from a female perspective, notes the infantile psychology inherent in economic theory and financial actions, based on sibling rivalry and the tyranny of want ('A Portrait of *Homo economicus* as a Young Man' 1999; Hutchinson 2010: 44). The art of acquisition is developed out of all proportion by financial institutions and companies, and the institutionalised indulging of childish acquisitiveness runs completely out of control, especially when one considers the revolving doors which lead to and fro between high political office and top jobs/lucrative consultancies in the big corporations and banks. Both Tony Blair and Sir Ratan Tata are presently (2010-11) listed as consultants to J.P. Morgan for example; and the top economists who before 2008 put the weight of their opinion—for a fee—behind financial policies that promoted derivatives trading and Icelandic bank investments, illustrate a corrosion of independent thought deep within their discipline.

Neoclassical economics traces its roots back to 18th century 'Age of Enlightenment' philosophers, such Locke, Hume and Adam Smith, who made self-interest the key to economic behaviour. Could it be that these eminent thinkers performed a profound disservice to human thinking, and to humans' role as guardian of the earth we live from, by elevating selfishness and acquisitiveness to such a central role? People from a tribal background often perceive this particularly clearly, from a tradition that grounds the spiritual more firmly in nature.

To re-ground ourselves in nature, intellectually, ecological economics offers models of analysing monetary flows in a way that connects them with the larger picture of material energy flows and Human Appropriation of Net Primary Production (HANPP).[20] But a more holistic way of thinking needs to be cultivated too, that reconnects nature with society, and thinking with feeling, 'thinking like a mountain' (John Seed 1988). Educational and professional norms often require one to separate one's feelings from one's thought process. Has this led to a split that actually prevents expert economists and engineers from comprehending the impacts of their projects?

There is a strong tradition of alternative economics, supplementing the Marxist tradition, and many wonderful models for living sustainably in the true sense (e.g. Lietaer's *The Future of Money* 2001; Greco's *The End of Money* 2009; Korten 2009, 2011). At the level of planning and politics, there seems to be an urgent need for transition towards *planned de-growth*— even though this means confronting the power structures entrenched around money. Otherwise the crash from the collective cycle of derivatives/speculation and national debt bubbles that have built up around the world could make the crashes of 1929 and 2008 seem small. In a way, ever since 1929, the crash has been staved off, by ballooning the bubble yet further in a method tightly controlled by central banks, yet fundamentally completely out of control.

For one, the crash has been staved off through incessant

wars—the very wars that have caused such big jumps in debt!—and what feeds the wars? The military industrial complex, whose extent and complexity escalated through the two world wars and then from 1951. The arms industry is bang in the centre of most countries' economies, yet little analysed as such, and known to be highly corrupt, highly polluting in terms of GHG emissions; and a major customer for mining/metals companies (Clairmont 1995: 15-18, Padel 2008, Padel and Das 2010: Chapter 10).

'Is there anything worth keeping in standard microeconomics?' Guerrin's article (2002), which questions entrenched assumptions about pricing, is intended to shock economists into new ways of seeing, demonstrating a divorce between the complex formulae in economics and 'stories' based on unproven assumptions. Several much older economics texts have been to all effects and purposes airbrushed out of economics teaching, such as Henry George's *Progress and Poverty* (1879) was considered more dangerous and subversive than *Das Kapital* in its time, which exerted a major influence in moulding mainstream theory into a form that would discredit George's 'single tax arguments', that were highly influential in the US (applied for a few years in Oregon), and among the radical wing of the Liberal Party in Britain, between 1901 and 1924.[21]

Clifford Hugh Douglas's analysis of the economic system came from his analysis of spending during the First World War, and how, from 1914 to 1919, Britain's national debt rose from £660 million to £7,700 million. Douglas produced several highly influential texts, including *Social Democracy* (1920) and *Social Credit* (1924), the name given to his theory, which was put into practice in the Canadian Province of Alberta from 1935 to 1940, by an elected Social Credit-oriented government, despite bitter attacks in print and politics, and a series of groundbreaking Acts (in effect nullified by the Federal Government), including a Banking Taxation Act, a Reduction and Settlement of Debts Act, and an Act to Ensure Publication of Accurate News, in a context where corporate ownsership of media often reduces 'freedom of the press' into a freedom to distort and conceal.

During this government's first three years in office, the Province's debt was reduced by $3 million ($900,000 the first year, $700,000 the second, and $1,400,000 the third), while every other Province's debts increased (Hutchinson 2010).

Many of the major proposals for an economic system not based on debt have tax as their focus (see also *Artha Kranti*, at www.arthakranti.org). All agree that present systems tend to tax the poor much more relatively than the rich, while in effect giving big subsidies to the rich. To simplify, the Georgist system wants a single tax on land, Social Crediters wish to tax banks and financial transactions, the Tobin Tax (first set forth by James Tobin in 1972, and invoked e.g. by the Commissioner of the European Union in September 2011, to the chagrin of London bankers and Treasury officials), targets currency conversions among other financial transactions, while many environmentalists want a system of carbon tax, instead of the fraudulent system of carbon-trading in place (CDM).

Politically, the way to introduce such taxes is fraught with difficulty, though Australia has opened the gateway. Recently, an Australian Prime Minister who tried to raise the tax on mining companies was removed by a mining-orchestrated coup. His successor has managed to introduce carbon and mining taxes (November 2011), that may pave the way towards governments imposing the kind of strong taxes needed, though such taxes will continue to be politically difficult, not least because they are bound to raise the price of petrol.[22]

Among solutions offered to India's agrarian crisis are radical decentralisation (considered under PESA), and the kind of land reforms that were intended after independence, but sidelined through the Green Revolution and policy inputs from the Ford Foundation and USAID. Prabhat Patnaik (2011: 131-2) also recommends a de-linking from global capital, in order to avoid the pernicious takeovers and manipulation from foreign finance.

On a small scale, examples of different models of development are numerous and diverse in India. There is no lack of alternatives (Kishen Pattnayak 2000). Literally hundreds of models are available from the Indian context, and from probably every country and region on earth. The question is, can we transform the role of money and debt, from a domination-oriented power structure based on competition and exploitation into a system based on sharing the earth's natural wealth? Can we, as a global species, develop beyond the paradigm of growth bubbles based on debt?

REFERENCES

Bera, Sayantan (2011). 'POSCO Unplugged', in *Down To Earth,* February 11.

Bhaduri, Amit (2009). *The Face You Were Afraid to See: Essays on the Indian Economy,* New Delhi: Penguin.

Bhaduri, Amit (2010). *Essays in the Reconstruction of Political Economy,* Delhi: Aakar.

Bidwai, Praful (2011). 'Scorching the Earth', in *Frontline,* Vol. 28 Issue 4, February 12-25.

Bose, Prasenjit (2011). 'The Three Stories of *Capital* and their Relevance Today', in *Marx's Capital: An Introductory Reader* by V. Athreya et al. pp. 77-103.

Burkett, Peter (2009). *Marxism and Ecological Economics: Towards a Red and Green Political Economy,* Chicago: Haymarket.

Caufield, Catherine (1998) [1996]. *The World Bank and the Poverty of Nations,* London: Pan.

Cernea, Michael (2011). 'Broadening the Definition of "Population Displacement": Geography and Economics in Conservation Policy', in Mathur (ed.) (2011), pp. 85-119.

Clairmont, Frederic F. (1996) [1995]. *The Rise and Fall of Economic Liberalism: The Making of the Economic Gulag,* Goa: The Other India Press.

Daly, Herman (2008). 'Towards a Steady State Economy', paper presented at UN Commission on Sustainable Development, available at http://www.theoildrum.com/node/3941. Originally in book form as *Steady State Economy,* 1977.

Das, Amarendra and Samarendra (2005). *Matiro Poko, Company Loko* (Earth Worm, Company Man, in Odia with English subtitles and commentary), about movements against mining in Odisha (from sdasorisa@gmail.com).

Douglas, Clifford Hugh (1974) [1920]. *Economic Democracy,* London: Cecil Palmer.

Douglas, Clifford Hugh (1933) [1924]. *Social Credit,* London: Eyre and Spottiswoode.

Esteva, Gustavo (1992). 'Development', in Wolfgang Sachs, (ed.) *The Development Dictionary: A Guide to Knowledge as Power*, pp. 6-25. London: Zed.

Feiner, Susan (1999). 'A Portrait of *Homo Economicus* as a Young Man', essay no. 9 in Martha Woodmansee and Mark Osteen (eds.). *The New Economic Criticism: Studies at the Intersection of Literature and Economics*, London: Routledge.

Ferguson, Charles (2010). *Inside Job* (about the economic crisis of 2008). Sony Pictures.

Foster, John Bellamy and Peter Burkett (2004). 'Ecological Economics and Classical Marxism', *Organisation and Environment*, Vol. 17, No. 1, pp. 32-60.

Foster, John Bellamy and Peter Burkett (March 2008). 'Classical Marxism and the Second Law of Thermodynamics: Marx/Engels, the Heat of the Universe, and the Origins of Ecological Economics, *Organisation and Environment*, Vol. 21, No. 1, pp. 3-37.

Gadekar, Sanghamitra and Surendra (1993). *Anumukti—A Journal Devoted to Non-nuclear India: Special Issue on Rawatbhata*, Vol. 6, No. 5, April-May 1993. Vedchhi, Gujarat: Sampoorna Kranti Vidyalaya.

Gaffney, Mason and Fred Harrison (1994). *The Corruption of Economics.* London: Shepheard-Walwyn with Centre for Incentive Taxation, Georgist Paradigm Series.

Galbraith, John Kenneth (1992) [1954]. *The Great Crash 1929,* London: Penguin.

George, Henry (1879). *Progress and Poverty,* New York: Robert Shalkenbach Foundation. Abridged edition.

George, Susan (1992). *The Debt Boomerang,* London: Pluto Press.

Ghanekar, Nikhil M. (September 18, 2010). 'The nuclear park at Jaitapur will be huge: So will the human cost', *Tehelka.*

Ghanekar, Nikhil M. (January 18, 2011). 'Villagers Up the Ante Against Jaitapur's N-plant', *Tehelka.*

Ghosh, Jayati (2011). 'Reading *Capital* in the Age of Finance', in *Marx's Capital: An Introductory Reader* by V. Athreya et al, pp. 38-50.

Giljum, Stefan, Christian Lutz and Ariane Jungnitz (2007). 'Quantifying indirect material flows of traded products with a multi-regional environmental input-output analysis', presented at the 7th conference of the European Society for Ecological Economics, Leipzig, Vienna: Sustainable Europe Research Institute, available at http://seri.at/wp-content/uploads/2009/09/ESEE-2007-PETRE-Presentation.pdf.

Graham, Ronald 1982. *The Aluminium Industry and the Third World,*

London: Zed.

Greco, Thomas (2009). *The End of Money and the Future of Civilization*, Green Press Initiative.

Guerrin, Bernard (2002). 'Is there anything worth keeping in standard microeconomics?' *Post-autistic Economic Review* Issue No.12, at http://www.autisme-economie.org/article115.html.

Henderson, Hazel (1988). *The Politics of the Solar Age: Alternatives to Economics*, Indiana: Knowledge Systems.

Henderson, Hazel (1996). *Building a Win-Win World: Life Beyond Global Economic Warfare*, San Francisco: Berrett-Koehler.

Herman, Edward S. (1995). *Triumph of the Market: Essays on Economics, Politics and the Media*, Boston: South End Press.

Haberl, Helmut, F. Krausmann and S. Gingrich (2006). 'Ecological Embeddedness of the Economy: A Sociological Perspective on Humanity's Activities 1700-2000', *Economic & Political Weekly* 25, November, pp. 4896-4904.

Higgins, Polly (2010). *Eradicating Ecocide: Laws and Governance to Prevent the Destruction of our Planet*, London: Shepheard-Walwyn.

Hinterberger, Friedrich, Stefan Giljum and Mark Hammer (2003). 'Material Flow Accounting and Analysis (MFA)', in *Encyclopaedia of Ecological Economics*, Vienna: Sustainable Europe Research Institute.

Hutchinson, Frances (2010). *Understanding the Financial System: Social Credit Rediscovered*, Charlbury, UK: Jon Carpenter.

Jagota, Mukesh and Abhrajit Gangopadhyaya (January 14, 2011). 'World Bank Pledges Nearly $2 Billion to India', *Wall Street Journal*, New York.

Krishna, Gopal (November 24, 2010). 'At Play in the Fields of the Lord', in *Tehelka*.

Korten, David (2009). *Agenda for a New Economy: From Phantom Wealth to Real Wealth*, San Francisco: Berrett-Koehler.

Korten, David. New Economy Working Group 2011. *How to Liberate America from Wall Street Rule.* Online edition at http://neweconomyworkinggroup.org/report/how-liberate-america-wall-street-rule.

Kumar, Arun (1999). *The Black Economy in India*, London and Delhi: Penguin.

Lietaer, Bernard (2001). *The Future of Money: Creating New Wealth, War, and a Wiser World*, New Falls (US): Century.

McKinsey & Company (2005). *Building India: Transforming the Nation's Logistics Infrastructure*, McKinsey India: Mumbai and Gurgaon (available at McKinsey website).

Mahariya, Baba (2001). 'Development at Whose Cost? An Adivasi on Dislocation and Displacement', in K.C. Yadav (ed.) *Beyond Mud Walls: Indian Social Realities,* Gurgaon: Hope India.

Martinez-Alier, Joan (2002). *The Environmentalism of the Poor: A Study of Ecological Conflicts and Valuation,* Cheltenham: Edward Elgar.

Martinez-Alier, Joan (2010). 'Environmental Justice and Economic Degrowth: An Alliance between Two Movements' (available at http://www.greencanal.eu).

Marx, Karl (2010, 1887). *Capital [Das Kapital]: A Critical Analysis of Capitalist Production,* Delhi: Leftword. Translated from the third German edition by Samuel Moore and Edward Aveling and edited by Frederick Engels. [1st German edition 1867].

Mathur, H.M. (ed.) (2011). *Resettling Displaced People: Policy and Practice in India,* Delhi: Council for Social Development & Routledge.

Mining Zone People's Solidarity Group October (2010). *Iron and Steal: The Posco-India Story,* At http://miningzone.org/.

Mittal, Tusha (February 1, 2011). 'Loopholes in Ministry's Posco Verdict?' *Tehelka.*

Nostromo Research (2011). *From Money to Metals: Tracking Global Mining Deals,* London: Nostromo, and Germany: Heinrich-Böll-Stiftung. Updated repeatedly, at http://moneytometal.org/index.php/From_Money_to_Metals.

Padel, Felix (February 2008). 'Mining as a Fuel for War', in *The Broken Rifle* Issue No. 77, p. 1, War Resisters International, at www.wri-irg.org/node/3576.

Padel, Felix and Samarendra Das (2008). 'Cultural Genocide: The Real Impact of Development-Induced Displacement', in H.M. Mathur (ed.), pp. 103-15, Delhi: OUP.

Padel, Felix (2010). *Out of This Earth: East India Adivasis and the Aluminium Cartel,* Delhi: Orient BlackSwan.

Padel, Felix 2011. 'Resettlement Realities: The Gulf between Policy and Practice', in H.M. Mathur (ed.). *Resettling Displaced People,* pp. 143-180. Delhi: Council for Social Development and Routledge.

Patnaik, Prabhat (2011). 'A Marxist Perspective on the World Economy', in *Marx's Capital: An Introductory Reader* by V. Athreya et al., pp. 120-33.

Pattnayak, Kishen (2000). *Bikalpaheen nahi hai duniya,* Delhi: Rajkamal.

Perry, Kevin E.G. (December 7, 2010). 'Secrets and Lies: Tackling HIV Among Sex-workers in India', in *The Guardian,* UK.

Rich, Bruce (1994). *Mortgaging the Earth: The World Bank, Environmental Impoverishment and the Crisis of Development,* London: Earthscan.

Ramakumar, R. (2011). 'Agriculture and Rural Society in Capital', in

Marx's Capital: An Introductory Reader by V. Athreya et al., pp. 51-76.

Ramesh, Jairam (2010). 'The Two Cultures Revisited: The Environmental Development Debate in India', *Economic & Political Weekly*, Vol. xlv, No. 42, October 16.

Robins, Nick (2006). *The Corporation that Changed the World: How the East India Company Shaped the Modern Multinational*, London: Pluto.

Roubini, Nouriel and Stephen Mihn (2010). *Crisis Economics: A Crash Course in the Future of Finance*, New York: Penguin.

Rowbotham, Michael (1998). *Grip of Death: A Study of Modern Money, Debt Slavery and Destructive Economics*, Charlbury, UK: Jon Carpenter.

Sahu, Subrat Kumar (2010). *DAM-aged*, in Odia with English subtitles and commentary, about the Upper Indravati Dams and Reservoir, Odisha (from subrat69@gmail.com).

Sainath, P. (1996). *Everybody Loves a Good Drought: Stories from India's Poorest Districts*, London: Penguin.

Samadrusti, October (2009). 'Nolia Sahi – A Fishing Village' (video on youtube).

Singh, Kavaljit (2010). *Fixing Global Finance: A Developing Country Perspective on Global Financial Reforms*, Delhi and Amsterdam: Madhyam and SOMO.

Soddy, Frederick (1926). *Wealth, Virtual Wealth, and Debt: The Solution of the Economic Paradox*, London: George Allen & Unwin.

Soddy, Frederick (1934). *The Role of Money*, London: Routledge.

Stiglitz, Josef (2002). *Globalization and its Discontents*, London: Penguin.

TERI (The Energy & Resources Institute) (March 2011). *India's Coal Reserves are Vastly Overstated: Is Anyone Listening?* Delhi: TERI.

NOTES

1. Padel and Das 2010: 148, 372.
2. 'Warren Buffet's Company has Stake in Posco Project', *India Today* 25.3.2011.
3. http://www.survivalinternational.org/news/6875, 21.1.2011.
4. Padel and Das 2010: 455, quoting Caufield 1998: 226-7.
5. Padel and Das 2010: 484-7, Stiglitz 2002: 22-23.
6. *Fiscal and Governance Reforms* (2001), Finance Department, Government of Orissa.
7. Graham 1982; Padel and Das 2010: 238-44.

8. National Alliance of People's Movements, Press Release 11.5.11'Rahul Sneaks into Land Row Village on Bike', *Times of India* May 12, 2011.
9. 'Proposed Power Plant in Dhenkanal in Trouble', *The Hindu*, 13.5.2011.
10. Rowbotham 1998, Padel and Das 2010: 529.
11. Nostromo Research: *From Money to Metals*, 2011.
12. Padel and Das 2010: 530-1.
13. Rowbotham 1998: 10-12, quoting H.D. McLeod, *The Theory of Credit*, 1894.
14. Rowbotham 1998: 24-27.
15. On the Occupy Wall Street Movement, see the movement's online journal, *The Occupied Wall Street Journal*, at http://www.occupiedmedia.org/ and 'How to Liberate America from Wall Street Rule' (Korten/New Economy Working Group, July 2011), activist-oriented online sequel to Korten 2009.
16. World Bank, Development Policy Review, July 14, 2003, Report No. 25797-IN, p. vi.
17. Ibid., 56.
18. 'Niyogi Murder Case: Life Sentence for Main Accused', *Times of India*, 20.1.2005.
19. Hinterberger *et al* 2003, Haberl *et al* 2006, Giljum *et al* 2007.
20. http://www.youtube.com/niyamgiri#p/a/u/1/ipHmVee_uXw.
21. *The Corruption of Economics* (Gaffney and Harrison 1994), presents George's thinking for a modern readership.
22. 12 October 2011, at http://www.globalpost.com/dispatches/globalpost-blogs/down-under/julia-gillard-australia-mining-carbon-tax-down-under; 23 November 2011, at http://www.guardian.co.uk/world/2011/nov/23/mining-tax-australia-passes-house.

10

Land Acquisition Laws and the State in the Neoliberal Era: Some Observations on the Constitutional Imperatives, Legislations and Judicial Interventions

V. Krishna Ananth

In the twenty years after the new economic policy was put in place in July 1991, we have found the state playing a more active role than in the past in the area of acquisition of private land. It is no exaggeration to say that the state resorted to force to facilitate industrial and other commercial activities during this period than during the four decades since the Constitution came into force. One does not come across such instances where the armed might of the state was used to assert its right to acquire private property for a 'public purpose' during the four decades after January 26, 1950 as in the several instances in the past two decades.

It is not as if that land acquisitions are only a feature of our recent past. On the contrary, land acquisition as such and compulsory acquisition of property by the state has been a part of our short history (in independent India). Article 31 of the Constitution (and Article 300-A since 1978) provides the Constitutional sanction for the various laws in this regard; to be precise, all laws in this area, will have to be consistent with the Constitutional provision and where a law is found to violate this, such laws will remain a nullity. It may be added that the

Land Acquisition Act, 1894 as well as the acquisition laws in the various states, draw its sanction from the Constitution. The Act, laying down the procedure for acquisition of land, is of colonial vintage.[1]

It is necessary to note that Article 300-A (as was the case with Article 31 until it was deleted) of the Constitution is clearly an injunction against the state from acquiring private property. In that sense, the makers of our constitution had recognised the concept of eminent domain only in a limited sense of the term. The specific context in which Article 31 of the Constitution came into being had to do with providing an injunction against indiscriminate acquisition of private property by the state. It is also significant to note here that the roots of Article 31 can be traced to Section 299 of the Government of India Act, 1935. Notwithstanding this, it will be idle to argue that the concept of eminent domain was laid to rest in our jurisprudence. On the contrary, it was invoked and embedded into our constitutional scheme by the Supreme Court from as early as in 1951 itself.

This essay is an attempt to place in context the various provisions and injunctions—Constitutional and Statutory—in the area of land acquisition from a historical perspective and locates its relevance in the context of the neoliberal state. Such an attempt cannot be restricted to a pedantic narrative but will necessarily involve drawing a distinction in the context between the times then and the present. Any discussion on the law of land acquisition cannot gloss over the substantial changes that the definition of "public purpose" has suffered during the sixty years of the Constitutional scheme. It will be pertinent, hence, to deal with our experience with Article 31 of the Constitution till it was deleted in 1978 by way of the Constitution (Forty-Fourth Amendment) Act, 1978. This period was marked by a catena of challenges against attempts by the state to acquire private property with a view to distribute the same and thus effect the ideals pronounced in Article 39 (b) and (c) of the Constitution. And in the subsequent phase, we find a substantial change in the process with the state asserting its powers for purposes that are quite the opposite and the challenges to these. It may be added that while the contestations in the previous era happened in the higher judiciary, the terrain for contest in the present times is most often on the streets and at times in the law courts too.

I

It may be noted, at the outset, that Article 31 of the Constitution, was the outcome of a serious debate in the Constituent Assembly. The provision, as it was in the Draft Constitution (Article 26) was for most parts a verbatim reproduction of Section 299 of the Government of India Act, 1935.[2] Article 31, thus, bore the Nehruvian imprint and in that sense had gone miles ahead from Section 299 of the 1935 Act. However, even after all these changes that put Nehru's ideals against private property in place, Article 31 remained an injunction against the state from acquiring private property. And the very fact that Article 31 found a place in Part III of the Constitution and thus the status of a Fundamental Right made it a substantive injunction than it was as in Section 299 of the 1935 Act.

It is imperative from the concerns of this paper that the specific context in which Section 299 became part of the Government of India Act, 1935, is recalled. The Indian National Congress, since 1917 (with the *satyagraha* campaign in Champaran and Kheda) had internalised the demand for security of tenure to the peasants as part of the national struggle for independence and the Fundamental Rights Resolution at Karachi marked a culmination of this process.[3] It is also relevant to point out the democratisation of the national movement in this phase and the emergence of a strong peasant movement, which in some instances, went beyond the control of the Indian National Congress. This happened in parts of United Provinces and Bihar and the roots of a radical agrarian political mobilisation in other parts such as Bengal and Malabar lay in this phase.

This indeed set the stage for the colonial law makers to add Section 299 into the Government of India Act, 1935. And the Joint Committee on Indian Constitutional Reforms laid bare this concern in its report.[4] The purpose of such an injunction was to ensure that the elected assemblies did not pass legislations against the zamindari and other forms of land-ownership and in favour of the rights of the peasants. Meanwhile, it is important to note that the Indian National Congress-led Provincial Government in the United Provinces did defy this injunction in a manner by enacting the United Provinces Tenancy Act, 1939 by which the landlords were deprived of their right to evict tenants therein on the ground that they had defaulted paying rent. The validity of this law was challenged on the ground that it was in violation of Section 299 of the Government of India Act. The challenge, however, was dismissed both by the Federal Court and subsequently by the Privy Council.[5] The fact is that the Constituent Assembly, while discussing Article 24 of the Draft Constitution, was certainly aware of this experience and the implication of Section 299 of the Government of India Act, 1935 and the potential for trouble in the event the government, in independent India, embarked upon any reforms in the agrarian sector.

For these reasons, when the draft Constitution was introduced on May 2, 1947, the Constituent Assembly deferred discussion on Article 24 to a later date. It was taken up, at last, on September 10, 1949, when Jawaharlal Nehru initiated the debate along with an amended version of the Draft Article.[6] In his long speech in the Constituent Assembly, Nehru dwelt on the question of compensation and he distinguished between acquisition of property (property in that debate primarily connoted to land) of small bits of property for public use (such as construction of post offices, schools and other such projects) where the acquisition shall be accompanied by full compensation to the land owner and acquisitions for large schemes of social reforms. In this, Nehru did suggest that acquisitions for such large schemes cannot be treated with the same standard as in the cases of public purposes.[7] It may be noted here that Vallabhbhai Patel too, while introducing the Draft in the earlier instance on behalf of the Advisory Committee of the Constituent Assembly, had spoke at length in the same way.[8]

In short, the makers of the Constitution were aware of the concept of Eminent Domain and in fact meant that even while having the Right to Property as a Fundamental Right and thus placed in Part III of the Constitution. They had also assumed, at that stage, that the land reforms programme and the necessary legislations for that will be in place even before the Constitution came into force. Clauses 4 and 6 of Article 31 were indeed the necessary guarantee in that regard. In the same way, there was clarity, in the Constituent Assembly on the implication of having the laws in this regard exposed to the concept of the due-process-of-law as it was done in Article V of the American Constitution. This, in fact, was dealt with in extensive detail in the sub-committee on Fundamental Rights of the Constituent Assembly itself. The makers of the Constitution decided against setting such acts for acquisition of property in conformity with the due-process-of- law and preferred to lay it down in conformity with the procedure established by law. Alladi Krishnaswamy Ayyar placed the difficulty in adopting the principle of the due-process-of-law in this context. He said:

> There is all the danger that it may stand in the way of what may be called expropriatary legislation. If you have got a set of judges who are more inclined to property, then they might put a wide construction upon the words so as to hamper what may be called a social legislation and if you have another set of judges who are imbued with modern ideas, they might put a more liberal interpretation. There is that danger inherent in 'due process' whatever provision of law may be made in the different provinces in India.[9]

All these issues, however, were reopened in less than a year after the Constitution was adopted on November 26, 1949.

II

Within months after the Constitution came into force on January 26, 1950, the Patna High Court struck down the Bihar Land Reforms Act, 1950, on grounds that it violated provisions of Article 14 of the Constitution. It may be stressed here that the case arose out of a petition by Kameshwar Singh, the Raja of

Darbhanga and a member of the Constituent Assembly too under Article 226 of the Constitution.[10] The fact is that here was a case of a member of the propertied class seeking redress from a Constitutional provision—Article 14—that ordained against inequality. It was revealed that the immunity to such a challenge that Article 31 (4) and (6) provided were insufficient insofar as the task of land reforms were concerned. The Nehruvian regime responded to this by way of the Constitution (First Amendment) Act, 1951 by which Article 31A and 31B along with the Ninth Schedule were inserted. As many as 13 legislations from the various provinces were included in the Ninth Schedule by this. And all the 13, pertained to abolition of zamindari or other such rights over land.[11] The Constitution (First Amendment) Act, 1951, that saved the laws from being struck down by the Supreme Court where the Bihar Act, along with similar legislations from Madhya Pradesh and the United Provinces was upheld as valid by a Constitution Bench.[12] And when the Bihar Act came up for scrutiny, the Supreme Court held it valid and struck down the decision by the Patna High Court.

The significant aspect of the judgment in this case, where Kameshwar Singh was among the respondents, from the concerns of this paper is what Justice S.R. Das had to say on what public purpose meant. He said:

> From what I have stated so far, it follows that whatever furthers the general interests of the community as opposed to the particular interest of the individual must be regarded as a public purpose. With the onward march of civilisation our notions as to the scope of the general interest of the community are fast changing and widening with the result that our old and narrower notions as to the sanctity of the private interest of the individual can no longer stem the forward flowing tide of time and must necessarily give way to the broader notions of the general interest of the community...
>
> The ideal we have set before us in Article 38 is to evolve a State which must constantly strive to promote the welfare of the people by securing and making as effectively as it may be a social order in which social, economic and political justice shall inform all the institutions of the national life. *Under Article 39 the State is enjoined to direct its policy towards securing, 'inter alia' that the ownership and*

> *control of the material resources of the community are so distributed as to subserve the common good and that the operation of the economic system does not result in the concentration of wealth and means of production to the common detriment... If therefore, the State is to give effect to these avowed purposes of our Constitution we must regard as a public purpose all that will be calculated to promote the welfare of the people as envisaged in these directive principles of State Policy whatever else that expression may mean.*[13] (emphasis added)

And on the specific issue of legislations on land reforms, Justice Das went on to say:

> In the light of this new outlook what, I ask, is the purpose of the State in adopting measures for the acquisition of the *Zamindaries* and the interests of the intermediaries? Surely, it is to subserve the common good by bringing the land, which feeds and sustains the community and also produces wealth by its forest, mineral and other resources, under State ownership or control. This State ownership or control over land is a necessary preliminary step towards the implementation of the directive principles of State policy and it cannot but be a public purpose. *It cannot be overlooked that the directive principles set forth in Part IV of the Constitution are not merely the policy of any particular political party but are intended to be principles fixed by the Constitution for directing the State policy whatever party may come into power.*[14] (emphasis added)

It thus emerged that the Supreme Court had held the Directive Principles of State Policies in general and Article 39 of the Constitution in particular as the premise from which public purpose would be determined insofar as land reforms legislations were concerned. It will be appropriate, however, to hasten to say that this mandate was reversed by the Supreme Court soon. In the Bela Banerjee case[15] where compensation was defined as just equivalent of the property acquired. The immediate fallout of this was a Calcutta High Court decision that held the Bengal Land Revenue Sales (West Bengal Amendment) Act, 1950 as unconstitutional. The amendment, as such, prohibited eviction of under-tenants for non-payment of rents and thus restricted the power of the landlords who were vested with such rights in the law as it existed. Such a restriction was warranted in the context of the sharp increase in land prices at that time (in the immediate aftermath of independence), particularly around Calcutta, and eviction suits had become the order of the times.[16]

The Nehruvian regime responded to this with the Constitution (Fourth Amendment) Act, 1955[17] by which the adequacy of compensation was declared as non-justiciable. The Constitution (Seventeenth Amendment) Act, 1964, subsequently, excluded such land under cultivation for personal consumption of the landlord from acquisition under Article 31 unless the compensation paid in such cases was not less than the market value of the property.[18] Article 31B too was amended to include 44 more laws to the Ninth Schedule taking the total number of Acts in the Schedule to 64. It may be added that not all of them related to land reforms and that it included a couple of acts that related to acquisition of property other than land. The Supreme Court upheld both the amendments to the Constitution in the Sajjan Singh case.[19]

III

All these, notwithstanding, and the Supreme Court threw the spanner in the works again: compensation was defined as 'just equivalent' again in the Vajravelu Mudaliar case.[20] This decision put the clock back and the law was taken to a position as laid in the Bela Banerjee case and the Constitution (Fourth Amendment) Act seemed to stand nullified. In other words, the impact of the decision came to be seen in the Supreme Court's verdict in the Bank Nationalisation case and the Privy Purses case; similarly, the apex court would soon over-rule the settled law from Shankari Prasad Deo and Sajjan Singh case while deciding the Golaknath case and soon take the Constitution to where it stood prior to the Constitution (Fourth Amendment) Act, 1955 insofar as the Right to Property was concerned.[21] An eleven-member bench, in the Bank Nationalisation case, similarly invoked the right of the judiciary to judge on the adequacy of compensation and struck down, by majority, the law nationalising 14 private sector banks.[22]

In response to this, the regime amended the Constitution further. The Constitution (Twenty-Fourth Amendment) Act,

1971[23] and the Constitution (Twenty-Fifth Amendment) Act, 1971[24] tackled this without mincing words and thus intended to overwhelm the decisions in the Golaknath case as well as the Bank Nationalisation Case. In addition, there was the Constitution (Twenty-Ninth Amendment) Act, 1972, that included two land reforms laws passed by the Kerala Legislative Assembly in the Ninth Schedule. All these amendments were challenged on grounds that these were invalid in the Kesavananda Bharati case.[25] The decision in this case is indeed the most significant in the history of Constitutional Law in India; and its importance from the concerns of this paper is that the Supreme Court upheld most parts of the amendments and in doing so, underscored the importance of Article 39(b) and (c), as integral in ensuring the rights guaranteed in Part III of the Constitution. The majority, in this case, put forth the Basic Structure Doctrine and thus set right the law and held the decision in the Golaknath case as incorrect.[26]

While a detailed analysis of the Kesavananda judgment will not be possible here, it is important, however, to deal with such aspects in the judgment where the judges dealt with the question of private property in relation to Article 39(b) and (c) to hold the Constitution Amendments impugned in this case as valid. The fact is that the majority in the Kesavananda case invoked the Preamble of the Constitution as a tool to identify the Basic Structure. And Justice H.R. Khanna, whose judgment tilted the bench's decision in a substantial manner, established a strong link between the Preamble and Article 38 of the Constitution. In his words,

> It would be seen that the first of the objectives mentioned in the Preamble is to secure to all citizens of India justice, social, economic and political. Article 38 in Part IV relating to the Directive Principles of State Policy recites that the State shall strive to promote the welfare of the people by securing and protecting as effectively as it may, a social order in which justice, social, economic and political, shall inform all the institutions of the national life.[27]

Having laid this as the premise and recalling the resolutions passed by the Indian National Congress' sessions at Lahore and

Karachi, Justice Khanna went on to say:

> So far as the question is concerned as to whether the right to property can be said to pertain to basic structure or framework of the Constitution, the answer, in my opinion, should plainly be in the negative. Basic structure or framework indicates the broad outlines of the Constitution, while the right to property is a matter of detail. It is apparent from what has been discussed above that the approach of the framers of the Constitution was to subordinate the individual right to property to the social good. Property right has also been changing from time to time. As observed by Harold Laski in *Grammar of Politics*, the historical argument is fallacious if it regards the regime of private property as a simple and unchanging thing. The history of private property is, above all, the record of the most varied limitations upon the use of the powers it implies. Property in slaves was valid in Greece and Rome it is no longer valid today...[28]

The importance of the Kesavananda case and the decision thereof, lay in this aspect insofar as the concerns of this paper are concerned. It may be added that two different Constitution Benches, subsequently held the Basic Structure Doctrine as well as the premise that the Preamble where Justice is defined in such clear terms as Social, Economic and Political shall form the basis of the law insofar as property rights were concerned. The two cases—Minerva Mills and Waman Rao—involved were decided after the Constitution (Forty-Fourth Amendment) Act, 1978. The Constitution bench, in these two cases, had also pronounced on the validity of the deletion of Article 31 of the Constitution and the insertion of Article 300A; the amendment by which the Right to Property ceased to be a Fundamental Right and rendered into a mere Constitutional Right. In the Waman Rao case, where the impugned law involved acquisition of land for redistribution and where the basis for fixing of ceiling was altered, Justice Y.V. Chandrachud said:

> Indeed, if there is one place in an agriculture-dominated society like ours where citizens can hope to have equal justice, it is on the strip of land which they till and love, the land which assures to them the dignity of their person by providing to them a near decent means of livelihood.[29]

It may be noted here that this sense was evident in the judgments, by the Supreme Court, almost three decades later while deciding cases involving acquisition of land in the name of public purpose. Between March and July 2011, the Supreme Court struck down land acquisition orders by the Government in Uttar Pradesh. It is necessary to add that while this was an argument in support of the government's right to acquire land in the name of public good, the context in 2011 was to save the farmers and their right to their property. It is important to note here that the Supreme Court had paved the path to this end by interpreting the elongated scope of Article 21 of the Constitution to include the Right to Livelihood as an integral part of the Right to Life and thus a Fundamental Right. This began with the judgment in the Olga Tellis case.[30] These happened in the decade after 1980 when the political establishment seemed to withdraw from the welfare state agenda and in a sense the beginning of a phase in our short constitutional history and the formal adoption of such a shift by way of the New Economic Policy resolution in Parliament in July 1991. The institution of Public Interest Litigation (PIL) by the higher judiciary in this period thus opened a phase when the Supreme Court began donning the mantle of enforcing the welfare agenda. In doing this, the Supreme Court effected a movement of some of the Directive Principles of State Policy into Part III of the Constitution and turned them into enforceable rights in the process.

The earliest instance when this spirit was evident in the neo-liberal age was a decision by the Supreme Court in the Samatha case. That was in July 1997. The issue, in that case, was transfer of land in tribal areas to private mine companies and that it militated against the Fifth Schedule of the Constitution. A three-member bench, by majority, set aside a decision to issue mine licenses to private companies. It will be relevant, from the scope of this paper, to cite Justice K. Ramaswami, who spoke for the majority in that case. He said:

> Justice is an attribute of human conduct. Law, as a social engineering, is to remedy existing imbalances, as a vehicle to establish an egalitarian social order in a Socialist Secular Bharat Republic... Welfare State is a rubicon between unbridled

> individualism and communism. All human rights are derived from the dignity of the person and his inherent worth. Fundamental Rights and Directive Principles of the Constitution have fused in them as fundamental human rights as indivisible and inter-dependent. The Constitution has charged the State to provide facilities and opportunities among the people and groups of people to remove social and economic inequality and to improve equality of status. Article 39(b) enjoins the State to direct its policy towards securing distribution of the ownership and control of the material resources of the community as best to subserve the common good. The founding fathers with hind sight, engrafted with prognosis, not only inalienable human rights as part of the Constitution but also charged the State as its policy to remove obstacles, disabilities and inequalities for human development and positive actions to provide opportunities and facilities to develop human dignity and equality of status and of opportunity for social and economic democracy. Economic and social equality is a facet of liberty without which meaningful life would be hollow and mirage.[31]

This approach, consistent though it was with the larger import of the majority judgment in the Kesavananda case and further strengthened by the decisions in the Minerva Mills case and in the Waman Rao case, appeared to be the lone voice of dissent against the indiscriminate resort to the provisions of the Land Acquisition Act, 1894, by the various state governments, cutting across the spectrum during the neo-liberal era. Of all those provisions that were so invoked, the most abusive was Section 17 of the 1894 Act [32] by which compulsory acquisition of land is possible even without providing the land owner an opportunity to object to such acquisition. In legal language, Section 17 of the 1894 Act provides for a denial of an enquiry mandated under Section 5A of the Land Acquisition Act, 1894.[33]

IV

In the neoliberal context, state governments have been empowered to negotiate private investments directly with domestic and foreign investors rather than having to depend on the Union for industrial development. There is, however, less of empowerment in this framework. The quest for industrialisation in this context has rendered the state governments weaker, so to say, while they negotiate with the potential investor. The fact is that investors, both domestic and foreign, engage in discussions with more than one state government at any given time for any given proposal. As is the logic in such a framework, investors manage to set the terms before the state government.[34] It is also a fact that industrialisation, in the neoliberal era, is more in the nature of investments in technology that are less labour intensive in comparison with that in the earlier phase. Investment in ICT far outstrips that in manufacturing sectors and this in turn has led to an exponential rise in investments around the urban centres and green-field projects have become a thing of the past. It has implications on the nature of employment generation too.[35]

A third aspect that has come as a challenge, in the neoliberal context, is the quest for land for housing for the burgeoning middle and upper middle classes, thanks to the nature of growth in employment around the cities and distinct from the several green-field projects that marked the industrial development in the earlier phase in independent India. Rather than townships that sprang up in remote locations, the quest now is to locate industrial activities around big cities. And that has meant the state, across the nation, setting out on a land acquisition spree. A case in point, in this regard, has been the conversion of land around the National Capital from agricultural to residential. And after a period when it appeared that the case of the farmer was lost forever, the Supreme Court, in a series of decisions in three cases involving such acquisition of agricultural land in Noida (in Uttar Pradesh) between March 7, 2011 and July 6, 2011, struck down such acquisition and has set the stage for a new look at the issues.[36]

It is important to note a statement by the judges (Justice in one of the three cases:

> Before concluding, we consider it necessary to reiterate that the acquisition of land is a serious matter and before initiating the proceedings under the 1894 Act and other similar legislations, the

> concerned government must seriously ponder over the consequences of depriving the tenure holder of his property. *It must be remembered that the land is just like mother of the people living in the rural areas of the country. It is the only source of sustenance and livelihood for the landowner and his family. If the land is acquired, not only the present but the future generations of the landowner are deprived of their livelihood and the only social security. They are made landless and are forced to live in slums in the urban areas because there is no mechanism for ensuring alternative source of livelihood to them. Mindless acquisition of fertile and cultivable land may also lead to serious food crisis in the country.* In the result, the special leave petitions are dismissed.[37] (emphasis added)

The importance of this judgment, in a case where land was compulsorily acquired under the garb of public purpose and promptly handed over to a host of private developers and builders, the judges spoke of the nexus between using the excuse of an emergency to acquire land and the vested interests behind acquisition. The land, in this instance, was initially acquired for industrial development and later converted to housing purposes. The Court, in fact, probed into the actual purpose that the land was put to use and in that sense it was a significant shift from the position in the past that the courts would not delve into the actual use that the acquired land is put to. The position, hitherto, was that an enquiry into the specifics of the public purpose is best left to the executive. This, indeed, is an evidence of a paradigm shift from the procedure-established-by-law framework to the due-process-of-law approach. The makers of the Constitution had preferred the procedure established by law because they were convinced, at that time, that the due-process-of-law framework would only lead agrarian reform legislations to protracted legal squabbles. However, in the context of the neoliberal era, the due-process-of-law framework has helped achieving the objectives of the preamble of the Constitution. This shift is very significant.

V

In conclusion, it may be said that inasmuch as the tussle during the 1950s between the judiciary, the executive and parliament over land acquisition took place in the context of the State's attempts to abolish zamindari and implement land reform, the neoliberal era sought the judiciary's intervention against acquisition of land from the small farmer and thus foregrounding livelihood concerns of the owners of small pieces of land. While in the earlier phase, the judiciary engaged itself in deciding on the validity of the many land reforms legislations passed by the various state governments with a view to elongate the scope of the ideals set in the Preamble of the Constitution, the two decades of neoliberal policies brought to the fore the abuse of provisions in the Land Acquisition Act, 1894.

It may be added that the issues raised in the earlier phase were settled in favour of Parliament that showed a sense of determination to give effect to Article 39(b) and (c) of the Constitution. Such insertions in the Constitution as Articles 31-A, 31-B and 31C and the fact that the apex court upheld them as valid were in another context where Public Purpose had a different meaning from what it is construed in the neoliberal context. These Articles were placed in the Constitution to remove the hurdles in the path of land acquisition for agrarian reform and in that sense, the objective was the very opposite of depriving the small farmer of his land. The debates in the Constituent Assembly on zamindari abolition and later the various judgments by the apex court upholding different legislations for compulsory acquisition of land and other property do point to a clear sense of purpose: To ensure that the ownership and control of the material resources of the community are so distributed as best to serve the common good. If the Constitutional amendments of the time and the legislation enacted during the 1950s and 60s was about facilitating and protecting the transfer of resources from the rich to the poor, the state and central governments have now been using provisions in the law to transfer land from the poor to the rich!

In as much as the earlier position of the courts was justified in the context of the land acquisition law being put to use to abolish landlordism, the current process of judicial intervention is very much welcome. In fact, the courts should have taken notice earlier of the manner in which agricultural land was being acquired by the various state governments and the resistance to such measures by farmers, especially when there is a threat to their livelihood. In now doing so, the apex court has only picked up the thread from the trend set by the higher judiciary in the 1980s when the scope of some of the provisions listed in the Constitution as Fundamental Rights were expanded to include some of the ideals proclaimed in the Directive Principles of State Policy. Like it did in the Olga Tellis case, the Supreme Court has now rightly read into the recent development in land acquisition a threat to the livelihood of the farming community and has asserted the right of the judiciary to intervene and ensure that the Right to Life, guaranteed by Article 21 of the Constitution, is not denied to the small, middle and marginal farmers in the name of public good.

NOTES

*** This paper is part of a larger research project undertaken as part of a fellowship with Nehru Memorial Museum and Library, New Delhi between May 2009 and 2011. I record my gratitude to E.K. Santha with whom I had several rounds of discussion before the draft of this paper was written. Her suggestions added value. The paper was completed before the state government in West Bengal, under Mamata Banerjee, legislated to restore the land in Singur to its original owners. The implications of this have not been dealt with here. The paper, however, points to the political dimensions and the law in this context.

1. The Indian Penal Code, the law that determines criminal jurisprudence in India is older than the Land Acqusition Act, 1894. The IPC was enacted in 1860 has suffered the least number of amendments in the 151 years of its existence. This is no commentary on the goodness of either of the two laws. The Land Acquisition Act, 1894, in fact, has been amended many times and the Land Acquisition and Rehabilitation & Resettlement Bill, 2011, introduced in Parliament, intend to replace the 1894 law.
2. This was clarified, in so many words, by Alladi Krishnaswamy Ayyar, a member of the Fundamental Rights sub-committee of the Constituent Assembly, informed the sub-committee that the article "closely followed Section 299 of the Government of India Act" and that the only difference lay in that while Section 299 of

the 1935 Act used 'just compensation' the Draft Constitution left it at 'compensation'. See B. Shiva Rao (ed.), *The Framing of India's Constitution – Select Documents,* Universal Law Publishing Company, Delhi, 1967 (Reprint 2010), Vol. 2, p. 273.

3. The Karachi resolution rendered a meaning to *swaraj* in such terms that it involved the rights of the different socio-economic groups and defined freedom in a manner where the aspirations of the various subaltern groups were internalised and declared as rights in independent India; the relevant aspect of the resolution from the concerns of this paper reads as follows: "The system of land tenure and revenue and rent shall be reformed and an equitable adjustment made of the burden on agricultural land, immediately giving relief to the smaller peasantry, by a substantial reduction of agricultural rent and revenue now paid by them, and in case of uneconomic holdings, exempting them from rent, so long as necessary, with such relief as may be just and necessary to holders of small estates affected by such exemption or reduction in rent, and to the same end, imposing a graded tax on net incomes from land above a reasonable minimum." (See Karachi Resolution, P. Sitaramayya, *The History of the Indian National Congress,* Vol. 1, Padma Publications, Bombay, 1946 (Reprint), pp. 463-65. It may be noted, in this context, that resistance to eviction for default of land rent had become a part of the Indian National Congress' agenda
4. The report, in paragraph 369, said: "We think that some general provisions should be inserted in the Constitution Act safeguarding private property against expropriation, in order to silence doubts which have been aroused in recent years by certain Indian utterances. It is obviously difficult to frame any general provision with this object without unduly restricting the powers of the Legislature in relation particularly to taxation. ... We do not attempt to define with precision, the scope of the provision we have in mind, the drafting of which will require careful consideration for the reasons we have indicated; but we think that it should secure that legislation expropriating or the authorisation of expropriation of the property of particular individuals should be lawful only if confined to expropriation for public purposes and if compensation is determined, either in the first instance or on appeal, by some independent authority. General Legislation, on the other hand, the effect of which would be to transfer to public ownership, some particular class of property, or to extinguish or modify the right of individuals in

it ought, we think to require the previous sanction of the Governor General or Governor (as the case may be) to its introduction; and in that event, he should be directed by his Instrument of Instructions to take into account as a relevant factor the nature of the provisions proposed for compensating those whose interests will be adversely affected by the legislation." (See C.L. Anand, *Constitutional Law and History of Government of India*, Universal Law Publishing Company, Delhi, (Eighth Edition) 2008, p. 812.

5. Justice Gwyer, at the Federal Court held as follows: The answer to this is that a law which regulates the relation of landlord and the tenant and thereby diminishes the rights which the landlord has hitherto exercised in connection with his land does not authorise the compulsory acquisition of the land for public or any other purpose; and, therefore, the question of compensation does not arise...We desire, however, to point out that what they are now claiming is that no legislature in India has any right to alter the arrangements embodied in their *sanads* nearly a century ago; and for all we know, they would deny the right of Parliament to do so. We hope that no responsible legislature or government would ever treat as of no account solemn pledges given by their predecessors; but the readjustment of rights and duties is an inevitable process, and one of the functions of a legislature in a modern state is to effect that re-adjustment, where circumstances have made it necessary, with justice to all concerned. It is, however, not for this court, to pronounce upon on the wisdom or the in the broader sense of legislative acts;..." (See AIR-1943-FC-49). The case was then taken on appeal to the Privy Council where Lord Wright held as follows:

   "In the present case, there is no question of confiscatory legislation. To regulate the relations of landlord and tenant and thereby diminish rights, hitherto exercised by the landlord in connection with his land is different from the compulsory acquisition of land..." (See AIR-1946-PC-127)

6. The amendment moved by Nehru was a substantial one and it contained at least two provisos that clearly protected land reforms legislations already in the process of becoming laws in the various Provincial Assemblies. The article, as amended, was adopted by the Constituent Assembly to become Article 31 of the Constitution as it was adopted on November 26, 1949. Clauses 4 and 6 of Article 31, were in fact, provisos that protected legislations by the various Provincial Assemblies abolishing

landlordism and acquisition of zamindaris and the redistribution of such property among the tenants. Nehru was explicit on this and he said: "It has been not today's policy, but the old policy of the National Congress laid down years ago that the zamindari institution in India, that is the big estate system must be abolished. So far as we are concerned, we, who are connected with the Congress, shall give effect to that pledge naturally completely, one hundred percent and no legal subtlety and no change is going to come in our way. That is quite clear. We will honour our pledges" (See *Constituent Assembly Debates*, Lok Sabha Secretariat, New Delhi, Vol. IX, p. 1197).

7. Ibid., p. 1195.
8. On May 2, 1947, Patel held: "Land will be required for many public purposes, not only and but so many other things may have to be acquired. And the state will acquire them after paying compensation and not expropriate them. That is the real meaning of the clause. But the zamindars or some of their representatives thought that their interest must be safeguarded by moving an amendment or by making a speech here. But they are not going to safeguard these interests in this way. They must recognise the times and move with the times. This clause here will not become the law tomorrow or the day after; it will take at least a year more, and before that, most of the zamindaris will be liquidated. Even under the present acts or laws in the different provinces legislation is being brought in to liquidate zamindaris either by paying just compensation or adequate compensation or whatever the legislatures there think fit. Therefore, it is wrong to think that this clause is intended really for them. It is not so. The process of acquisition is already there and the legislatures are already taking steps to liquidate the zamindaris..." (See CAD, Vol. III, p. 522)
9. B. Shiva Rao, op. cit., p. 241.
10. Section 24 of the Act provided the manner of determination of the compensation. It laid down a sliding scale for the assessment of compensation. Where the net income did not exceed Rs. 500, the compensation payable was twenty times the net income and where the net income computed exceeded Rs. 1,00,000, it was at three times the amount. In the case of the Maharaja of Darbhanga, the estate acquired also comprised land purchased by him by spending about a crore of rupees and also comprised mortgages to the tune of half a crore. All these vested in the Bihar State along with the inherited zamindaris of the Maharaja and arrears

of rent amounting to Rs. 30,00,000 while the total compensation payable was nearly a sum of Rs. 9,00,000.

11. The amendment bill was moved by Jawaharlal Nehru on May 12, 1951. It may be noted that this happened in the Provisional Parliament that consisted of the members of the Constituent Assembly itself.
12. Shankari Prasad Deo vs Union of India (AIR-1951-SC-458). In this case, the Supreme Court held that Parliament had seamless powers to amend the Constitution and that the Fundamental Rights too were amendable.
13. AIR-1952-SC-0-252. paragraph 106.
14. Ibid., paragraph 106.
15. State of West Bengal vs Mrs. Bela Banerjee and Others (AIR-1954-SC-0-170). It may be pointed out that the case, as such, did not flow out of a land reforms law. It involved the principles for compensation for urban land acquired for construction of houses for the repatriates from Bangladesh and the Supreme Court struck down the law on grounds that the compensation fixed was inadequate.
16. It may be noted that the Calcutta High Court, in this instance, had gone against the decision by the Federal Court and upheld by the Privy Council in the Jaganath Baksh Singh case. However, it may be stressed here that the High Court's decision drew the law as laid down in the Bela Banerjee case. Meanwhile, the Supreme Court too held the law as violative of Article 31(2) which guaranteed compensation as a necessary ingredient to compulsory acquisition. The principle, then, was that compensation and its adequacy were justiciable.
17. By this amendment, Article 31 (2), for instance, was amended to read as follows:

(2) No property shall be compulsorily acquired or requisitioned save for a public purpose and save by authority of a law which provides for compensation for the property so acquired or requisitioned and either fixes the amount of the compensation or specifies the principle on which, and the manner in which, the compensation is to be determined and given; *and no such law shall be called in question in any court on the ground that the compensation provided by that law is not adequate*. (emphasis added)

(2A) "Where a law does not provide for the transfer of the ownership or right to possession of any property to the State or to a corporation owned or controlled by the State, it shall not be deemed to provide for the compulsory acquisition or requisitioning of property, notwithstanding that it deprives any person of his property." (See Subhash Kashyap, *Constitution Making Since 1950: An Overview*, Universal Law Publishing Company, Delhi, Vol. 6, p. 25). It may be added that this was also the time when the Congress Party was beginning to commit itself explicitly to the idea socialism and the culmination of that in its Avadi session in 1955. Jawaharlal Nehru's speech in the Lok Sabha while moving the Bill was evidence of this. He said: "The responsibility for the economic and social welfare policies of the nation should lie with Parliament and not with the courts... The decisions of the Supreme Court shows an inherent contradiction between the Fundamental Rights and the Directive Principles. *It is upto this Parliament to remove this contradiction and make the Fundamental Rights subserve the Directive Principles of State Policy.*" (emphasis added) [See Lok Sabha Debates, March 14, 1955]

18. Subhash Kashyap, op. cit., p. 66. Article 31 A (1) (i), inserted by the amendment, read as follows: "Provided further that where any law makes any provision for the acquisition by the State of any estate and where any land comprised therein is held by a person under his personal cultivation, it shall not be lawful for the State to acquire any portion of such land as is within the ceiling limit applicable to him under any law for the time being in force or any building or structure standing thereon or appurtenant thereto, unless the law relating to the acquisition of such land, building or structure, provides for payment of compensation at a rate which shall be less than the market value thereof."
19. Sajjan Singh vs State of Rajasthan (AIR-1965-SC-0-845). It may be added here that the thrust in this challenge, like in the Shankari Prasad Deo case was on whether Parliament had the powers to amend Articles in Part III of the Constitution and whether the Fundamental Rights could be abridged at all. The Bench declared that Parliament's powers were seamless and thus upheld the amendments.
20. P. Vajravelu Mudaliar vs The Special Deputy Collector for Land Acqusition, Tamil Nadu and Another (AIR-1965-SC-0-1017). The Vajravelu Mudaliar case, where the Supreme Court declared the Land Acquisition (Madras Amendment) Act, 1961 as invalid was decided on October 5, 1964; the Sajjan Singh case was decided on October 30, 1964. It may be pointed out here that Justice K. Subba Rao, speaking for the bench, in the Vajravelu case, held

the Madras Act void on grounds that Article 31 A of the Constitution, even after the Constitution (Fourth Amendment) Act, 1955, saved acquisitions only in case of such laws related to agrarian reforms. In this case, acquisitions were done for purposes of slum clearance and hence compensation had to be 'just' and take into consideration the market value of the property acquired. Speaking for the bench as a whole, Chief Justice K. Subba Rao held as follows: "The fact that Parliament used the same expressions, namely, 'compensation' and 'principles' as were found in Article 31 before the Amendment is a clear indication that it accepted the meaning given by this Court to those expressions in Mrs. Bela Banerjee's case, 1954 SCR 558: (AIR 1954 SC 170). It follows that a Legislature in making a law of acquisition or requisition shall provide for a just equivalent of what the owner has been deprived of or specify the principles for the purpose of ascertaining the "just equivalent" of what the owner has been deprived of." (See AIR-1965-SC-0-1017, paragraph 14).

21. It may be noted that the thrust in the Golaknath case was on Parliament's power to amend the Constitution and it was held that any amendment to the provisions in Part III were beyond Parliament's power. The 11-member bench, in that case, even while striking down the Constitution Seventeenth Amendment, held the laws as passed hitherto (and protected by the first, fourth and seventeenth amendments) as valid, invoking the principle of stare decisis. (See AIR-1967-SC-1643. Paragraph 44).
22. R.C. Cooper vs Union of India (AIR-1970-SC-0-564). Even if this case did not pertain to land acquisition, it assumes relevance to the concerns of this paper in that the Supreme Court invoked Article 31(2) to strike down the Act. In that sense, it followed the trend set by the apex court in the Vajravelu Mudaliar case as well as in the Golaknath case.
23. Two changes were introduced in the Constitution by this: Article 13(4), inserted, read as: "Nothing in this article shall apply to any amendment of this Constitution made under Article 368."

    And Article 368 was amended to read as follows: "Article 368 of the Constitution shall be renumbered as clause (2) thereof, and- For the marginal heading to that article, the following marginal heading shall be substituted, namely:

    "Power of Parliament to amend the Constitution and procedure thereof." Before clause (2) as so re-numbered, the following clause shall be inserted, namely:

(1) "Notwithstanding anything in this Constitution, Parliament may in exercise of its constituent power may amend by way of addition, variation or repeal any provision of this Constitution in accordance with the procedure laid down in this article."

In clause (2) as so re-numbered, for the words "it shall be presented to the President for his assent and upon such assent being given to the Bill", the words "it shall be presented to the President who shall give his assent to the Bill and thereupon" shall be substituted;

After clause (2) as so renumbered, the following clause shall be inserted, namely:

(3) "Nothing in Article 13 shall apply to any amendment made under this article."

24. Two changes were made to the Constitution as such by this. One was that Article 31(2) was amended in such a way that the word 'compensation' was replaced by the word 'amount'. And second was the insertion of Article 31C that read: "31C. Saving of laws giving effect to certain directive principles.-Notwithstanding anything contained in article 13, no law giving effect to the policy of the State towards securing the principles specified in clause (b) or clause (c) of Article 39 shall be deemed to be void on the ground that it is inconsistent with, or takes away or abridges any of the rights conferred by Article 14, Article 19 or Article 31; *and no law containing a declaration that it is for giving effect to such policy shall be called in question in any court on the ground that it does not give effect to such policy;...*" It may be noted here that the portion highlighted was struck down by the Supreme Court in the Kesavananda case even while the other part was upheld as valid.
25. Kesavananda Bharati vs State of Kerala (AIR-1973-SC-1451).
26. On April 24, 1973, the bench put out a summary of its decision. It read as follows: "The view by the majority in these writ petitions is as follows:
    1. Golaknath's case is overruled;
    2. Article 368 does not enable Parliament to alter the basic structure or framework of the Constitution;
    3. The Constitution (Twenty-Fourth Amendment) Act, 1971 is valid;
    4. Section 2a and 2b of the Constitution (Twenty-Fifth Amendment) Act, 1971 is valid;
    5. The first part of Section 3 of the Constitution (Twenty-Fifth

Amendment) Act, 1971 is valid. The second part, namely, "and no law containing a declaration that it is for giving effect to such policy shall be called into question in any Court on the ground that it does not give effect to such policy" is invalid;

6. The Constitution (Twenty-Ninth Amendment) Act, 1971 is valid."

The summary was signed only by nine of the 13 judges. This had become necessary after the 11 separate judgments in that case. This, however, did not dilute the effect of the decision and the law, as interpreted by this decision holds to this day. (See Introductory Editorial Note, AIR-1973-SC-1461; pp. 1461-62).

27. Ibid., paragraph 1486-87. Justice Khanna also held that "I find that although it gives a prominent place to securing the objective of social, economic and political justice to the citizens, there is nothing in it which gives primacy to claims of individual right to property over the claims of social, economic and political justice. *There is, as a matter of fact, no clause or indication in the Preamble which stands in the way of abridgement of right to property for securing social, economic and political justice. Indeed, the dignity of the individual upon which also the Preamble has laid stress, can only be assured by securing the objective of social, economic and political justice.*" (emphasis added) (See Ibid., paragraph 1492)
28. AIR-1973-SC-1461. Paragraph 1496. Justice Khanna quoted Harold Laski's citing John Stuart Mill in this regard: "The idea of property is not some one thing identical throughout history and incapable of alteration .... at any given time it is a brief expression denoting the rights over things conferred by the law or custom of some given society at that time, but neither on this point, nor on any other, has the law and custom of a given time and place, a claim to be stereotyped forever. A proposed reform in laws or customs is not necessarily objectionable because its adoption would imply, not the adaptation of all human affairs to the existing idea of property, to the growth and improvement of human affairs."
29. Waman Rao and others vs Union of India and Others (AIR-1981-SC-271I Paragraph 28. It may be noted here that this sense was evident in the judgments, by the Supreme Court, almost three decades later while deciding cases involving acquisition of land in the name of public purpose. Between March and July 2011, the Supreme Court struck down land acquisition orders by the Government in Uttar Pradesh. It is necessary to add that while

this was an argument in support of the government's right to acquire land in the name of public good, the context in 2011 was to save the farmers and their right to their property. We shall discuss this in detail in the following chapter. Suffice to say here that there was a pro-people tilt in both these instances.

30. Olga Tellis vs Bombay Municipal Corporation (AIR-1986-SC-180). The scope of Article 21 of the Constitution was further elongated in a catena of cases since then. Some of the important cases of this kind were: In Bandhua Mukti Morcha v. Union of India (AIR 1984 SC 802) the Supreme Court held that right to live with human dignity enshrined in Article 21 derives its life breath from the Directive Principles of State Policy and that opportunities and facilities should be provided to the children to develop in a healthy manner and in conditions of freedom and dignity. Adequate facilities, just and human conditions of work etc. are the minimum requirements which must exist in order to enable a person to live with human dignity and the State has to take every action. In Subhash Kumar v. State of Bihar,(AIR 1991 SC 420), the Court held that the right to life includes the right to enjoyment of pollution free water and air for full enjoyment of life. In Olga Tellis v. Bombay Municipal Corporation, (AIR 1986 SC 180) as we have discussed in the previous chapter, the Court had held that right to livelihood is an important facet of the right to life. In C.E.S.C. Ltd. v. S. C. Bose (1992 AIR SCW 202) it was held that the right to social and economic justice is a fundamental right. Right to health of a worker is a fundamental right. Therefore, right to life enshrined in Article 21 means something more than mere survival of animal existence. The right to live with human dignity with minimum sustenance and shelter and all those rights and aspects of life which would go to make a man's life complete and worth living, would form part of the right to life. Enjoyment of life and its attainment—social, cultural and intellectual—without which life cannot be meaningful, would embrace the protection and preservation of life guaranteed by Article 21. In C.E.R.C. v. Union of India (AIR1995-SCW-2834), the court held that the right to health and social justice as a fundamental right to workers. In Life Insurance Corporation v. Consumer Education and Research Centre (1995-AIR-SCW-2834). Right to economic equality was held to be a fundamental right in Dalmia Cement Bharat Ltd. v. Union of India (1996 AIR SCW 3652). Right to shelter was held to be a fundamental human right in P. G. Gupta v. State of

Gujarat, (1995 AIR SCW 1540) and in such other cases as M/s. Shantistar Builders v. Narayan Khimlal Totame (AIR 1990 SC 630), Chameli Singh v. State of UP (1996 AIR SCW 542) and Ahmedabad Municipal Corporation v. Nawab Khan Gulab Khan (1996 AIR SCW 4315). In Delhi Transport Corporation vs D.T.C. Mazdoor Congress, (AIR 1991 SC 101) the Supreme Court had held that right to life would include the right to continue in permanent employment which is not a bounty of the employer nor can its survival be at the volition or mercy of the employer. The court had held that income is the foundation to enjoy many fundamental rights and when work is the source of income, the right to work would become as much a fundamental right.

31. AIR-1997-SC-3297. paragraph 73. The learned judge relied upon an earlier judgment in this context by a nine-member bench of the Supreme Court. In the State of Karnataka vs Ranganatha Reddy (AIR-1978-SC-215). In that case,where the nationalisation of contract carriages was upheld as constitutional, the judges dealt with Article 39 (b) of the Constitution and said: "it was held that one of the principal aims of socialism is the distribution of the material resources of the community in such a way as to subserve the common good. This principle is embodied under Art. 39(b) of the Constitution as one of the essential directive principles of State polity. The key word is distribution and the genus of the Article, if we may say so, cannot but be given full play as it fulfils the basic purpose of restructuring the economic order. Each word in this Article has a strategic role and the whole Article is a social mission. It embraces the entire material resources of the community. Its task is to distribute such resources, its goal is to undertake distribution as best to subserve the common good. It reorganises by such distribution the ownership and control." In another case, Sanjeev Coke Manufacturing Company vs Bharat Coking Coal Limited (AIR-1983-SC-239), the Supreme Court had held as follows: "While considering Article 39(b) of the Constitution, that the broad egalitarian principle of economic justice was implicit in every directive principle and, therefore, a law designed to promote a Directive Principle, even if it came into conflict with the formalistic and doctrinaire view of equality before the law, would most certainly advance the broader egalitarian principle and desirable constitutional goal of social and economic justice for all. If the law was aimed at the broader egalitarianism of the Directive Principles, Article 31C protected the law from needless,

unending and rancorous debate on the question whether the law contravened Article 14's concept of the equality before the law. The law seeking the immunity afforded by Article 31C must be a law directing the policy of the State towards securing a Directive Principle and the connection with the Directive Principle must not be some remote or tenuous connection. The object of the nationalisation of the coal mine is to distribute the nation's resources."

32. Section 17 of the Act provides for emergency acquisitions that can be effected after a mere 15 days after the notification and without an enquiry. The emergency can be both on the basis of a natural calamity/cause (such as a river changing course) as well as a public purpose that may be deemed emergent by the authority.
33. Section 5 A reads: (1) Any person interested in any land which has been notified under Section 4, sub-section (1), as being needed or likely to be needed for a public purpose or for a company may, within thirty days form the date of the publication of the notification, object to the acquisition of the land or of any land in the locality, as the case may be. (2) Every objection under subsection (1) shall be made to the Collector in writing and the Collector shall give the objector, an opportunity of being heard in person or by any person authorised by him in this behalf or by pleader and shall, after hearing all such objections and after making such further inquiry, if any, as he thinks necessary, either make a report in respect of the land which has been notified under Section 4, subsection (1), or make different reports in respect of different parcels of such land, to the appropriate government containing his recommendations on the objections, together with the record of the proceedings held by him for the decision of that government. The decision of the appropriate government on the objections shall be final. (3) For the purposes of this section, a person shall he deemed to be in load who would be entitled to claim an interest in compensation if the land were acquired under this Act.
34. The Singur experience is a case in point. The factory was shifted to Gujarat where the state government could dance to the tunes of the corporate investor because the resistance to land acquisition could be muted the regime there.
35. As for instance, unlike a steel plant that came up in the 1950s and 1960s, where a large number of workers, skilled and unskilled were employed in the plants as 'workers', the neo-

liberal era is dominated by ITES where those employed are 'employees' rather than workers. In a society where access to education, from primary levels to higher education, is driven by a casteist bias and thus excludes a large section of the socially backward classes, the scope for absorbing these sections into the class of workers is severely restricted. Even if it is true that there is a large potential for growth in the ancillary sectors to the ITES, such as security services, transport, construction and others, in the ITES driven growth, the fact is that such employment avenues are not the same as those where a large number of unskilled workers being engaged in the factories and thus drawn into the mainstream industrial workforce as then. In simple language, a security guard in the present context will not be able to send his children to schools from where the centres of excellence in the higher education sector from where the corporations draw their technical and management professionals.

36. It may be stressed here that the judgments in the three cases and the implication on the law is only one dimension. The big picture, indeed, emanates from the organised resistance to land acquisition from across the country and the fact that the political establishment finds itself in a position of being sent into the oblivion. The defeat of the CPI(M)-led Left Front in the April-May 2011 elections to the State Assembly is a case in point and evidence that land acquisition to facilitate growth is indeed a serious challenge that political parties can gloss over only to their peril.
37. See (2011) 12 SCC 375. Greater Noida Industrial Development Authority vs Devendrakumar and Others (decided on July 6, 2011).

11

Will Neoliberal Policies and Regulations Resolve Our Water Sector Dilemmas? Learning from Maharashtra and Gujarat

P.K. Viswanathan

> Nothing is more useful than water; but it will purchase scarce anything; scarce anything can be had in exchange for it. A diamond, on the contrary, has scarce any value-in-use; but a very great quantity of other goods may frequently be had in exchange for it. (Smith, 1776: 33)

The world is known to be at the clasp of a serious water crisis. The first World Water Development Report (WWDR) published in 2003 by the UN raises several concerns adding to the water crisis, viz., a) rising population without adequate water and sanitation; b) growing gap between rich and poor as well as urban and rural populations in water and sanitation services; c) rising costs of mitigating water-related disasters; d) declining quality of water resources and ecosystems; e) under-financing of the water sector; and f) rising pressures on water with increasing agricultural and industrial demand and pollution (UN/WAAP, 2003). The imminent threat from the climate change impacts adds a new dimension to the water crisis putting the global water sector in a predicament, necessitating effective policies and actions to overcome the impasse. The problems of climate change risks on the global water sector seem to be precarious in view of the: i) prominence of water being a critical resource in the adaptation and mitigation strategies; ii) centrality of agricultural water management for food security especially in the wake of the recent global food crisis; and iii) risk of not meeting the water-related Millennium Development Goals by 2015 (World Bank, 2010).

Incidentally, the impending water crisis had also resulted in a radical transformation especially among the developed countries of the North and many of the developing countries in the South by way of evolving policies, legal frameworks and implementing regulatory reforms/ interventions in the water sector. But, by and large, it appears that there is a clear divide between the north and the south in terms of the implementation of policies and regulatory reforms. For instance, a number of developed countries have been somewhat successful in responding to the crisis by developing policies and appropriate market based instruments (MBIs) as well as management strategies for the water sector[1]. Whereas, many of the developing countries are hard-pressed by either the lack of, or poor implementation of such policy instruments or regulatory systems. It may be observed that in most parts of the Asian and African regions in particular, there are policy initiatives and institutional reforms without explicit impacts leading to effective institutional or governance regimes for sustainable development and management of the water sector through sector-sensitive dynamic and robust policies.

This irony of 'policies for the sake of policies and reforms for the sake of reforms in the water sector' as emerge in the south is an interesting episode that demonstrates the way in which water sector policies and reforms in the developing countries are explicitly influenced by the neoliberal policies/ ideas as well as market driven technological and institutional solutions as being tried in the developed regions[2]. The growing body of research on the discourse of neoliberalism advocates that neoliberal policies are integral aspects of global market integration and offers unprecedented opportunities for growth through market reforms, privatisation, financial disciplining and dismantling of the state bureaucracies (Erjavec and Erjavec, 2009). In the case of the water sector, the neoliberal policies urge the need to reform the existing institutions, devise new legislations and establish new governance systems to improve multi-stakeholder institutional coordination, regulatory functions, and service delivery in the water sector (Castro, 2008).

Thus, the stronghold of neoliberal policies and reforms in the water sector as observed in the developed countries seems to be bringing in radical changes in views reinstating the preeminence of market based instruments (MBIs) as effective mechanisms for resolving the multiple water sector challenges and conflicts in the developing countries. But, this romanticism about the neoliberalism and the replication of neoliberal policies to countries in the south raises important issues, especially when there is a clear divergence in the trajectories of water use, the policies, investment priorities and development strategies within the water sector between the semi-arid north and the semi-arid south as observed by Allan (2005). For instance, in the neoliberal north, there has been a shift in policies especially since the 1980s towards putting water back into the environment. In sharp contrast, in the south, there remains a predictable commitment to taking more water out of the environment in order to further increase the food output to meet rising food demands, to avoid dependence on imports, and to increase the wealth of the respective economies as a whole (Allan, 2005).

Set in the broader perspective of the neoliberal policies and reforms impacting governance of the global water sector, this paper examines the responses, status and implications of the policy innovations and regulatory reforms in the regional context of India with particular reference to Maharashtra and Gujarat states. In doing so, the paper tries to engage in discussion on three pertinent issues, viz. a) what are the national and state-level responses towards the neoliberal policies and their immediate outcomes on reforms in the water sector?; b) whether the neoliberal policies and the regulatory systems as evolved in the developed country contexts would help resolve the burgeoning challenges and conflicts confronting the water sector in India?; and c) what are the critical issues and challenges that the policies and regulatory systems face in achieving the goals of integrated water resources development and a sustainable water future for the country?

The paper is organised into four sections. Section 2 provides an overview of the national and state level responses to the neoliberal policies which have taken the shape of national water policies of 1987 and 2002 and the subsequent enunciation of water policies by individual states. It then makes a critical review of the contrasting scenarios of policy and regulatory reforms in Maharashtra and Gujarat states, which are distinct in terms of the growth dynamism having serious implications on the water resources by way of over extraction of groundwater and ever growing industrial and urban demands for water. Maharashtra in particular has been in the forefront for launching various water sector reforms, mostly guided by the neoliberal policies. Section 3 examines the major outcomes and challenges or the dilemmas in the implementation of water sector reforms in Maharashtra and Gujarat. Section 4 concludes the paper by posing some important concerns on the very relevance and robustness of the neoliberal reforms in the water sector in addressing the multi-faceted water sector challenges in India.

Water Policies and Regulatory Regimes in India: An Overview

The history of water sector development in India reflects that the national policies and priorities have been highly obsessed with the development of multi-purpose river valley projects (MRVP). Both the national and state governments have been engaged in formulating and implementing policies and programmes for development of water systems aimed at irrigation, flood control, hydro-power generation, drinking water supply and industrial and other uses. Over the past five decades, India had spent more than $50 billion for infrastructure development in water sector, comprising a large number of small, medium and large dams, barrages, hydropower schemes, canal networks, etc. Indeed, this resulted in tremendous achievements in terms of assured irrigation in the command areas, water supply for hydropower and thermal power development as well as the drinking water supplies. As many parts of post-independent India were facing serious problems of frequent famines and droughts, the construction of large dams for irrigation and other purposes has been certainly justified by the planners and policy makers. Irrigation development has been highly instrumental in the success of Green Revolution (GR) technologies leading to expansion of HYVs of food crops (mainly wheat and rice) in the entire northwest region of the Indo-Gangetic Plains (Chand, 2010).

However, despite the notable achievements, India's water sector has been beset with serious problems of under-performance with poor realisation of irrigation potential. The seriousness of the sub-optimal performance of surface irrigation systems in the country has been further compounded by the parallel developments in extracting the groundwater resources beyond sustainable levels. Today, the groundwater resources are in a critical state in most parts of the country, especially in Gujarat, Maharshtra, Punjab and Tamil Nadu and groundwater also forms the largest source of irrigation water supplies (65-70 percent) and 80 per cent of the domestic water supplies (World Bank, 2005). Besides, the Water Quality Assessment Authority (WQAA) reports several problems about the poor quality and delivery of drinking water and sanitation services in the country[3].

Thus, the sorry state of affairs of India's water sector points to a crisis emerging from policy dilemmas and governance failure compounded by several other challenges, viz. a) perceptible gap in the provisions of water across competing sectors, especially safe drinking water in rural and urban areas; b) issues of legitimisation of rights to water as a fundamental right; c) growing water markets even in the rural fringes; d) absence of institutional and regulatory systems for effectively addressing the dynamic agrarian changes in the canal commands; e) varying degrees of implementation and success of participatory water management interventions; and f) the growing environmental and human health-related concerns along with socio-economic impacts of poorly implemented rehabilitation/resettlement programmes, to mention a few.

If we consider the contextual relevance of launching of policies and regulatory reforms in the India's water sector, it may seem that the situations were quite demanding for a paradigm shift in policies and regulatory regimes in the light of the policy interventions that happened among the countries in the north. But it is yet intriguing that how the policies and regulatory reforms as developed in the North could be effective in resolving the policy dilemmas and the governance crises of the sorts in India as described above.

The Indian Constitution provides a solid foundation for evolving legal and policy frames required for the water sector in the country. Water is also a state subject with 'irrigation' being entry 17 of the state list. 'Water rights' irrespective of the limitations due to definition and implementation are derived from the fundamental rights of the Constitution under Article 21. State governments are obviously empowered to legislate on water related matters and ensure good governance.

Water sector development, which assumed centre-stage of the planned development programmes in the country, has been perceived and implemented in a highly 'centralised and top down' framework even by the states. Since water resources are considered as nature's free gift, formal water sector policies were either non-existent or rudimentary. The institutional and or regulatory mechanisms that existed have always been dominated by the centralist decision-making powers. However, the scenario had undergone some changes since the 73rd and 74th amendments in the Constitution passed in 1992, which empowered the Panchayati Raj Institutions (PRIs) to administer water sector development programmes. Since then, there were series of enactments, legislations and policy interventions within the water sector (surface, groundwater and drinking water sub-sectors) marking a paradigm shift in policies, perspectives and approaches mostly confining to the micro level contexts of the Indian states. But, in most cases, these legislations, enactments and policy formulations seemed mere refinements or modifications or additions to the pre-existing legal and regulatory regimes of the colonial era.

The National Water Policies: 1987 and 2002

Of late, the two national water policies, viz., Water Policy 1987 and Water Policy 2002 have been quite instrumental in introducing the legal/ policy initiatives and regulatory reforms in the water sector in the country. The first National Water Policy (NWP) adopted in September 1987 underlined that 'water is a prime natural resource, a basic human need and a precious national asset'. This policy intended promoting a standardised national information system, data collection, establishment of basin-wise organisations with multi-disciplinary approach to planning, formulation, clearance and implementation of projects, rehabilitation, groundwater development, water zoning, flood and drought management, R & D and training (Kumar and Seth, 2000). In the planning and operation of water resource systems, the priorities of water allocation were set as: a) drinking water; b) irrigation; c) hydro-power; d) navigation; and e) industrial and other uses. The policy also addressed several areas of intervention, viz., assessment of water resources, ground water hydrology and recharge, prevention of salinity ingress, etc.

Though the 1987 NWP covered wide ranging aspects of the water sector, a number of challenges emerged in due course of its implementation. Reportedly, the Ministry of Water Resources (MWR) has not been well-equipped in implementing the policy[4]. To overcome some of the discrepancies in implementing the 1987 policy, the NWP 2002 was announced as a modified version of the 1987 policy. The 2002 policy was set in the backdrop of the impending water crisis and the severe droughts in the country. Hence, provision of drinking water assumed topmost priority in the 2002 policy as well. With the inclusion of provision of water for ecological services, the 2002 policy set the priorities as: a) drinking water; b) irrigation; c) hydro-power; d) ecology; e) agro-industries and non-agricultural industries; f) navigation and other uses. In the remaining areas and provisions, the 2002 policy appears to be a replica of the 1987 policy.

A notable difference in the 2002 policy has been its focus on privatisation[5]. The policy put forth supply side solutions in terms of institutional mechanisms, technological options, innovations and corporate management strategies for ensuring better financial returns through market-driven water pricing solutions. Thus, there has been a big push towards the neo-liberal idea of promoting private-public partnerships in the provision of water, especially, rural water supplies, which was anchored by the international development agencies, such as the World Bank and eminently supported by the then national government. But, the two national water policies seem to be mere statement of intentions or pontifications as they have not been complemented by supportive legislations or action plans at the national level.

Nevertheless, following the 2002 policy, a series of legislations and policies have been introduced by the states, in the arenas of rural and urban drinking water and the irrigation water sectors. Many of the states have also come up with respective state water policies. Prominent among them include: Tamil Nadu Water Policy 1994; Uttar Pradesh State Water Policy 1999; Karnataka State Water Policy, 2002; Maharashtra State Water Policy 2003; Madhya Pradesh State Water Policy 2003; Kerala Water Policy, 2007 and Orissa State Water Policy in 2007 (MOWR, 2010).

Incidentally, many of these policy and regulatory reforms invariably seem to be similar in setting their priorities and legitimising the neoliberal approach of market based solutions for the water sector governance. This reasoning is only logical as there are many questionable issues concerning the manner in which the water sector reforms are implemented in several of these states, particularly, Maharashtra and Gujarat. In particular, Maharashtra seems to have gone far ahead in implementing water sector reforms with several policy initiatives pertaining to distribution and management of water for irrigation and other competing uses. In contrast, the state of Gujarat has a notorious legacy in the development and management of water resources. Despite the plethora of challenges facing the water sector, the state still remains somewhat closed to the idea of a formal enactment or implementation of water policy and regulatory reforms.

Rest of the section critically examines the diverging scenarios of the status of implementation of water sector reforms in Maharashtra, as against the virtual laxity of Gujarat in initiating any such reform process, when the water sector in the state is beset with increasing problems of over-extraction of groundwater, growing demand for urban and industrial consumption, etc.

Water Policies and Related Regulatory Reforms in Maharashtra

Maharashtra is the third largest state in the country with a geographical area of 30.8 million hectares covering a population of 112.37 million as per the 2011 Census (GOI, 2011). The growing population together with booming industrial sector exerts great pressure on the water resources. Agriculture employing 70 per cent of the labour force continues to be the largest sector drawing the state's freshwater, especially groundwater. The state remains as socially and politically dynamic with the presence of a powerful farmers' lobby and several other factors ultimately influencing the governance of water sector. The state also has a long tradition of community water management. A case in point is the 300-year-old system of water management—the *Phad system*—a community managed irrigation system prevalent in northwestern Maharashtra.

The history of legislative/ institutional reforms in water sector in Maharashtra may be traced back to 1960 when the state implemented the Maharashtra Fisheries Act, 1960. This was followed by various other important enactments in the 1970s, viz. a) Water (Prevention and Control of Pollution) Act, 1974; b) Maharashtra Irrigation Act, 1976; and c) Maharashtra Kharland Improvement Act, 1979. In 1972, the state had set up a Groundwater Surveys & Development Agency (GSDA), especially for the development of minor irrigation schemes based on groundwater. But, many of these legislations were essentially to discipline the water sector and to ensure its optimum development for fulfilling the water needs of different users.

Nevertheless, after a long silence of almost a decade during the 1980s, the state had introduced a number of policy and regulatory reforms in the 1990s which were more radical in terms of restructuring the institutional and governance systems followed until then. Prominent among these reforms were implementation of the Maharashtra Groundwater (Regulation for Drinking Water Purposes) Act, 1993, followed by enactments for setting up of five major river basin/ irrigation development corporations, viz., a) Krishna Valley Development Corporation Act, 1996; b) Vidarbha Irrigation Development Corporation Act, 1997; c) Tapi Irrigation Development Corporation Act, 1997; d) Konkan Irrigation Development Corporation Act, 1997; and e) Godavari Marathwada Irrigation Development Corporation Act, 1998. Notably, the setting up of the irrigation development corporations may be seen as a radical step towards breaking the conventional 'command and control' model of water regulation through privatisation of water control systems in the state.

The last decade witnessed more of radical reforms in the state's water sector. In 2003, the state announced the Maharashtra State Water Policy (MSWP). This was followed by two major enactments, viz., the Maharashtra Water Resources Regulatory Authority Act, 2005 (MWRRA) and the Maharashtra Management of Irrigation Systems by Farmers Act, 2005 (MMISFA), which have been regarded as quite path breaking in the realm of water sector reforms in the state.

The Maharashtra State Water Policy (MSWP) 2003 was mainly based on the NWP 2002 and the Maharashtra Water and Irrigation Commission's Report. The basic objectives of the MSWP are "to ensure the sustainable development and optimal use and management of the State's water resources, to provide the greatest economic and social benefit for the people of the State and to maintain important ecological values within rivers and adjoining lands." The important objectives and the strategies for achieving those objectives as proposed in the MSWP are presented in Box 1.

Box 1: Maharashtra Water Policy: Objectives and Strategies

Objectives	*Strategies*
1. Create an enabling environment for equitable and productive water management in an environmentally sustainable manner to promote growth, reduce poverty and minimise regional imbalances.	1. River Basin Agencies (RBAs): Delineate the five river basins into 25 sub-basins for integrated planning, development and management of water resources and watersheds in respective river basins. 2. Participatory water management: To comply with this, farmer management of irrigation systems has been made mandatory along with formation of WUAs. Water will be supplied on a volumetric basis to WU As only.
2. Create incentives for efficient use of water and empower WUA to participate in management; to grant the WUAs entitlements to water so as to enable them decide on best use without bureaucratic interference.	3. WUAs and bulk water entitlements: The concept of 'bulk water entitlements' was introduced mainly to effect water allocations through WUAs. WUAs hold bulk entitlement to water on behalf of their members. WUAs will be formed as federations at the distributary level and will be responsible for the O&M of canals and other structures and facilities.
3. Create new institutional arrangements at river basins to guide and regulate water management; to decentralise the responsibility at river basins and sub-basins	4. Water for domestic and industrial use: To launch a perspective plan to integrate the provision of drinking water both to the rural and urban sectors with the multi-purpose projects. Suggests a pricing policy to cover at least the O&M costs of the water supply.

4. Place a high priority on promoting the development, adaptation and dissemination of new technology to improve efficiency and productivity encouraged.	5. Private sector participation: Encourages participation of corporate, commercial enterprises and water service providers in preparing the river basin plans. Similarly, partnerships between the state and the private sector in financing for and introduction of new technologies.
5. Enact appropriate legislation and enabling rules to effect the above strategies: For this, the state will adopt three critical items of legislation including: a) an act to authorise farmers' management of irrigation systems; b) an act to create a state water authority; c) and river basin authorities.	6. Priorities in water allocation: Priorities include: a) drinking, cooling, hygiene and sanitation needs including livestock; b) industrial, commercial use and agro-based industrial use; c) agriculture and hydropower; d) environment and recreation uses; and e) all other uses. 7. Transfer of water use entitlements: "Transfer of all or a portion of water entitlement between entitlement holders in any category of water use and priority shall be permitted on both annual and seasonal basis based on fair compensation of the entitlement.

Source: State Water Policy, Maharashtra.

The Maharashtra Water Resources Regulatory Authority Act, (MWRRA) 2005

The state water policy prescribed setting up of two major regulatory instruments, viz., (i) a state water resources regulatory authority and river basin authorities; and (ii) an act to authorise farmers' management of irrigation systems. Accordingly, the state passed the Maharashtra Water Resources Regulatory Authority (MWRRA) Act, 2003 (Mah. Act No. XVIII of 2005), which was adopted in 2005. The MWRRA is supposed to regulate the state's water resources by engaging into multiple tasks: a) facilitate and ensure judicious, equitable and sustainable management, allocation and utilisation of water resources; b) fix water rates for agriculture, industrial, drinking and other purposes; and c) perform matters connected therewith or incidental thereto. The MWRRA Act also sanctions the formal setting up of the River Basin Agencies (RBAs) or River Basin Development Corporations (RBDCs).[6]

The MWRRA is also the designated authority to issue the bulk water entitlements (BWE) to WUAs or other entities. The Act also lays down the criteria of allocation and provision of BWEs issued by the RBAs based on the category of use subject to the priority assigned. BWEs are issued for uses, such as irrigation, drinking, municipal and industries to relevant user entities, mainly WUAs and others and not individual farmers per se. Individual Water Entitlements will be issued only for the construction and operation of individual lift irrigation schemes using surface water sources through bore-wells, tube wells or other facilities for extraction of sub-surface water. In all cases the BWE will be measured volumetrically and with respect to time of delivery and flow rate of delivery. The Act also suggests criteria in matters of transfer or trading of water entitlements.

The Maharashtra Management of Irrigation Systems by Farmers' Act, 2005

The second and perhaps the most important legal instrument as prescribed by the 2003 Water Policy in Maharashtra is the Act authorising farmers' management of irrigation systems (FMIS) in the state. Thus, the policy seems to give greater emphasis for involving farmers, the dominant segment of water users, in the process of management of water resources. This step might help in creating new, and strengthening of the existing WUAs in the state. This could be an important step especially in a context when the performance of the water sector is undermined by serious issues of underutilisation of irrigation potential. In fact, this initiative of management of irrigation systems by farmers may be considered as reinventing the economic significance of the WUAs as critical instruments for achieving efficiency in irrigation management transfer (IMT) and the participatory irrigation management (PIM). These are being tried in countries including India, though with limited success.

Thus, while there are serious apprehensions about the success and effectiveness of such participatory interventions in the country, the government of Maharashtra seems to have taken a bold step by making legislation for farmer management in irrigation systems. Besides, new regulatory systems are put in place by way of introducing water auditing, benchmarking of water resources projects, water entitlements, etc. A Project Level Association is made responsible for water budgeting, in the absence of which, the Canal Officer is held responsible. Further, the SWP claims that a well-defined transparent system for water entitlements will be established, so that these cannot be changed unilaterally by any state agency or authority. However, a critical analysis of BWEs underlies the limitations in both the conceptualisation as well as the broader policy context in which they are situated. Firstly, the entitlements refer to authorisation granted to use water, i.e. usufruct rights. But this is not linked to any notion of *inherent* rights of farmers over water (Upadhyay, 2005). In fact, even with the new changes in the state, there is no enforceable guarantee offered by the state for access to either drinking or irrigation water. Secondly, the policy permits transfer of all or a portion of water entitlement between entitlement holders in any category of water use, and priority on both annual and seasonal basis based upon fair compensation of the entitlement. However, it is not clear whether only the quota for a particular season or year is transferable, or whether a permanent transfer of the entitlement is also feasible. Further, there is no provision for transfer of entitlements to non-entitlement holders (such as the landless), a provision which may adversely affect women.

Fixation of Bulk Water Tariff

One of the major interventions by the MWRRA is the introduction of a market based instrument, i.e., the fixation of bulk water tariffs[7] (BWT) and this may be regarded as the first of its kind in the country. The MWRRA claims that the fixation of the criteria based water tariff has been found on 'sound economic principles and informed economic choices'. Several incentives/ concessions have also been proposed to the agriculture, industry and drinking water sectors to: (i) give relief to the economically weaker sections including marginal and small farmers and tribal farmers; (ii) to encourage adoption of micro irrigation techniques; (iii) to paddy areas for switching to volumetric tariff; (iv) to rural drinking water users and agro industries; (v) to encourage adoption of recycling by industries and usage of treated effluent for irrigation. The "polluter pays" principle has been introduced for errant industries (MWRRA, 2009).

Thus, seemingly, the regulatory reforms have been overtly keen on streamlining the institutional structures involved in the governance of the water sector by way of segregating the sectoral administration of water distribution. Accordingly, while irrigation management is administered through CADA and the Irrigation Development Corporations, drinking water supplies are regulated by the Water Supply and Sanitation Department (WSSD), the Maharashtra Jeevan Pradhikaran (MJP) and the Municipal Corporations (MCs). The Maharashtra Industrial Development Corporation (MIDC) takes care of the industrial and domestic water needs (retail and/or bulk sale) in MIDC areas, and in non-MIDC areas, either Municipal Corporations supply water to the industries or the industries themselves manage it through dedicated pipe lines (MWRRA, 2009). However, the sectoral water allocations as well as the implementation of bulk water tariffs have been beset with various operational level constraints in Maharashtra, as we discuss further.

Water Policy and Regulatory Regime in Gujarat

Gujarat occupies about 6 per cent of the land resources and roughly 3 per cent of India's freshwater resources, and 5 per cent of its population as per the 2011 provisional Census (GOI, 2011). The state has low per capita rainwater availability as compared to several others and hence, most parts of the state remain "water starved". Almost 70 per cent of the freshwater resources in the state are concentrated in the south and central regions. Water problems are acute and are manifest in the form of depletion and pollution of groundwater aquifers, polluted water bodies, water-logging and salinity in canal commands, salinity ingress in coastal areas, fast growing competition between non-conventional water consumptive sectors, such as rural and urban drinking water as well as the industrial sectors.

The future of Gujarat's water sector seems to be bleak in view of the growing water demand and the threat of potential conflicts between competing sectors. Water pollution caused by industrial effluents is a prominent problem. Besides, the growth of urbanisation especially since the last ten years has also been seriously affecting the water sector in the state. Incidentally, there has been a surge in empirical research undertaken by institutional agencies, including government and international bodies, such as the IWMI as well as individual researchers examining the magnitude of the impending water crisis in Gujarat as caused by the rapid changes.

While a review of the empirical studies is beyond the scope of the paper, it may be observed that there is a consensus on the virtual absence of overarching policies and regulatory systems governing the water sector in the state[8]. Of the many studies, mention may be made of the White Paper on Water in Gujarat prepared by IRMA/ UNICEF in 2001, which brought out the status report on water resources in the state. It identifies the pertinent issues and the emerging challenges in Gujarat's water sector and outlines strategies for resolving the issues including identification of options for future action for drought-proofing. The white paper had underlined the need for expediting the announcement of a water policy, which is to be backed by a facilitating law, and buttressed by an appropriate organisational structure and governance system. The White Paper also recommended the setting up of an autonomous Water Development and Management Board at the state level, to plan, coordinate and direct water management projects (IRMA/UNICEF, 2001).

Though the White Paper made a candid case for formulating the State Water Policy, there has not been any such initiative for developing a comprehensive policy or legislative framework to address the woes of the water sector in Gujarat. However, recently, there have been some efforts in recent years in the state for introducing certain legislations/ policy reforms in the water sector. In particular, the State has introduced two specific policy-cum-regulatory interventions, viz., a) the Gujarat Water Regulatory Commission (GWRC); and b) the Gujarat Water Users' Participatory Irrigation Management (GWUPIM) Bill, 2007.

Gujarat Water Regulatory Commission Bill 2006

The State has been in the process of setting up the Gujarat Water Regulatory Authority (GWRA) following the MWRRA Act 2005. The Government of Gujarat (GoG) with the help of the Tata Energy and Resources Institute (TERI) has prepared draft legislation for setting up of independent regulatory authority for the water and sanitation sectors. The Gujarat Water Regulatory Commission Bill 2006 aims to bring different departments under one umbrella for the purpose of water distribution, rationalisation of water supply and fixation of tariffs. It is claimed by the officials that the proposed water regulatory authority (WRA) will work towards bringing clarity to the roles of various government bodies involved in water distribution, boost private sector investment, improve productivity and efficiency in the sector and also address the cost aspects. Aiming at an economic costing of water, the Bill includes municipal bodies and industrial users in its ambit. Apart from the Gujarat Water Regulatory Commission (GWRC), the Bill also provides for the setting up of the State Water Regulatory Council (SWRC) (chaired by the Chief Minister, with 10 other ministers as members) and a State Water Regulatory Committee (chaired by the Chief Secretary, with 13 other secretaries). The proposed Bill also recommends setting up of a 15-member consultative committee including local bodies, academia, industry, agriculture and labour sectors, NGOs/ civil society organisations (CSOs) and research bodies to advise the

GWRC on policy and tariffs and protect the consumer interests. While no timeline has been set for the formation of the Commission, it was envisaged that the Bill may get official sanction in due course of time.

Nevertheless, it may be observed that even if the proposed WRA is established in Gujarat it need not be as effective as envisaged in addressing the various water sector challenges of the state. It is quite likely that the WRA would turn into a 'monopoly provider', thus questioning the legitimacy of the WUAs in enforcing the rights of people over water. Moreover, the Bill by and large, calls for a radical transformation in the existing legal, regulatory, financial and administrative frameworks to facilitate for private sector participation in the provision of drinking water, especially in the urban areas. The proposed Bill also commits to provide adequate returns through creating an attractive tariff regime that would facilitate the entry of private sector players in the water sector in the state. Such a decision, as one official feels, stands justified as "over the years, public investment in water infrastructure, particularly in cities, has gone down. Given this, it becomes evident that private investment can salvage the situation. And once private money comes in, we have to address issues like pricing, competition and regulation. That is why this Bill."

Further, there are ambiguities as regards the fixation of tariff rates for various services. For instance, on the one hand, the Bill proposes to set a tariff that progressively reflects the cost of supply of water and sewage services at improving levels of efficiency and quality in case of consumers apart from agriculture. On the other hand, it also proposes to set a tariff that progressively reflects only the cost of operation and maintenance in case of irrigation water supply system, taking into consideration the area, the cropping pattern and seasonal rainfall variations. The Bill also lacks clarity when it proposes to set a tariff that progressively reduces cross subsidies and eventually eliminate them. For example, there is no clear mention as to: 'what modalities will have to be used for implementing the cross subsidisation' and 'which sectors and segments of population to be benefited by the cross subsidisation policy?'.

The Gujarat Water Users' Participatory Irrigation Management Act, 2007

The second major aspect of legislative reform in the water sector is the Bill called the Gujarat Water Users' Participatory Irrigation Management (PIM) Bill 2007, enacted on September 17, 2007. The Act seeks scaling up PIM by giving statutory support to the combined efforts of the Water Resources Department, farmers and NGOs. As per the Act, WUAs shall be formed by a competent authority for each service area, consisting of land holders in the command area. However, membership in the WUA is not binding.

Particularly since the enactment of the PIM Act, there has been notable progress in the implementation of the act in Gujarat as indicated by the formation of WUAs. For instance, till 2009, over 1266 WUAs have been formed covering 3.48 lakh hectares of command area. The experience so far indicates that PIM programme has resulted in changes in water allocation, distribution and management in almost all areas served by the WUAs (DSC, 2006). The significance of PIM lies in that it aims at improving the performance and financial viability of irrigation structures through a system of cost recovery and turnover of operations and maintenance to local water users themselves. One of the important expectations of PIM is the long run benefit to the government through a reduction in its expenditure. This, however, pre-supposes that WUAs will be self-sufficient in maintaining and operating the irrigation system (Parthasarathy, 2010).

Implementation of Water Sector Reforms: Outcomes and Dilemmas

In a way, water policies as they emerge in the neoliberal format in India are integral to the efficiency drive adopted by the states depicting the dynamic responsiveness of the governance systems towards achieving allocative and distributive efficiencies within the water sector. Such an efficiency drive may be imperative given the stark realisation that agriculture, the dominant water consuming sector, has been mainly responsible for the critical state of affairs of the water sector in

India. This may further be evident if we examine the contradictions in the inter-sectoral water allocation and the enforcement of the bulk water tariff in Maharashtra, in particular.

Maharashtra's Water Sector Dilemmas

Hence, this section looks at the major outcomes and the resultant dilemmas following the implementation of water sector reforms in Maharashtra and Gujarat. It critically examines the posthoc performance of water sector in the event of introduction of BWT and the concerns emerge from the stakeholder consultations on the implementation of BWT and bulk water entitlements in Maharashtra. It then discusses the emerging issues and dilemmas in Gujarat's water sector.

Table 1 presents the trends in sectoral water consumption in Maharashtra in the last decade of water sector reforms. It shows that irrigation water demand constituted the dominant water user (77-83 per cent), followed by the fast growing drinking water demand (13-20 per cent).

Table 1

Trends in Water Consumption by Different Sectors in Maharashtra (Mm³)

Year	Irrigation	Drinking/ Domestic	Industries	Total
2002-03	13980 (80.4)	2643 (15.2)	773 (4.4)	17396 (100.0)
2003-04	10951 (77.4)	2579 (18.2)	623 (4.4)	14153 (100.0)
2004-05	12327 (79.3)	2554 (16.5)	657 (4.2)	15538 (100.0)
2005-06	15564 (81.7)	2808 (14.7)	677 (3.6)	19049 (100.0)
2006-07	16497 (83.2)	2624 (13.2)	712 (3.6)	19833 (100.0)
2007-08	18158 (80.5)	3719 (16.5)	681 (3.0)	22558 (100.0)
2008-09	17186 (77.3)	4383 (19.7)	668 (3.0)	22237 (100.0)

Note: Mm³- Million Cubic Metres. Figures in parentheses are respective shares in total water consumption. *Source*: MWRRA

Ironically, industrial water consumption figures are reported to be 3-4 per cent of the gross water consumption in the state, which itself is a contradiction, as Maharashtra is known for its fastest growing industrial sector in the country. In absolute terms, demand for irrigation has increased by about 23 per cent from 13980 million cubic metres (Mm^3) in 2002-03 to 17186 Mm^3 in 2008-09. The drinking water demand increased substantially by almost 66 per cent during the same period. It is quite strange to see that the industrial water consumption has been stagnating during most years with a decline in absolute terms after 2006-07, which is certainly illogical.

In fact, the above water consumption figures raise several questions about the methodological and the political economy issues underlying the assessment of the sectoral water demand in Maharashtra. The observed high water consumption (75-80 per cent) by the irrigation sector itself may be erroneous given the huge water losses (60-75 per cent) reported from surface irrigation systems due to seepage and other operational factors (MWRRA, personal communication).

In sharp contrast, the BWT levied by the MWRRA indicate that the highest amount of tariff has been levied on the industrial sector, which increased by more than 88 per cent from Rs. 174 crores (2002-03) to Rs. 328 crores (2007-08) as seen from Table 2. Interestingly, the BWT levied on the irrigation sector had

Table 2

Trends in BWT Levied from Different Sectors in Maharashtra (Rs. Crores)

Year	Irrigation	Drinking/ Domestic	Industries	Total
2002-03	90 (24.9)	97 (26.9)	174 (48.2)	361 (100.0)
2003-04	88 (21.5)	99 (24.1)	223 (54.4)	410 (100.0)
2004-05	77 (16.6)	118 (25.4)	270 (58.1)	465 (100.0)
2005-06	68 (17.1)	125 (31.5)	204 (51.4)	397 (100.0)
2006-07	98 (20.0)	114 (23.6)	273 (56.4)	485 (100.0)
2007-08	113 (18.4)	172 (28.1)	328 (53.5)	613 (100.0)
2008-09	118 (17.9)	246 (37.5)	293 (44.6)	657 (100.0)

Note: Figures in parentheses are respective shares in total water tariff levied by the state. *Source:* MWRRA

increased only by about 31 per cent from Rs. 90 crores to Rs. 118 crores during the period with a relatively lower contribution to the total BWT levied (say, 18%). The share of domestic/ drinking water sectors had increased by two and a half times from Rs. 97 crores to Rs. 246 crores.

An interesting dimension of tariff implementation in Maharashtra pertains to the differential tariff structure as suggested for the irrigation and non-irrigation (domestic/ drinking and industrial) sectors. Based on the actual tariffs levied and realised, the unit water tariffs may be derived for three major uses as shown in Table 3.

Table 3

Trends in Unit Water Tariffs Levied and Realised Across Sectors (Rs/ 10 kilo litres)

Year	Drinking Water		Industrial Water		Irrigation Water		Total Water Sector	
	Levied	Realised	Levied	Realised	Levied	Realised	Levied	Realised
2002-03	3.67	2.11	22.51	18.87	0.64	0.16	2.08	1.29
2003-04	3.84	2.72	35.78	26.94	0.80	0.22	2.90	1.85
2004-05	4.62	2.79	41.12	35.92	0.62	0.23	2.99	2.16
2005-06	4.45	2.85	30.11	26.87	0.44	0.22	2.08	1.56
2006-07	4.34	3.43	38.33	33.27	0.59	0.27	2.44	1.88
2007-08	4.62	3.68	48.16	41.70	0.62	0.20	2.72	2.03
2008-09	5.62	2.66	43.89	40.61	0.69	0.21	2.96	1.91

Source: MWRRA

Among the three sectors, the irrigation water tariffs levied are abysmally low (Rs. 1/kilo litres). Whereas, industrial water tariffs have more than doubled between 2002-03 (Rs. 22.21/kilo litres) and 2007-08 (Rs. 48.16/kilo litres), the tariff levied on drinking water increased by one and a half times from Rs. 3.67 to Rs. 5.62 during the period.

Some important issues emerge here are: (a) 'whether the differential water tariffs as implemented in the state are reflective of the sensitiveness of water use in each sector; (b) whether the decision to keep abysmally low tariffs for irrigation water are politically motivated; and (c) whether the seemingly exorbitant water tariffs for industries are vehemently opposed by the industrial sector?'. Apparently it seems that the water tariffs are differentiated across sectors in response to their sensitiveness to demand. For instance, irrigation water tariffs are kept reasonably low in consideration of equity, timeliness and adequacy in its distribution. Whereas, industrial water tariffs are the highest in view of the affordability of the sector. Industries can afford to pay the water charges, as water tariffs are always included as input costs, burden of which could eventually be transferred to the consumer. Further, industries get water at 90 per cent reliability while the irrigation sector is deprived of water at times of shortage.

Thus, the Maharashtra water policy justifies the differential tariff system by keeping high tariffs for industrial sector, which in turn gets the highest priority in allocation than the irrigation sector. Though irrigation tariffs are kept the lowest, the political economy of neoliberal policy twist becomes apparent here as irrigation water supplies are cut during drought seasons. On the other hand, industries and domestic sectors get full quota and hence, there is little opposition from these sectors for the higher water tariffs. Seemingly, "pay more to get more reliable supply is the market principle that guides this tariff fixation." But, this over prioritisation of water supplies to the industrial sector creates ripples in the whole process of water distribution as water supplies to the agriculture sector are adversely affected at critical phases of crop growth.

Probably, this certainty in allocation and distribution of water for the industrial and drinking water sectors could be a major factor that explains the better realisation and collection efficiency in water tariffs, especially in the case of the industrial sector as evident from Figure 1. It shows that the irrigation sector is highly crippled with the problem of inefficiency in the collection and realisation of BWT despite the lower levels of tariff levied on the sector. The efficiency in the collection of water tariff in the irrigation sector has been the lowest at 31 per cent as compared to drinking water (47 per cent) and the industrial (93 per cent) sectors.

The poor realisation of water tariffs in the case of irrigation sector may also be attributed to reasons other than the affordability and willingness of the farmers per se. For instance, it has been reported that most of the irrigation systems in the state suffer from serious problems of poor conveyance efficiency caused due to seepage and other operational factors, resulting in lower irrigation efficiencies of 25-30 per cent.

Thus, the trends in the allocation/consumption as well as fixation, collection and realisation of water tariffs bring out contradicting outcomes of implementation of the water sector reforms in Maharashtra. In fact, it is yet a matter of debate as to what factors explain this diverging pattern of performance in the allocation of water and tariff imposition and collection across the three sectors. Similarly, it is also important to dig out the real political economy issues underlying the dynamics of lower water allocation to industries as reported, when the industrial water demand is slated to be very high in the state following massive industrial expansion.

Figure 1: Trends in Efficiency in the Collection of Water Tariffs in Maharashtra

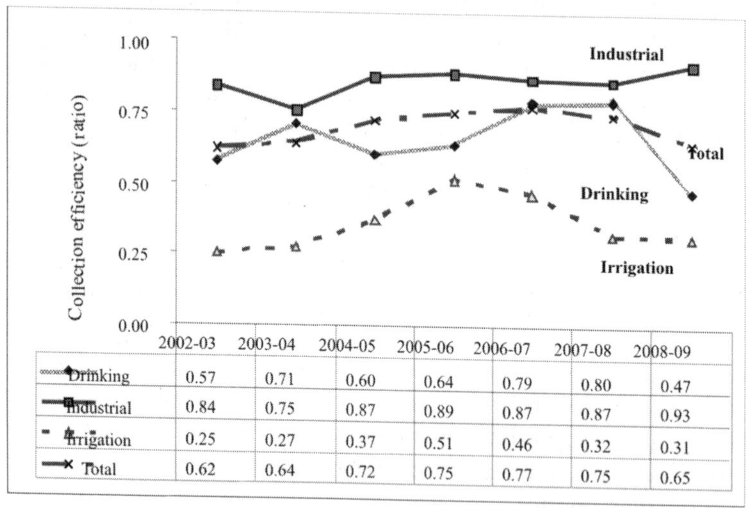

	2002-03	2003-04	2004-05	2005-06	2006-07	2007-08	2008-09
Drinking	0.57	0.71	0.60	0.64	0.79	0.80	0.47
Industrial	0.84	0.75	0.87	0.89	0.87	0.87	0.93
Irrigation	0.25	0.27	0.37	0.51	0.46	0.32	0.31
Total	0.62	0.64	0.72	0.75	0.77	0.75	0.65

Note: Efficiency in the collection of BWT is measured in terms of the ratio of tariff collected to the tariff levied on each sector. *Source*: MWRRA (estimated)

The bulk water tariff system as being implemented in Maharashtra has also been beset with several operational issues and the approach paper on the fixation of bulk water tariff has been heavily criticised by the major stakeholders on various counts as evident from Box 2.

Box 2

Summary of Points of Stakeholder Consultations on the MWRRA Approach Paper on Bulk Water Tariff Fixation Held at Various Locations in Maharashtra

No.	*Points Raised/Comments Made*
1.	Problems of water losses have not been considered in the approach paper. If the system is run more effectively and losses reduced, cost can be recovered without giving any 'tariff shock' to the consumers. Losses due to leakages and water theft should not be loaded on tariff.
2.	Review of tariff structure in other states is not done. Maharashtra already has higher water rates than others. Hence, farmers do not reveal the actual irrigated area, report low value crops in place of cash crops and also engage in water thefts. This adversely affects water use efficiency as evident from the Water Audit reports.
3.	The Approach paper does not consider assessment of exact area of crops, improved billing system, reducing water losses and thefts, for increasing revenue. Better management of recovery of tariff might help increase the tariff outturn rather than an increase in tariffs per se. Large amounts of arrears from big farmers, industries and Municipal Corporations are yet to be collected. Given these discrepancies, a higher water tariff will only mean further violations by the users by not adhering to pay water tariffs, creating several defaulters.
4.	That the water tariffs for irrigation are quite high is acting as a major deterrent in the formation/ functioning of WUAs. Responsibilities of WUAs are still not properly defined or worked out for them.
5.	Until the experiment of volumetric supply for 286 irrigation projects is not complete, tariff fixation exercise may not be much useful. MWRRA should force the government/ irrigation departments for the time-bound implementation of volumetric supply-based tariff system.

6. The difference between created irrigation potential and actual irrigation is a complex issue. There should be in-depth consideration of this issue while making the regulations for determination of bulk water tariff.
7. The proposal for levying fixed water tariff for non-users of water may not be acceptable to the tail enders, who are always deprived.
8. Uniform application of the volumetric-based tariff system is not possible in Maharashtra, because, currently, the proportion of volumetric supply is only 15 per cent and for 85 per cent area, area based water allocation method is prevalent. This means that of the 45 lakh ha, only 7 lakh ha could be brought under volumetric based tariff and the remaining 38 lakh ha will continue with the area-based tariff system. It will require huge investments for a transition from the area-based to the volumetric-based tariff system in the state.
9. Recycling and reuse of water by industries is encouraged by the MWRRA. But, since treatment is costly, persuading industries to recycled reuse is rather difficult. On the other hand, industries would not mind even paying higher tariff if they get adequate water in time. Industries, such as steel and paper are water-intensive with paper industries causing severe pollution problems. This contradicts when the farmers are deprived of water during periods when they want it most. They are also compelled to adjust their crops to suit water availability.
10. Issue of equity is not considered for tariff regulation and social policy consideration for life-line water services is ignored. Environmental consideration is not incorporated as part of tariff regulations. Principle of Transparency-Accountability-Participation-Capacity Building (TAP-C) is neglected completely.
11. There are no field observations made apart from the published data. Experience of increasing water tariff vis-à-vis, net increase in revenue in irrigation sector needs consideration.
12. There are nine agro-climatic regions in Maharashtra. Hence, uniform tariff across the state will not be appropriate owing to significant variations on account of soil, crops, climate

and availability of water. Further, irrigated area in the state needs a reality check in view of the agro-climatic divisions. Most of the western region still remains to be rainfed without irrigation facilities.

13. Reject the current approach paper submitted by ABPS Infrastructure. Stop forthwith the public consultation system including public hearing scheduled on the basis of the approach paper. Direct the consultant to revise entire approach paper in compliance with TOR and taking cognisance of various lacunas pointed out by several organisations and individuals during consultations. Ensure adequacy and quality of the approach paper by circulating it among experts, social activists, research organisations, etc.
14. For arriving rates of unit quantity of water, some important factors needing consideration are: a) quality of service; b) reliability of water supply; c) economic use of water; d) sector of water use (primary/ secondary/tertiary); e) social importance; f) No. of families benefit; g) equitable distribution of resources.

Source: Review of Stakeholder Consultations Conducted by the MWRRA.

As evident from the above, the MWRRA approach paper prepared by a private consultancy firm (ABPS Infrastructure) did not involve important stakeholders. The approach paper seems to be unrealistic in terms of fixation of BWT and the norms suggested for its implementation are ambiguous. Only the report has been kept in the public domain (MWRRA website) for stakeholder viewpoints, which in most cases were not properly considered while revising the approach paper. It is also apprehended that the consultant suggested the BW tariffs across sectors without adequate field studies reflecting the willingness and ability to pay among the agriculturists, non-farm sectors, and the urban-rural areas.

An important concern as raised during the consultations was the high cost of establishment for irrigation management, including the salaries of the employees in the department of water resources. The approach paper thus ceases to be a neoliberal policy tool which cuts short the jurisdiction of the

MWRRA as a cost recovery agency without addressing issues concerning equity, efficiency and sustainability of water distribution as well as pollution of water bodies and the concomitant water losses.

Gujarat's Water Sector Dilemmas

As observed, the water governance scenario in Gujarat is much more complex as the state seems to tread on a feeble and insensitive water regulatory regime. The dilemma is that there is no single agency in the state that is concerned with the overall governance of water that deals with legal, policy and rights apart from allocation and pricing-related issues (Kumar, 2004). Interestingly, the water sector in the state lacks a comprehensive policy framework and an overarching and integrated regulatory system with institutional systems in place to deal with the multi-pronged crisis surfacing the segment. Water sector development in the state has been quite contradictory in terms of the sub-optimal performance of the surface water sector as against the ruthless exploitation of the groundwater sector, driven by the rapid expansion of tubewells. While this contradiction points to the urgency of a comprehensive water policy and regulatory institutions in the state, the regional disparities in the access to water are serious issues meriting region-centric planning and policies for management of water resources. In addition to proper planning of water resources management, the distribution of intra-state water resources and optimum utilisation of water resources are equally important.

In fact, the launching of neoliberal economic reforms has caused radical transformation in almost all spheres of governance and administration in the state, including the enunciation of several reforms in the water sector, mainly in terms of increased privatisation of lead government portfolios on the administration of water. This radical move towards privatisation has been promoted in the state on the pretext of achieving performance efficiency in the water sector, especially to achieve better outcomes in the allocation and recovery of water tariffs. However, this paradigm shift raises concerns of equity in water delivery as well as effective implementation of water sector reforms among the heterogeneous farmers who by now have adopted a highly dynamic and water-intensive cropping pattern in the state with a heavy dependence on the already depleted groundwater sources. The expanding commercial agriculture calls for increased investments for intensification and expansion of coverage of canal irrigation systems (as in the case of SSP). Similarly, the provision and improvements in the quality of drinking water distribution would require significant investments in the sector. In fact, the increasing water demand from the growing urban population along with the over-extraction of groundwater for irrigation and the domestic as well as industrial uses signal the deepening water governance crisis in the state. While this calls for alternate paradigms for development of water harvesting structures and management of water resources in the state, it needs reconciliation that whether large-scale entry of the private sector in the provision of water services would be an alternative as propounded by the draft water policy legislation as designed by TERI.

One of the major challenges for the water sector in Gujarat is the rising industrial water demand. There has been tremendous expansion in the industrial activities (Viswanathan and Parikh, 2010) in the state which puts a heavy toll on the already depleted water resources in terms of increasing extraction of freshwater (surface and groundwater) as well as causing high levels of salinity in groundwater sources. There are also severe problems of groundwater contamination caused by solid and liquid waste disposal from industries and human settlements. The regions around the major industrial centres like Vadodara, Bharuch, Ankleshwar, Vapi, Valsad, Surat, Navsari, etc. have polluted water sources, which have adversely affected their drinking water sources as well. Perhaps, this hints at a major policy failure, as the state's industrial expansion strategies do not seem to have given proper consideration on imposing stricter vigilance measures in imposing measures for harvesting and management of water used for industrial and drinking water purposes[9]. That said, it seems that of late, the state has been thinking in terms of developing an industrial water policy. The urge for such a policy drive also comes from the huge infrastructure investments taking place in the state towards development of the 11 plus Special Investment Regions (SIRs), Special Economic Zones (SEZs) and several industrial parks, besides other industrial clusters, all of which would have tremendous implications on the shrinking levels of water resources (Dave, 2011).

One of the important reform steps initiated by the state has been the launching of the Swarna Jayanti Mukhya Mantri Shaheri Vikas Yojana (SJMMSVY) to provide water through the Narmada canal in response to the worsening scenario of urban drinking water supply. This scheme targets to ensure adequate water supply to meet the norms of 100 lpcd of water for all urban local bodies (ULBs) with full coverage of household access to piped water in the next 3-5 years. Essentially, this seems to be an ambitious plan as the urban areas post a tremendous growth in terms of population and urban amenities and infrastructure. Moreover, in view of the shrinking freshwater resources and the emerging climate change induced risks, it may be observed that the provision of drinking water through the Narmada canal would only lead to increased conflicts over sharing or distribution of water between the rural and urban areas in the state.

The neoliberal economic reforms have also been impacting the farmers in Gujarat in terms of a dramatic shift in agriculture driven by the market forces, which in turn have promulgated them to adopt a highly water-intensive cropping pattern (Shah et al., 2011). In fact, there have not been any dynamic policy responses in the state to address the challenges and constraints posed on the water front by such an agriculture growth paradigm. The virtual failure of surface water systems in delivering water to the fields, farmers have increasingly relied either on lifting water directly from the canals or deepening their groundwater aquifers to grow those water intensive crops, especially, Bt cotton, wheat, sugarcane, etc. Despite the availability of technological solutions in the form of sprinkler and drip irrigation systems, the diffusion and intake of these solutions have been far from satisfactory in the state. All these eventualities essentially point at the policy and governance failures which should have been dealt by the state through appropriate legislations (including groundwater) or enactments or even regulatory interventions. The criticality of a comprehensive water policy in the context of Gujarat also stems from the fact that much of the recent droughts in the state have been related to hydrological factors rather than those related to climatic risks ensuing from monsoon failures (Dave, 2011).

This raises the imperative of devising robust policies and effective models of water governance for the state. More specifically, there rises the question that "what types of institutional systems or regulatory processes have to be put in place to achieve the larger goals of sustainable water production/ harvesting and management as well as equity along with the new prioritisation strategies as promulgated by the neoliberal policy regime?". Apparently, there are several evidences suggesting that the conventional state-centric or the 'command and control' style of management of water sector has been proven to be highly disastrous in most of the states, including Gujarat.

Concluding Observations

This paper critically examines how the neoliberal policies as emerged in the west in the post-liberalisation era have influenced the water sector reform policies and interventions in the Indian states, particularly, Maharashtra and Gujarat. It observes that the policy responses and regulatory reforms in the case of Maharashtra have been somewhat proactive in sensitising the issues concerning allocation and distribution of water across competing sectors. Nevertheless, the legislations and regulatory systems that came into being are far from internalising the ground level realities concerning the critical issues of equitable distribution and conservation of water harvesting systems in a sustainable manner. The analysis reveals that the incompatibility between the neoliberal policies and the water sector interventions in the Indian context may be explained in terms of the fact that India tried experimenting the macro-economic policy reforms as in many other developed countries without giving proper consideration to the internal restructuring required for making the water sector institutions perform better in the new policy environment. As may be seen from the water sector reforms elsewhere, the models in most cases have been found to be following 'one-size fits all' type of approach with only minor modifications on a case by case basis. Further, many of these models, say, the US, Chile, Mexico, China and Morocco, are found to have been prescribed by the external funding agencies, as water sector reforms in those countries were preceded by macro-economic reforms/policy changes or structural adjustment measures as suggested by such agencies.

As many argue, the physical/economic scarcity as loom large in the country should have been a major trigger for water sector reforms in India rather than the macro-economic policies emerging from the globalisation process. For instance, Shah et al., (2004) observes that the institutional reforms already taken place in the water sector are vague and not adequate to manage India's scarce water resources and the real institutional reforms is still a cry in wilderness. This underlies that meaningful institutional reforms be sensitive to water scarcity issues—be it surface or groundwater related (Shah et al., 2004). The micro level issues that loom large adversely affecting the harnessing, distribution and sustainable management of water resources should have been instrumental in driving policies and institutional interventions in the Indian context.

There are also growing concerns that the inclusion of neoliberal perspectives in framing water sector policies in India has by and large ignored the IWRM approaches. Though the 2002 National Water Policy tried adopting the IWRM approach and introducing water rights for managing water resources at the river basin level (Shah and Van Koppen, 2006), only very few states are found to follow the IWRM principles in view of the several problems as embedded in the approach. For example, the MWRRA has been created to implement IWRM in Maharashtra and facilitate creation and trading water entitlements, so that these entitlements can be transferred, bartered, bought or sold on an annual or seasonal basis within the market system. However, due to lack of information and guidance, the prospect of the authority to effectively regulate the water markets has become grim. Also, many fear that tradable water rights (TWR) suggested in the IWRM approach will lead to allocation of water to economically powerful people (Dharmadhikary, 2007, cited in Venkatachalam, 2008) and therefore, there will be stiff resistance, especially from the resource poor users of water (Kumar, 2007).

A greater challenge confronting the emergent water policy and regulatory regimes in the country in general and Maharashtra and Gujarat in particular is their complete sense of ignorance or lack of appreciation of the multifarious water sector (especially in the arena of drinking water) interventions by the grass roots level agencies, especially, the NGOs and other community based organisations and their impacts on water use and conservation.

There is plethora of other issues for which the neoliberal water policies do not provide adequate explanations. Some of them, inter alia, include:

a) What are the specific legal/ethical/political/socio-economic, agriculture and external trade policy environments within which these policies and interventions have been evolved and operating in Indian context?
b) How best these policies are informed to and understood by the varied actors/stakeholders and how these actors respond to varying scenarios of water governance and institutional regimes?
c) How realistic and cohesive have been the national as well as the state-specific water policies in respect of context-specific choice of technological solutions, institutional forms and allocation and pricing instruments and regulatory mechanisms?
d) Do the state-specific water policies adequately capture: (i) the gender roles/gendered dimensions of water management, access to water and control over the decision-making processes; and (ii) spatial vs temporal vs inter and intra-generational distributions and concerns of equity and sustainability?

An important question that still remains unclear in the neoliberal water policy discourse in India is, "what is water right and how is the water entitlement defined?". For water rights to be effectively implemented, two other concepts have to be defined on operational terms: one is access to water and the other is allocation principles of the resource per se. Since the water allocation principle laid down by the MWRRA considers the WUAs as the prime custodians of water transaction, the individual farmers would face serious difficulties in legitimising their individual water rights, especially in cases where the WUAs are either non-existent or weaker in performance. The legitimisation and enforcement of individual water rights may also largely depend on the egalitarian or democratic ways in which the WUAs function, without being badly influenced by the local dynamics.

With a lack of clarity on vital elements of managing water resources, the state setting up a plethora of regulatory institutions may apparently make the concept of people's (community) participation a major casualty. It becomes evident that in many of the natural resource management regimes there is a need to intercede the management of the resources and the users' interests with clearly defined legal framework and access rights. It also appears that in most states (except Maharashtra and Andhra Pradesh) who have launched water sector reforms, including enactment of water policies, the half-hearted attempts to reverse engineer the process of providing legal support to isolated cases of water distribution (not management) have neither led to improvements in resource management nor in legitimising users' stake in the resource or its management domains. Therefore in the present context, the adaptation of neoliberal policy prescriptions to the water sector endorsing the involvement of the private sector in water resource development and management would only be seen as a means for legitimising the role of market forces in addressing the vast social complexities around water, which is more than an economic commodity with immense socio-cultural and environmental significance.

This is not to suggest that the neoliberal ideas as they have shaped the formulation of water sector reforms in India seem to be highly detrimental to the larger goals of sustainability of the water resources. Rather, we would argue that the neoliberal perspective that water, if treated and marketed as an economic good should also coincide with an enormous amount of economic and social activism on the part of the state or the private sector to ensure that the policy reforms improves the efficiency in water allocations along with fulfilling inter as well as intra-generational equity in distribution. Fulfilment of inter and intra-generational equity in water distribution would help achieve sustainability of the resource base through institutional and pricing mechanisms (reflecting the scarcity/economic value) for effective enforcement of water rights among the multiple stakeholders. Thus, while emphasising the primacy of market-based instruments, especially, competitive water pricing, the neoliberal policies should also set the stage for effecting stricter enforcement of water rights, community/stakeholder participation, decentralisation, privatisation of particular functions in water delivery and a thorough overhaul of the roles of the state pertaining to governance of water resources, especially, the regulation of the market or private sectors as well as regulation of the resource exhaustive water management regimes.

Finally, it has become imperative now to launch a new water policy[10] for the country and the states, which is more holistic and realistic of the imminent crises surmounting the water sector of the country from multiple dimensions. The deliberate choice of a neoliberal policy approach as originated in the west that only addresses the issue of cost recovery or pricing based on market driven policies would only augment the crisis in India's water sector.

REFERENCES

Allan, J.A. (2005). *Water in the Environment/Socio-Economic Development Discourse: Sustainability, Changing Management Paradigms and Policy Responses in a Global System*, London: Blackwell Publishing, pp. 181-99. www.aquastress.net/share/img.../16_Allan-

WaterEDGov Oppn.pdf (accessed on September 30, 2010).

Bharwada, Charul and Vinay Mahajan (2002). 'Drinking Water Crisis in Kutch: A Natural Phenomenon', *Economic and Political Weekly*, November 30, pp. 4859-66.

Burke, Jacob J. and Marcus H. Moench (2000). *Groundwater and Society: Resources, Tensions and Opportunities*, United Nations.

Castro, José Esteban (2006). *Water, Power and Citizenship: Social Struggle in the Basin of Mexico*, New York: Palgrave Macmillan.

Castro, José Esteban (2008). 'Neoliberal Water and Sanitation Policies as a Failed Development Strategy: Lessons from Developing Countries', *Progress in Development Studies*, 8 (1): 63-83 (January).

Cullet, Philippe (2006). 'Water Law Reforms: Analysis of Recent Developments', *Journal of the Indian Law Institute*, 48(2), http://www.ielrc.org/conent/a0603.pdf.

Cullet, Philippe (2007a). Water Law in India: Overview of Existing Framework and Proposed Reforms, *IELRC Working Paper, 2007-01*, Geneva: International Environmental Law Research Centre.

Cullet, Philippe (2007b). *The Sardar Sarovar Dam Project: Selected Documents*, Hampshire, UK: Ashgate Publishing Company.

Dave, Kapil (2011). Thrust on Industry, 50-year-old Water Supply Plan in Pipeline, *The Indian Express*, February 21, Gandhinagar, Gujarat.

Davis, J., A. Kang, J. Vincent and D. Whittington (2001). 'How Important is Improved Water Infrastructure to Micro Enterprises? Evidence from Uganda', *World Development*, 29 (10): 1753-1767.

Dharmadhikary, Shripad (2007). A Flawed Model for Water Regulation, India Together, www.indiatogether.org/2007/may/env-mwrra.htm.

DSC (Development Support Centre) (2006). *Proceedings of the Regional Workshop on Participatory Irrigation Management*, January 20-21', Ahmedabad: Ahmedabad Management Association.

DFID (2001). Addressing the Water Crisis: Healthier and More Productive Lives for Poor People: Strategies for Achieving the International Development Targets, Department for International Development, London: DFID.

Dubash, Navroz K. (2002). *Tubewell Capitalism: Groundwater Development and Agrarian Change in Gujarat*, New Delhi: Oxford University Press.

Erjavec, Karmen and Emil Erjavec (2009). 'Changing EU Agricultural Policy Discourses? The Discourse Analysis of Commissioner's Speeches 2000-2007', *Food Policy*, 34 (2009): 218-226.

GOI (1987). *National Water Policy, 1987*. Government of India, Ministry of Water Resources.

GOI (2002). *National Water Policy, 2002*. Government of India, Ministry of Water Resources.

GOI (2011). *Provisional Population Tables and Annexures, Census of India 2011*. Government of India

Goswami, Subhrangsu (2011). 'Revisiting Sardar Sarovar Canal Based Drinking Water Project in Gujarat', in Parthasarathy, R. and Ravindra H. Dholakia (2011). *Sardar Sarovar Project on the River Narmada, Vol. 3: Impacts So far and Ways Forward*, New Delhi: Concept Publishing Company for CEPT University, Ahmedabad, pp. 693-726.

Gujarat Ecology Commission (2001). *State of the Environment-Gujarat*, Vadodara: Gujarat Ecology Commission, March.

Hirway, Indira and Subhrangsu Goswami (2008). 'Functioning of the Drinking Water Component of the Narmada Pipeline Project in Gujarat', *Economic and Political Weekly*, March 1, 2008, pp. 51-59.

Hope, R.A. (2004). Water Policy and Poverty Reduction in a Semi-arid Catchment, Unpublished doctoral thesis, UK: University of Newcastle-upon-Tyne.

Hope, R.A. (2006). 'Evaluating Water Policy Scenarios Against the Priorities of the Rural Poor', *World Development*, 34(1): 167–179.

Iyer, Ramaswamy R. (2007). 'The National Water Scene', *ORF Discourse*, Vol. 2, No. 2, pp. 1-9, February.

Iyer, Ramaswamy R. (2010). 'Approach to a New National Water Policy', *The Hindu*, October 29, 2010, http://www.thehindu.com/2010/10/29/stories/2010102963801 400.htm (accessed on May 10, 2011).

IRMA/UNICEF (2001). White Paper on Water in Gujarat, Institute of Rural Management, Anand, report prepared for Narmada Water Resources and Water Supply Department, Government of Gujarat.

Kumar, Bhisham and S.M. Seth (2000). Isotope Hydrology—Present Status and Future Prospects in India, paper presented at the International Conference on Integrated Water Resources Management, Organised by National Institute of Hydrology, December 20-22, New Delhi (http://www.nih.ernet.in/iso_stat_pap.htm, accessed on March 7, 2008).

Kumar, M. Dinesh (2005). India's Water Economy: Bracing Up for a Turbulent Future, *Workshop Report, IWMI-Tata Water Policy Programme*, Annual Partners' Meet 2005, pp. 36.

Kumar, M. Dinesh and O.P. Singh (2001). 'Market Instruments for

Demand Management in the Face of Scarcity and Overuse of Water in Gujarat, Western India', *Water Policy*, 3(2001): 387-403.

Kumar, M. Dinesh (2004). 'Roof Water Harvesting for Domestic Water Security: Who Gains and Who Loses?', *Water International*, 29 (1): 43–53 (March).

Kumar, M. Dinesh, O.P. Singh, Rahul Singh and Tushaar Shah (2004). 'Virtual Water Trade in Dairy Economy: Irrigation Water Productivity in Gujarat', *Economic and Political Weekly*, 39 (31): 3492-3497 (July 31).

Kumar, M. Dinesh and O.P. Singh (eds.), (2007). *Groundwater Management in India: Physical, Institutional and Policy Alternatives*, New Delhi: Sage Publications.

Kumar, M. Dinesh (2007). Towards Evolving Institutional Arrangements for Managing Groundwater, in M. Dinesh Kumar and O.P. Singh (eds.), *Groundwater Management in India: Physical, Institutional and Policy Alternatives*. New Delhi: Sage Publications. pp. 288-320.

Mehta, L. (2000). 'Water for the 21st Century. Challenges and Misconceptions', *IDS Working Paper No. 111*. Sussex, UK: Institute of Development Studies (IDS).

Mehta, Lyla (2003a). 'Contexts and Constructions of Water Scarcity', *Economic and Political Weekly*, 38 (48): 5066-5072 (November 29).

Mehta, Lyla (2003b). 'Problems of Publicness and Access Rights: Perspectives from the Water domain', in Lyla Mehta (ed.) *Providing Global Public Goods: Managing Globalisation*, Oxford: Oxford University Press.

MOWR (2006). *Performance Budget 2005-06*, Ministry of Water Resources, Government of India. http://www.wrmin.nic.in/writereaddata/linkimages/Chapter19633955671.pdf (accessed on October 8, 2010).

MOWR (2010). Background Note for Consultation Meeting with Policy Makers on Review of National Water Policy, Ministry of Water Resources, Government of India.

MWRRA (2009). 'Approach Paper on Preparation of Criteria for Bulk Water Pricing in the State of Maharashtra', Vol. I, Maharashtra Water Resources Regulatory Authority, Mumbai, November 2009, pp. 154.

ODI (2002). *The "Water Crisis": Fault Lines in Global Debates, Water Policy Programme*, London: Overseas Development Institute, http://www.odi.org.uk (accessed September 28, 2010).

Oza Apoorva (2007). 'Irrigation and Water Resources: Part I: Irrigation: Achievements and Challenges', in 3iNetwork (2007): *India*

Infrastructure Report 2007: Rural Infrastructure, New Delhi: Oxford University Press, pp. 178-196.

Parthasarathy, R. (2000). 'Participatory Irrigation Management Programme in Gujarat: Institutional and Financial Issues', *Economic and Political Weekly*, 35 (35 and 36), August 26-Spetember 2.

Parthasarathy, R. (2004). Decentralisation and Institutional Dynamics: The Case of PIM Programme in India, Gujarat Institute of Development Research *Working Paper 147*, September.

Parthasarathy, R. (2005). 'Objects and Accomplishments of Participatory Irrigation Management Programme in India: An Open Pair of Scissors', in R. Parthasarathy and Sudarshan Iyengar (eds.) *Developmental Paradigms and Challenges for Western and Central Regional States in India*, New Delhi: Concept Publishing Company.

Parthasarathy, R. (2010). 'The Role of Irrigation in the Growth Story of Gujarat', in Ravindra H. Dholakia and Samar K. Datta (eds.). *High Growth Trajectory and Structural Changes in Gujarat Agriculture*, Delhi: Macmillan Publishers India Limited, pp. 114-135.

Parthasarathy, R. and Ravindra H. Dholakia (2011). *Sardar Sarovar Project on the River Narmada, 3 Vols., Vol. 1: History of Design, Planning and Appraisal; Vol. 2. History of Rehabilitation and Implementation; Vol. 3: Impacts So Far and Ways Forward*, New Delhi: Concept Publishing Company for CEPT University, Ahmedabad.

Pathak, M.D., A.D. Gadkari and S.D. Ghate (1999). Groundwater Development in Maharashtra State, India, 25th WEDC Conference, 'Integrated Development for Water Supply and Sanitation', Addis Ababa, Ethiopia.

Planning Commission (2002). *Tenth Five Year Plan*, New Delhi: Planning Commission.

Planning Commission (2005). *Mid-Term Appraisal Plan, Water Resources. (2002-2005)*, New Delhi: Planning Commission.

Planning Commission (2007). *Report of the Expert Group on "Ground Water Management and Ownership"*, New Delhi: Planning Commission, September 2007, p. 61.

Phansalker, Sanjiv and Vivek Kher (2006). A Decade of the Maharashtra Groundwater Legislation: Analysis of the Implementation Process, *Law Environment and Development (LEAD)* Journal, Vol. 2, No. 1, pp. 69-83.

Prakash, Anjal and R.K. Sama (2006). 'Contending Water Uses: Social

Undercurrents in a Water-scarce Village', *Economic and Political Weekly*, February 18, 2006, pp. 577-579.

Ranade, Rahul and M. Dinesh Kumar (2004). 'Narmada Water for Groundwater Recharge in North Gujarat: Conjunctive Management in Large Irrigation Projects', *Economic and Political Weekly*, July 31, 2004, pp. 3510- 3513.

SANDRP (2007). 'Sardar Sarovar: Drinking Water Allocations Diverted to Industries, Non-Drought-Prone Areas', *Dams Rivers & People*, South Asia Network on Dams, Rivers and People (SANDRP), April 2007.

Sangameswaran, Priya (2007). 'The Right to Water in Different Discourses', in Sara Ahmed, Margreet Zwarteveen and Suman Gautam (eds.) *Engendering Integrated Water Management in South Asia: Policy, Practice and Institutions*, New Delhi: Sage Publications.

Sangameswaran, Priya (2010). 'Rural Drinking Water Reforms in Maharashtra: The Role of Neoliberalism', *Economic and Political Weekly*, 44 (4): 62-69 (January 23).

Shah, Tushaar (2004). 'Water and Welfare: Critical Issues in India's Water Future', *Economic and Political Weekly*, 39 (12): 1211-13 (20 March).

Smith, Adam (1776 originally). *An Inquiry into the Nature and Causes of the Wealth of Nations*, 1976 edition. Chicago: University of Chicago Press.

TERI (2001). Regulatory Framework for Water Services in the State of Gujarat, New Delhi, Tata Energy Research Institute, *TERI Project Report No. 2000ER61*, p. 228.

TISS (2008). 'Performance and Development Effectiveness of the Sardar Sarovar Project', Tata Institute of Social Sciences, Mumbai, August 2008, Pages xv+102, www.tiss.edu (accessed on March 30, 2011).

Tyagi, N.K. (1987). 'Managing Salinity through Conjunctive Use of Water Resources', *Ecological Modelling*, 40: 11-24.

UN (2003). *Water for People, Water for Life—UN World Water Development Report*, Paris: UNESCO.

UN/WWAP (2003). *1st UN World Water Development Report: Water for People, Water for Life*, United Nations/World Water Assessment Programme), United Nations Educational, Scientific and Cultural Organisation (UNESCO) and Paris, New York and Oxford: Berghahn Books.

Upadhyay, Videh (2005). 'Confusing Water Rights with Quotas', *India Together*, October 27. WHO, 2003, 'Right to water', World Health

Organization, France, also available at http://www.who.int/water_sanitation_health/rightowater/en/.

Van Koppen, Barbara, R. Parthasarathy and Constantina Safiliou (2002). 'Poverty Dimensions of Irrigation Management Transfer in Large-Scale Canal Irrigation in Andhra Pradesh and Gujarat, India', *Research Report 61*. Colombo, Sri Lanka: International Water Management Institute.

Venkatachalam, L. (2008). 'Market-Based Instruments for Water Allocation in India: Issues and the Way Forward', in M. Dinesh Kumar, et al., (2008). *Managing Water in the Face of Growing Scarcity, Inequity and Declining Returns: Exploring Fresh Approaches*, IWMI-Tata Water Policy Research Program: Proceedings of the 7th Annual Partners' Meet, ICRISAT Campus, Patancheru, Hyderabad, April 2-4, 2008, pp. 498-512.

Viswanathan, P.K. and R. Parthasarathy (2008). 'Are Water Policies a case of Reverse Engineering in India?', in M. Dinesh Kumar, et al. (2008): *Managing Water in the Face of Growing Scarcity, Inequity and Declining Returns: Exploring Fresh Approaches*, IWMI-Tata Water Policy Research Programme: Proceedings of the 7th Annual Partners' Meet, ICRISAT Campus, Patancheru, Hyderabad, April 2-4, 2008, pp. 692-707.

Viswanathan, P.K. and Jyoti Parikh (2010). *Impact of industrialisation and Related Activities on Marine Protected Areas: A Case Study of Marine National Park, Jamnagar District in Gujarat*, Unpublished Report submitted to IRADe, New Delhi, pages: vi+103 (July).

Wilder, Margaret (2008). 'Equity and Water in Mexico's Changing Institutional Landscape', in John Whiteley, Helen M. Ingram, and Richard Perry, (eds.), *Water, Place and Equity*, Cambridge, MA: Massachusetts Institute of Technology (MIT) Press.

Wood, John R. (2007). *The Politics of Water Resource Development in India—The Narmada Dams Controversy*, New Delhi: Sage Publications.

World Bank (2005). *India's Water Economy: Bracing for a Turbulent Future*, Washington: World Bank.

World Bank (2010). *Sustaining Water for All in a Changing Climate, World Bank Group Implementation Progress Report of the Water Resources Sector Strategy*. The International Bank for Reconstruction and Development/The World Bank, Washington DC, pp. xiii+105, http://siteresources.world bank.org/NEWS/Resources/sustainingwater.pdf (accessed September 28, 2010).

WWAP (2009). *The United Nations World Water Development Report 3: Water in a Changing World*, World Water Assessment Programme. 2009, Paris: UNESCO, and London: Earthscan, pages xxvi+318 http://www.unesco.org/water/wwap/wwdr/wwdr3/pdf/WWDR3_Water_in_a_Changing_ World.pdf (accessed September 29, 2010).

NOTES

This paper draws from the research undertaken by the authors to review the water sector reforms in India with special reference to Maharashtra and Gujarat. We express thanks to the IWMI-ITP for providing the financial support for undertaking this study. The usual disclaimers apply.

1. Often, the case of Mexico is shown to be one of the most successful in the effective implementation of water sector reforms. The core components of successful water policy reform in Mexico are: a) efficiency; b) decentralised management; c) participation; and equity/sustainability. Mexico's transition to the new policy regime was additionally influenced by a range of exogenous and endogenous factors, including the country's political opening, its turn to neoliberal economic restructuring, a greatly retrenched role for the state vis-a-vis markets, and the emergence of civil society actors demanding more voice over water allocation, services, pricing and quality (Wilder 2008; Castro 2006).
2. The characterisation of water as an economic good in the Dublin-Rio principles and the advocacy of water markets and the privatisation of water services by the World Bank and the Asian Development Bank have also been instrumental in popularising the neoliberal principles, particularly their long-term implications for financial disciplining through water pricing and the focus on rights to water (Mehta and Madsen, 2003).
3. For instance, only 89 per cent of the country's population has access to improved drinking water source with hardly 28 per cent having access to improved sanitation facilities. Further, about 2.17 lakh rural habitations in the country are affected by water quality problems. More importantly, 71 stretches on various rivers in the country have been identified as polluted (http://mowr.gov.in/wqaa/index.html).
4. This has also been revealed by Ramaswamy Iyer, who has been engaged in drawing out the 1987 water policy. He observes that "when we worked on the National Water Policy in 1985-86, we had a vague idea about shifting attention from big projects to a unified, focused water policy. Having converted the Department

of Irrigation into the Ministry of Water Resources, we discovered that the National Water Resources Committee, set up in 1980, had not met even once. We had a meeting, and that's where the National Water Policy originated. ..While the National Water Resources Council approved the National Water Policy in September 1987, there was no accompanying blueprint for making it operational, as originally envisaged....We did try to address the question of institutionalisation through periodic meetings at different levels, but over a period of time that initiative petered out, unfortunately" (Iyer, 2007:8).

5. The policy document observes that: "private sector participation should be encouraged in planning, development and management of water resources projects for diverse uses, wherever feasible. Private sector participation may help in introducing innovative ideas, generating financial resources and introducing corporate management and improving service efficiency and accountability to users. Depending upon the specific situations, various combinations of private sector participation, in building, owning, operating, leasing and transferring of water resources facilities, may be considered" (GOI, 2002).
6. The important functions of the RBDCs are to: a) determine and distribute bulk water entitlements for various categories of use; b) establish a water tariff system at sub-basin, river basin and State level based on consultations with stakeholders. Water charges so fixed should reflect full recovery of the cost of the irrigation management, administration, operation and maintenance of the project; c) administer and manage interstate water resources of the State; d) review and clear water projects at the sub-basin/ river basin levels and ensure the proposal is in conformity with Integrated State Water Plan; e) review entitlements after three years; f) establish a system of enforcement, monitoring and measurement of Entitlements; g) determine and ensure that the cross-subsidies between Categories of Use are totally offset; and h) develop the State Water Entitlement database.
7. Bulk tariff is the tariff levied by the service provider, viz. Water Resources Department (WRD) for volumetric supply of water to bulk users from its reservoirs, dams and canals. While water drawn by industries and drinking water users is volumetrically measured, as much as 90 per cent of the agricultural users in the State still get water from area-based supplies. Only in about 10

per cent of the irrigated area have water user associations, to whom volumetric supplies are possible, been formed (MWRRA, 2009).

8. The literature examining the critical issues affecting the water sector in Gujarat is very vast indeed. Prominent ones in this regard are the studies, viz. IRMA/UNICEF, 2001; Kumar and Singh, 2001; Dubash, 2002; Mehta, 2003 a,b; Ranade and Kumar, 2004; Kumar, et al., 2004; Prakash and Sama, 2006, TISS, 2008; Shah, 2004; Kumar, 2007; Parthasarathy and Dholakia, 2011; Cullet, 2007b; etc.
9. Despite promotion of water harvesting schemes for addressing the drinking water scarcities in the state, with changing lifestyles and burgeoning urban demand, it is a matter of serious concern that 'how far these water harvesting structures can help resolving the problems of water supply in Gujarat. Currently, much of the urban drinking water supplies are sourced from groundwater, which is a serious problem in the context of emerging groundwater depletion and contamination (Goswami, 2011).
10. Iyer (2010) puts forth the genuineness and the urgency for a radical overhaul in India's water sector, including the need for a new National Water Policy (NWP), which stems from the gross mismanagement of water, caused by a host of natural and human induced outcomes, viz., a) intermittent, unreliable, unsafe and inequitable water supply in urban areas; b) rivers turning into sewers or poison and contaminated aquifers; c) intractable water related conflicts between uses, sectors, areas, states; d) major and medium irrigation systems in disarray, rendering poor and unreliable service and characterised by inequities of various kinds; e) alarming depletion of aquifers in many parts of the country; f) inefficiency and waste in every kind of water-use; g) the environmental/ecological impacts of big water resource projects, poor EIAs, the displacement of people by such projects and the general failure to resettle and rehabilitate project-affected persons.

Notes on Contributors

Asok Kumar Ray, Visiting Faculty, OKD Institute of Social Change and Development, Guwahati.

Felix Padel, Freelance Anthropologist, Author.

Indraneel Dasgupta, Professor, Economic Research Unit, Indian Statistical Institute, Kolkata.

Joydeep Baruah, Assistant Professor, OKD Institute of Social Change and Development, Guwahati.

Neil DeVotta, Associate Professor of Political Science at Wake Forest University, Winston-Salem, North Carolina.

P.K. Viswanathan, Associate Professor, Gujarat Institute of Development Research, Ahmedabad.

Radhika Kumar, Assistant Professor, Department of Political Science, Motilal Nehru College, University of Delhi, Delhi.

Samir Kumar Das, Presently Vice-Chancellor, North Bengal University and former Professor and Chair, Department of Political Science, University of Calcutta, Kolkata.

Santanu Rakshit, Associate Professor, Department of Palli Charcha Kendra (Social Studies and Rural Development), Visva Bharati University, Santiniketan.

Sudipta Bhattacharyya, Associate Professor, Department of Economics and Politics, Visva Bharati University, Santiniketan.

V. Krishna Ananth, Associate Professor, Department of Journalism and Mass Communication, Sikkim University, Gangtok.